China's Digital Expansion in the Global South

For those wanting to understand implications for the Global South of China's emergence as a digital superpower, this book analyses China's digital impact in Latin America, North Africa and Asia, covering issues including platforms, e-commerce, technology transfer and digital surveillance. It also incorporates a major literature review that outlines a six-part future research agenda.

At the intersection of China's growing global presence and growing digital power lies its digital expansion in the low- and middle-income countries of the Global South. Worth billions of USD annually in trade and investment and having a significant impact on these countries' social and economic development, this phenomenon has been relatively ignored by researchers to date. This major new volume provides significant new insights that help advance our knowledge of this important topic. A systematic review of literature identifies key issues within the field and outlines a six-part future research agenda. Those issues are then explored in greater depth: reviewing the relationship between activities of Chinese platform firms, the state's Belt and Road Initiative, and local context in the Global South; investigating the activities of Alibaba as it has sought to grow its operations in Mexico; analysing whether two Chinese tech giants – Huawei and ZTE – are contributing to an upgrading of local technological capabilities in Algeria and Egypt; and digging behind portrayals of China exporting "digital authoritarianism" to understand the realities of surveillance system exports to countries in Latin America.

Overall, this book fills important gaps in our understanding of China's digital expansion in the Global South and challenges preconceptions and one-sided views of this major recent activity. It was originally published as a special issue of *The Information Society*.

Richard Heeks is Professor of Digital Development at the Global Development Institute at the University of Manchester, UK. He is Director of the University's Centre for Digital Development, with research interests around digital transformation, digital uplands and the geopolitics of AI.

Christopher Foster is a Senior Lecturer at the Global Development Institute at the University of Manchester, UK. His research focuses on the digital economy, digital governance and the implications of innovations on the global distribution of production, work and labour.

Ping Gao is a Senior Lecturer at the Global Development Institute at the University of Manchester, UK. His research focuses on IT innovation and policy, especially in the Chinese context and from a government perspective.

Xia Han is a Lecturer in International Business at the Alliance Manchester Business School at the University of Manchester, UK. Her research draws from political economy and international business to explain the expansion of emerging market multinational enterprises with a focus on Chinese firms. She looks at the implications of international relations for MNEs.

Nicholas Jepson is a Lecturer at the Global Development Institute at the University of Manchester, UK. His work examines the global political economy of the rise of China, particularly in relation to development in Latin America, sub-Saharan Africa and Eastern Europe. He leads the finance working group for the China in Europe Research Network (CHERN).

Seth Schindler is Professor of Urban Politics and Development at the University of Manchester, UK. He is also the co-founder of the Second Cold War Observatory. He previously coordinated the MA in Global Studies at the Humboldt University of Berlin, Germany.

Qingna Zhou obtained her PhD degree at the University of Manchester, UK. She is serving as an interdisciplinary lecturer across the International Business Group at the Alliance Manchester Business School and the Global Development Institute. Her research interests include digital multinationals, digital transformation and China's digital expansion in the Global South.

China's Digital Expansion in the Global South

Edited by
Richard Heeks, Christopher Foster, Ping Gao, Xia Han, Nicholas Jepson, Seth Schindler and Qingna Zhou

Routledge
Taylor & Francis Group
LONDON AND NEW YORK

First published 2025
by Routledge
4 Park Square, Milton Park, Abingdon, Oxon, OX14 4RN

and by Routledge
605 Third Avenue, New York, NY 10158

Routledge is an imprint of the Taylor & Francis Group, an informa business

British Library Cataloguing-in-Publication Data
A catalogue record for this book is available from the British Library

ISBN13: 978-1-032-94328-2 (hbk)
ISBN13: 978-1-032-94340-4 (pbk)
ISBN13: 978-1-003-57022-6 (ebk)

DOI: 10.4324/9781003570226

Typeset in Minion Pro
by codeMantra

Publisher's Note
The publisher accepts responsibility for any inconsistencies that may have arisen during the conversion of this book from journal articles to book chapters, namely the inclusion of journal terminology.

Contents

Citation Information vi
Notes on Contributors vii

Introduction: China's digital expansion in the Global South 1
Richard Heeks, Christopher Foster, Ping Gao, Xia Han, Nicholas Jepson, Seth Schindler and Qingna Zhou

1 China's digital expansion in the Global South: systematic literature review and future research agenda 5
Richard Heeks, Angelica V. Ospina, Christopher Foster, Ping Gao, Xia Han, Nicholas Jepson, Seth Schindler and Qingna Zhou

2 Chinese digital platform companies' expansion in the Belt and Road countries 32
Yujia He

3 Alibaba in Mexico: adapting the digital villages model to Latin America 56
Guillermo J. Larios-Hernandez

4 Learning along the Digital Silk Road? Technology transfer, power, and Chinese ICT corporations in North Africa 72
Tin Hinane El-Kadi

5 The Chinese surveillance state in Latin America? Evidence from Argentina and Ecuador 90
Maximiliano Facundo Vila Seoane and Carla Morena Álvarez Velasco

6 China's expansion into Brazilian digital surveillance markets 104
Esther Majerowicz and Miguel Henriques de Carvalho

Index 123

Citation Information

The following chapters were originally published in *The Information Society*, volume 40, issue 2 (2024). When citing this material, please use the original page numbering for each article, as follows:

Introduction
China's digital expansion in the Global South
Richard Heeks, Christopher Foster, Ping Gao, Xia Han, Nicholas Jepson, Seth Schindler and Qingna Zhou
The Information Society, volume 40, issue 2 (2024), pp. 65–68

Chapter 1
China's digital expansion in the Global South: Systematic literature review and future research agenda
Richard Heeks, Angelica V. Ospina, Christopher Foster, Ping Gao, Xia Han, Nicholas Jepson, Seth Schindler and Qingna Zhou
The Information Society, volume 40, issue 2 (2024), pp. 69–95

Chapter 2
Chinese digital platform companies' expansion in the Belt and Road countries
Yujia He
The Information Society, volume 40, issue 2 (2024), pp. 96–119

Chapter 3
Alibaba in Mexico: Adapting the digital villages model to Latin America
Guillermo J. Larios-Hernandez
The Information Society, volume 40, issue 2 (2024), pp. 120–135

Chapter 4
Learning along the Digital Silk Road? Technology transfer, power, and Chinese ICT corporations in North Africa
Tin Hinane El-Kadi
The Information Society, volume 40, issue 2 (2024), pp. 136–153

Chapter 5
The Chinese surveillance state in Latin America? Evidence from Argentina and Ecuador
Maximiliano Facundo Vila Seoane and Carla Morena Álvarez Velasco
The Information Society, volume 40, issue 2 (2024), pp. 154–167

Chapter 6
China's expansion into Brazilian digital surveillance markets
Esther Majerowicz and Miguel Henriques de Carvalho
The Information Society, volume 40, issue 2 (2024), pp. 168–185

Notes on Contributors

Miguel Henriques de Carvalho, Department of Economics, Rural Federal University of Rio de Janeiro, Brazil.

Christopher Foster, Global Development Institute, University of Manchester, UK.

Ping Gao, Global Development Institute, University of Manchester, UK.

Xia Han, Alliance Manchester Business School, University of Manchester, UK.

Yujia He, Patterson School of Diplomacy and International Commerce, University of Kentucky, Lexington, USA.

Richard Heeks, Global Development Institute, University of Manchester, UK.

Tin Hinane El-Kadi, Department of International Development, London School of Economics, UK.

Nicholas Jepson, Global Development Institute, University of Manchester, UK.

Guillermo J. Larios-Hernandez, Centro de Emprendimiento Universitario, Universidad Anahuac Mexico, Mexico.

Esther Majerowicz, Department of Economics, Federal University of Rio Grande do Norte, Natal, Brazil; Graduate Program in Economics, Federal University of Rio Grande do Norte, Natal, Brazil.

Carla Morena Álvarez Velasco, Institute of High National Studies, Quito, Ecuador.

Angelica V. Ospina, Global Development Institute, University of Manchester, UK.

Seth Schindler, Global Development Institute, University of Manchester, UK.

Maximiliano Facundo Vila Seoane, School of Politics and Government, National University of San Martín, Argentina.

Qingna Zhou, Alliance Manchester Business School, University of Manchester, UK.

Introduction: China's digital expansion in the Global South

Richard Heeks, Christopher Foster, Ping Gao, Xia Han, Nicholas Jepson, Seth Schindler and Qingna Zhou

In the past decade or so, China has emerged as a global digital superpower, with digital exports and activities reaching out around the world. This has naturally attracted attention from scholars but most research to date has focused on the digital economy within China or on impacts within the high-income countries of the Global North.

Much less-researched have been the implications for other low- and middle-income developing countries of the Global South, where China has a rapidly-growing digital presence. This presence is impacting across different areas:

- Infrastructure, for example, via Digital Silk Road (DSR) components of China's Belt and Road Initiative (BRI), and contributions to construction of smart cities;
- The economic sphere, for example, with Chinese e-commerce platforms allowing greater penetration of local markets;
- The social sphere, for example, via TikTok and other Chinese social media platforms; and
- The political sphere, for example, with export of Chinese surveillance systems, and growing influence on regional and global digital governance.

What little has been researched and written about China's digital involvement in the Global South has often taken one of two distinct positions. Either from the perspective of China itself, tending to put a positive gloss on activities, or from the perspective of the US, seeing China's digital growth as an economic or political threat. Scholarship from the Global South and/or from the perspective of Global South actors has been rare.

Recognizing this, the "China's Digital Expansion in the Global South" project was initiated, with funding from the School of Environment, Education, and Development and from the Faculty of Humanities, both at the University of Manchester. The development of this special issue began with a track at the Development Studies Association conference in 2021, a systematic literature review (included in this special issue), and a call for case studies that elicited more than 60 proposals from which five papers were ultimately developed.

Following rounds of internal feedback, we held an international workshop in 2022 at which case studies were presented and discussed, leading to production as working papers. These papers were then submitted into the review process for *The Information Society* and now form the basis for this special issue.

In the remainder of this editorial, we introduce the articles in this special issue. They offer a range of perspectives across the different spheres, as outlined above, and draw on research from Africa, Asia and Latin America.

The literature review – "China's Digital Expansion in the Global South: Systematic Literature Review and Future Research Agenda" by Richard Heeks, Angelica Ospina, Christopher Foster, Ping Gao, Xia Han, Nicholas Jepson, Seth Schindler, and Qingna Zhou – is based on analysis of 75 topic-specific papers. It reviews the general features of this literature, including its bi-modal (US- and China-based) distribution of authorship that correlates with Sino-phobic and Sino-philic perspectives, and its relative lack of primary data or theorization. It provides a chronological review of the gradual progression of China's exports to Global South countries up the digital stack, from telecom infrastructure to devices, data services, and platforms.

The review then analyses key emergent themes from the literature These include the synergies and tensions between the various Chinese state, public, and private actors involved; the digital expansion strategies adopted by these actors including Digital Silk Road and tech firm internationalization; and the more micro-level approaches taken to design and implementation of digital projects in Global South countries. Evidence about development impact is considered, with concerns raised in some sections of literature about cybersecurity, digital colonialism, and dependency, inequalities within and between countries, and environmental sustainability. The review also explores two domain-specific issues arising in the literature: whether China is exporting "digital authoritarianism", and the implications of China's growing digital presence for digital governance at both global and national levels.

A number of these themes – most of which emerge from a very limited base of literature and an even-smaller base of empirical evidence – are then explored in greater depth by the other articles in this special issue.

Yujia He's article, "Chinese Digital Platform Companies' Expansion in the Belt and Road Countries", investigates the relationship between three things: activities of Chinese platform firms in Global South countries, the Chinese state's Belt and Road Initiative (including its Digital Silk Road component), and local context. Global quantitative data shows growth of Chinese platform firms' investments to have been much stronger in non-BRI-participating countries compared to countries that are participating.

This matches results of an Indonesia-specific investment case study in He's article, which show Chinese firms perceiving BRI/DSR as a high-level brand or slogan that may be useful in some circumstances or avoided in others, but which has limited impact on investment decisions. Instead, those decisions are driven much more by local market factors such as market size, and are shaped by other local contextual factors including national policy (both policy content and the nature and extent of implementation) and the state of the labor market. These are shown to have prompted Chinese platform firms to localize their business operations, to seek local partners, and to invest in local capacity building. They have also adapted to local circumstances in other ways; sometimes finding ways to work around local policy. The findings here thus move beyond the simplistic notion that China's digital expansion is being directed by the Chinese government. Rather, they reorient attention to the interests and behaviors of the tech firms. The article also helps expose the importance of local policies and conditions in shaping that expansion; factors that have often been ignored in the literature to date.

The strategies adopted by Chinese tech firms in the Global South are also the topic of the article by Guillermo J. Larios-Hernandez, "Alibaba in Mexico: Adapting the Digital Villages Model to Latin America". He researched the activities of Alibaba as it sought to grow its operations in Mexico. Alibaba has been emblematic in China's broader digital expansion, with its "Electronic World Trade Platform" approach, said to epitomize the "inclusive globalization" vision – China's alternative to the type of globalization fostered by the US and other Western states and digital firms. Echoing the findings of the previous article, this one charts the way in which local context led Alibaba – via its Mexican subsidiary, Atomic88 – to customize its approach. Given it had only a nascent position in a local e-commerce market dominated by US and Latin American platforms, Alibaba did not seek to compete head-on, for example, by directly promoting sales via its e-commerce platforms. Instead, it adopted a longer-term perspective that focused first on the digitally-enabled development of a relatively neglected sector in Mexico: small enterprise. It neither directly funded nor provided its e-commerce platform services to these enterprises, but instead facilitated local actors, particularly universities, to develop a training and consultancy intervention model.

The long-term impact of its initiative on inclusivity is uncertain, but what it has done is to help Alibaba build relationships with key digital economy stakeholders in Mexico. These relationships will potentially provide a valuable foundation for next steps toward a larger and more direct presence in the market. The article demonstrates the importance of local factors and local actors and the ability of Chinese tech firms to customize growth strategies based on context. It again shows the way in which expansion can often occur with little overt role for the Chinese state.

After articles studying China's digital activities in two middle-income countries in Asia and Latin America, the next article turns attention to Africa; specifically North Africa. Where the two previous articles concentrated on the strategies adopted by Chinese tech firms, "Learning Along the Digital Silk Road? Technology Transfer, Power, and Chinese ICT Corporations in North Africa" by Tin Hinane El-Kadi focuses more on the development impact of those strategies. Specifically, it studies whether two Chinese tech giants – Huawei and ZTE – are contributing to an upgrading of local technological capabilities through their activities in Algeria and Egypt. These activities include not just major infrastructure contracts but also a manufacturing plant and a joint technology training center and innovation laboratory.

Despite this potential, the article finds that the two firms created no opportunities for knowledge transfers that could lead to meaningful technological upgrading in the two countries. There has been local skill building, particularly via relationships with North African universities, and a major diffusion of Chinese digital technologies but this has mainly served to reconfigure local digital ecosystems toward a domination of Chinese products, processes, and systems. This may well be a natural part of commercial competition for markets rather than part of a grand plan directed from Beijing, but it is creating a new set of dependencies on Chinese tech firms. Proactive local policies, which the two previous articles both showed to have an effect on the actions of Chinese firms, are therefore needed to promote stronger involvement of local organizations and greater knowledge spillovers.

The final two articles – "The Chinese Surveillance State in Latin America? Evidence from Argentina and Ecuador" by Maximiliano Facundo Vila Seoane and Carla Morena Álvarez Velasco, and "China's Expansion into Brazilian Digital Surveillance Markets" by Esther Majerowicz and Miguel Henriques de Carvalho – both provide new insights into a much-contested aspect of China's exports to Global South countries: the export of surveillance technologies. As discussed in the literature review paper, this has been painted, particularly by US-based sources, as the export of digital authoritarianism that is undermining democracy and strengthening autocracy. Anti-China rhetoric more broadly has also at times been replicated by politicians in Latin America.

Both articles present evidence that challenges partial and politicized views. Alongside the previous article on limits to Chinese tech firms' technology transfer and the initial literature review, they question the idea of Chinese exceptionalism; finding a number of similarities between the actions of Chinese and Western digital firms. They show that both historically and currently, Western firms have been supplying surveillance technologies to Latin America; sometimes as part of the very same systems in which Chinese technologies are involved. Those technologies may well be part of broader emergency response or e-government systems; the kind of system widely promoted in the international development activities of Western states.

As do all of the articles in this special issue, the two final articles challenge the image of the Chinese state as the puppet-master directing and controlling matters. In all cases, organs of the Chinese central government have played only a limited and background role. Instead, the core relationships are between Chinese tech firms (albeit some state-owned), local state actors in the Global South, and, to varying extents, local or even Western firms. Rather than fears about digital authoritarianism, it is those relationships which are the focus for local concerns, with accusations of corruption in procurement, and worries about lack of accountability in the use of surveillance systems. The Argentina/Ecuador article in particular recovers local agency, showing how procurement, design and implementation of the systems have been driven by local agendas rather than by Chinese actors.

Those local agendas cut across the political spectrum, and the two articles comprehensively debunk the association in some US-origin sources between Chinese surveillance technologies and autocratic and/or left-leaning national regimes. Polities of all stripes from right to left, from less to more democratic, and from national to local levels have all procured these technologies from Chinese firms. This once again reinforces how an understanding of local context, local politics, and local history is essential to any analysis of China's digital expansion in the Global South.

Overall, the articles presented here start to fill some important gaps in our understanding of China's digital expansion in the Global South, and they challenge some preconceptions and one-sided views of this major, recent activity. The articles in this special issue provide a valuable foundation for future and more research on this important topic. That research can potentially be guided by the six research agenda priorities identified in the literature review paper:

- More voices from the Global South, both as authors and subjects of research
- Updating the scope of research to encompass: a broader range of digital technologies, the role of data and human infrastructure in China's digital expansion, and the impact of recent trends in Chinese domestic digital policy
- Moving beyond the "Team China" monolith to understand the actual coherence, collaboration, competition, and conflict between different Chinese digital actors who are active in the Global South
- Steering between Chinese exceptionalism and identicalism, i.e. between the extreme positions that China is unique in its digital interactions with Global South countries, and that China is no different to other countries
- Evaluating the development impact of China's digital expansion in the Global South: the

distribution of benefits and disbenefits, the contribution or otherwise to the United Nations' Sustainable Development Goals, and specific impacts around sovereignty, dependency, inequality, and environmental sustainability
- Studying the role of local agency in the so-called "digital cold war" between the US and China, including room for maneuver of local policy-makers in both national and global digital governance, optimum strategies for local digital firms, and Global South countries as sites for learning by Chinese digital policy-makers and firms

Disclosure statement

No potential conflict of interest was reported by the author(s).

ORCID

Richard Heeks http://orcid.org/0000-0002-4551-2208
Christopher Foster http://orcid.org/0000-0001-7827-2485
Ping Gao http://orcid.org/0000-0002-9683-1989
Nicholas Jepson http://orcid.org/0000-0003-0163-3179
Seth Schindler http://orcid.org/0000-0003-2233-0628
Qingna Zhou http://orcid.org/0000-0002-7516-884X

References

El-Kadi, T. H. 2024. Learning along the Digital Silk Road? Technology transfer, power, and Chinese ICT corporations in North Africa. *The Information Society* 40 (2): 136–153.

He, Y. 2024. Chinese digital platform companies' expansion in the Belt and Road countries. *The Information Society* 40 (2): 96–119.

Heeks, R., A. V. Ospina, C. Foster, P. Gao, X. Han, N. Jepson, S. Schindler, and Q. Zhou. 2024. China's digital expansion in the Global South: Systematic literature review and future research agenda. *The Information Society* 40 (2): 69–95.

Larios-Hernandez, G. J. 2024. Alibaba in Mexico: Adapting the digital villages model to Latin America. *The Information Society* 40 (2): 120–135.

Majerowicz, E., and M. H. de Carvalho. 2024. China's expansion into Brazilian digital surveillance markets. *The Information Society* 40 (2): 168–185.

Vila Seoane, M. F., and C. M. Álvarez Velasco. 2024. The Chinese surveillance state in Latin America? Evidence from Argentina and Ecuador. *The Information Society* 40 (2): 154–167.

OPEN ACCESS

China's digital expansion in the Global South: systematic literature review and future research agenda

Richard Heeks, Angelica V. Ospina, Christopher Foster, Ping Gao, Xia Han, Nicholas Jepson, Seth Schindler and Qingna Zhou

ABSTRACT

At the intersection of China's growing global presence and growing digital power lies its digital expansion in the low- and middle-income countries of the Global South. Worth billions of US$ annually in trade and investment, and having a significant impact on these countries' social and economic development, this phenomenon has been relatively ignored by researchers to date. However, it has nonetheless now been sufficiently studied to warrant a systematic literature review, the results of which are reported in this article. The article has two aims: to identify what is already known about China's digital expansion in the Global South and, from this, to outline a future research agenda. After characterizing the features, research design, and perspectives within current literature, the article overviews China's digital expansion. It outlines this expansion's synergies, tensions, strategies, design and implementation approaches, and evidence about development impact on Global South countries. The article explores two domain-specific issues arising in the literature: whether China is exporting "digital authoritarianism," and the implications of China's growing digital presence for digital governance at both global and national levels. The article ends by laying out a six-part research agenda for future investigation of China's digital expansion in the Global South: more Southern voices, updating the scope of research, moving beyond the "Team China" monolith, steering between Chinese exceptionalism and identicalism, evaluating development impact, and local agency in a "digital Cold War."

Introduction

China has been engaged in digital initiatives such as telecommunications projects in the low- and middle-income countries of the Global South[1] since at least the 1980s (Luo 2019). The extent of this activity has increased significantly during the twenty first century starting with the digital components of the country's "Going Out" globalization strategy from 1999, which was succeeded by the "Belt and Road Initiative" (BRI) infrastructure investment strategy from 2013, and then the "Information Silk Road" which then became the "Digital Silk Road" component of BRI announced from 2015 onwards. In parallel, the remarkable growth of China's own digital economy – forming nine of the world's 20 largest Internet companies in 2022 (Clement 2022) – has partly driven, and to some extent been driven by, the overseas digital expansion of Chinese tech firms, including expansion in countries of the Global South.

This expansion is increasing with, for example, ambitious plans to grow China's digital trade (Shen 2021), a greater shift toward digital in China's international cooperation strategy particularly in the wake of Covid-19 (Buckley 2020; Wang 2022), and with some reorientation in Chinese digital investment focus from Global North to Global South amid China's "turbulent relationships with the major advanced economies" (Tanjangco et al. 2020, 6). China's digital expansion is not just driven by economic considerations but is also a central plank of China's foreign policy and global political ambitions: it is thus important of itself but also as the increasing foundational component of China's whole approach to globalization and international relations (Cheney 2019; Vila Seoane 2020). Some have therefore talked of China's "digital empire" and its strategies as "digital imperialism"

(Chalk 2019; Keane and Yu 2019). Whatever the terminology, China is now a major force in the digital development of Global South countries, with important implications for their digital economies, societies, policies, etc., and impacting critical dimensions of development including growth, inequality, sustainability, sovereignty, and security.

Yet literature to date on China and its role in the Global South has paid limited attention to the digital component of these growing interactions and there are calls for more research to be undertaken on this important issue given its significant development ramifications (see, among others, Cheney 2019; Erie and Streinz 2021; Hernandez 2019; Ly 2020; Shen 2018; Vila Seoane 2020). But what should the agenda be for this future research, based on what is already known? Despite the widespread agreement that the digital component of China's engagement with the Global South has been overlooked relative to other dimensions, the literature is growing. The literature has now reached the point where a systematic review is needed in order to understand the current state of knowledge, and to identify gaps that would represent future research priorities.

In this article, in seeking to achieve these twin aims, we first lay out the methods applied by this systematic literature review, and then present some general characteristics of the literature such as authorship, research design, and perspective. The main contribution of the article then follows. It outlines the different technologies and systems involved in China's digital expansion. It analyses current understanding of a set of cross-cutting issues emerging from the literature and of importance to Global South countries: synergies and tensions between different actors, strategies adopted by both state and business, approaches to design and implementation of digital systems, and the impact of China's digital expansion. In addition, it explicates two particularly contested issues affecting the relationship of Global South countries to China and the West: whether China is exporting "digital authoritarianism," and the implications of China's growing digital presence for digital governance at both global and national levels. The article ends by drawing out a six-part research agenda for future investigation of China's digital expansion in the Global South; a research agenda of growing import given the increasing scale and scope of this phenomenon.

Methods

In order to perform the literature search, keyword searches were undertaken on Google Scholar, using 20 separate searches based around different combinations of terms extracted from literature known to be relevant including "digital silk road" and "information silk road," together with more general terms such as "China" "digital economy," or "China" "digital trade" in combination with geographic terms "Africa," "Asia," and "Latin America." The search was first conducted in June 2021 and then updated in August 2022 selecting, in each case, the ten most highly-cited items for each of the 20 searches. In total, this produced 219 English-language items. We also contacted 18 scholars whose work appeared among highly-cited items, asking them for recommendations of key literature to include, which led to 22 items. This total of 241 items was reduced to 216 on elimination of duplicates.

The 216 items were then subject to an initial multi-researcher triage with 129 items eliminated due to being insufficiently relevant to the topic or – in a small number of cases – inaccessible, which reduced the number to 87 which were read in full. This step led to 12 items being eliminated on grounds that they were not specifically relevant to China's digital expansion in the Global South, with 75 items therefore being included in the full literature review. We do not claim that these 75 items represent the totality of all possible literature relating to the focal topic. However, given the search strategies and the ranking of Google Scholar items by citation, they will likely incorporate the more-influential literature in the field, and given the number of items included, they will likely be significantly representative of overall literature.

An analytical template was drafted based on three domains: the main theme of the paper, characteristics of the paper including authors and research design, and content of the paper including main findings. Initial analysis by the first and second authors was then undertaken for ten items using this template, as a result of which there was some further refinement. The finalized template was then applied the remaining 65 items by one author with cross-check of coding by a second author. The analyzed components were then compiled into the findings below.

Characterizing the literature on China's digital expansion in the Global South

General features

The identified literature on China's digital expansion in the Global South is all quite recent, with the earliest item being published in 2012 and roughly three quarters published in the three most-recent full years of the search, 2019-2021. Just over half of the items were journal articles[2], 20 were institutional publications with various labels (reports, briefings, working papers, etc.), 11 were book chapters, and the remaining six were two books, two short papers, a dissertation, and a conference paper.

The literature had a bi-modal distribution of author location with just over a quarter of first authors being US-based, a similar number being China-based, and the remainder drawn in small numbers from 20 different locations. As will be seen below, this bi-modality was also reflected to some extent in the perspectives expressed within the papers. There was a relative lack – 19% – of authors based in the Global South. As an instance, there were as many first authors based in Australia as there were in the whole of Africa, and most of the latter were located in South Africa.

Four disciplines dominated, as judged by the department or online profile of the first author. These were international studies including international relations, area/regional studies, business and management particularly international business, and communications and media studies. There were notably few – just five – from development studies despite its overwhelming focus on issues of the Global South; and none from information systems despite its overwhelming focus on digital technologies and systems.

Research design

In terms of the design of research within the literature surveyed, more than three-quarters of the sources used only secondary data. The minority (24%) using primary data split two-thirds:one-third between those including interviews and those undertaking text analysis. Empirical research has thus been a relative rarity. Of research based on text analysis, none of the sources was Global South-specific, and the interview-based research was strongly skewed toward interviews with Chinese actors. In total, only eight of the 75 papers included primary evidence from Global South sources, and only four drew the majority of their primary evidence from Global South sources.

The great majority (more than 85%) of papers made no explicit use of any theory or even conceptual framework. Of the ten that did, the application in four was light touch, meaning that the theory was mentioned within the findings of the paper but it was not used as the basis for the analysis. Two of the other six papers created a basic economic model linking the Internet to economic growth, and only four were in any way systematic in their application of a preexisting theory or framework to shape the analysis and findings of the paper.

The geographic focus of research design was generally quite broad in scope. Half of the studies covered many dozens of countries; encompassing all countries involved in BRI, for example. Conversely, and consistent with the limited extent of empirical research, there were relatively few studies focused on individual countries. Put another way, there were so far no country-specific studies for the great majority of Global South countries in which China is digitally engaged.

Turning to technological focus, about half of the literature was given over to general discussions covering all, or a significant spread, of the different technologies encompassed in China's digital expansion. Within this, the bulk of discussion was given over to the telecommunications infrastructure investments of the Digital Silk Road (DSR) programme. The remaining literature was split roughly evenly between items discussing infrastructure – particularly telecommunications infrastructure – and items discussing specific applications, most notably e-commerce and surveillance systems. Little specific attention was given so far to data other than in terms of data policy, and to emerging technologies such as 5G, Internet of Things, fintech, artificial intelligence, and autonomous vehicles which have been innovation priorities within China for some years (Bu et al. 2021). There was also a chronology here that reflects the history of Chinese digital engagement in the Global South. Earlier literature focused largely on telecommunications infrastructure, and only latterly have papers expanded beyond this to analyze the impact of platforms and applications like e-commerce and surveillance[3].

General perspective

Interpreting the perspective of a paper is a subjective process but this was undertaken on the basis of the descriptors attached to either China in general or to actions of the Chinese state or Chinese firms. Based on this, it can be argued that there are two contrasting clusters of literature: one Sino-philic, one Sino-phobic. One example of the former is a set of papers on the Digital Silk Road in *China International Studies*; a journal published under the sponsorship of China's Ministry of Foreign Affairs (Huang 2019; Luo 2019; Wang 2020). While analytical, these papers cast DSR in a solely positive light, summed up by one section heading, "China-Latin America Digital Silk Road: A Win-Win and All-Win Choice" (Luo 2019, 51). Others, too, ascribe positive characteristics and are largely uncritical of China and its digital expansion (e.g. Gong, Gu, and Teng 2019; Li 2019; Teng 2020; Zhao 2020) being what Wen (2020, 148) describes as "celebratory accounts."

The Sino-philic cluster is particularly – though not solely – associated with China-based authors. Conversely, and particularly emerging from US think-tanks, are accounts that largely characterize DSR and related actions by the Chinese state as part of a geopolitical strategy to maximize Chinese power by fair means or foul, to spread authoritarianism and undermine democracy, and to weaken US global power (e.g. Cheney 2019; Hemmings 2020; Hillman 2021a; Polyakova and Meserole 2019). As one example, DSR is described as being used by China "to increase geoeconomic competition and spread political illiberalism" (17) including "the deceptive use of information for hostile purposes" (18) such as "disinformation campaigns using big data" (19) (Cheney 2019).

While these two clusters did not form the majority of the literature analyzed here, both of these one-sided positions may be influential in setting a narrative. One sees the positions reflected in the media (e.g. Field and Smith 2021; Ren 2019) and they may also interact with policy. Papers published in a Ministry of Foreign Affairs-sponsored journal could conceivably influence policy in China and, in the US, Senate reports (e.g. Minority Staff, US Senate Committee on Foreign Relations 2020) have cited the think-tank authors and there are examples of the authors testifying before Congress (Hillman 2021b; Meserole 2022).

Whether at the two extremes in their views on China, or taking a more hybrid approach, the majority of the literature has been Sino-centric. That is, almost all papers focused on Chinese tech firms and/or on the Chinese state to the relative exclusion of Global South actors.

Overview of China's digital expansion

There is a tendency to associate China's digital activities in the Global South with the Belt and Road Initiative; specifically with its Digital Silk Road component, which was discussed under other terminology from 2015 (PRC 2015) but first explicitly mentioned at the May 2017 Beijing Belt and Road Forum (Xi 2017) and, subsequently, used with growing emphasis within BRI (Shen 2018; Triolo et al. 2020). However, as noted in the Introduction, this phenomenon long pre-dates Belt and Road's 2013 launch. Cooperation between China and Brazil on development of an earth resources satellite dates from 1988 (Luo 2019), while Huawei's first foray into the African telecommunications market came in 1998 (Jiang, Tonami, and Fejerskov 2016). Huawei and other Chinese ICT companies were supported as part of the "Going Out" internationalization strategy from 1999 (Gagliardone and Geall 2014), and ICT projects and investments continue to occur outside the Belt and Road Initiative (Tang 2020). The situation is therefore summarized stylistically by Figure 1.

China's digital activity in the Global South is sizeable, though figures vary widely and can be unclear whether they represent actual or intended investments, and just state or state plus private investments. For example, in specific relation to the Digital Silk Road[4], claims include: US$200bn overall invested by 2018 (Deeks 2018), US$17bn invested in projects completed by 2019 (Eder, Arecesati, and Mardell 2019), US$70bn committed in Africa in 2019 (Garcia 2019), US$8bn committed in Africa in 2021 (Chaudhury 2021). ICT broadly is the sector with the largest Chinese foreign direct investment with, for example, China's ICT investment in Latin America alone by 2017 said to be US$38bn (Hernandez 2019; Luo 2019). These investments, alongside direct sales, have led to equally huge revenue generation for Chinese tech firms. Again, as an example, "In 2018, Huawei generated $5.8 billion in revenue in Africa alone, 60% of which was through the sale of equipment and services and 40% through its phones" (Clémençot 2019). The importance of digital expansion to Chinese businesses varies across sectors: China's e-commerce giants make the great majority of their revenue in the Chinese market (albeit their vast size means their overseas operations are still sizeable) (Triolo et al. 2020), whereas telecommunications firms Huawei and ZTE make the majority of their revenue overseas (Agbebi, Xue, and Yu 2021; Das 2017).

The role of Chinese firms in the digital economies of Global South countries has also increased rapidly.

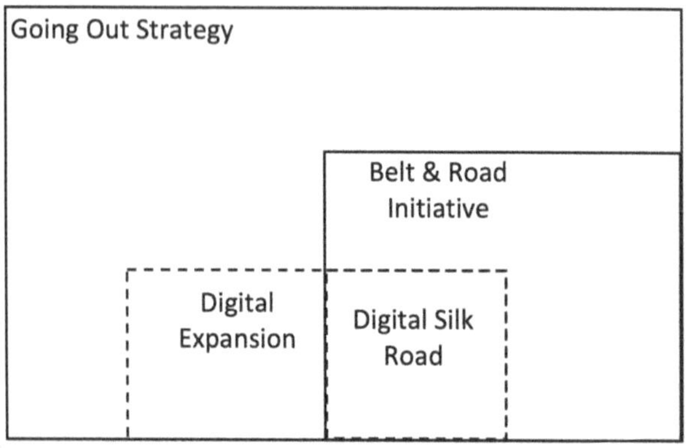

Figure 1. China's digital and global engagements with the Global South.

Looking at digital infrastructure projects specifically (see Figure 2's location map of major projects), firms such as Huawei and ZTE are dominant providers in a number of countries, with Huawei cited as "the foundation of Africa's telecom infrastructure" including 70% of the continent's 4G network (Djan and Owusu-Ansah 2020, 187; see also Ellis 2013, van der Lugt 2021, Wen 2020). Alongside this, state-owned firms such as China Telecom, China Unicom, and China Mobile have typically taken key responsibility for growth in strategic international telecommunications links such as land-based and undersea cables (Shen 2018; Wang 2020).

In all, Chinese firms and agencies have been involved in five main aspects of digital infrastructure (Gong and Li 2019; He 2019; Shen 2018; Shen 2020): international telecom infrastructure of "submarine, terrestrial, and satellite links" (Shen 2018); national telecom infrastructure such as 4G and 5G; retail digital devices such as modems and phones and tablets; data-oriented web services such as cloud, server, and data center infrastructure; and applications platforms such as e-commerce platforms, smart city (including surveillance) projects, and information-and-communication-technology-for-development (ICT4D) systems. These infrastructural layers plus underpinning institutional and physical and human infrastructure (particularly governance which covers standards, laws, norms, and policies, discussed separately below) are increasingly being understood as a package – a "Chinese technology stack" (see Figure 3) – that both benefits and requires the cooperation of multiple Chinese firms, and which creates cross-layer dependencies that raise barriers to competitors (Triolo et al. 2020).

The chronological shifts in literature noted above reflect a real historical progression in relation to the technology stack. The main focus of China's digital activity during the 1990s and 2000s was telecom infrastructure and then phones, with web services and applications platforms starting to emerge only during the later years of the 2010s (Hernandez 2019; Keane and Yu 2019; van der Lugt 2021). e-Commerce has been a particular concentration of the more-recent activity with one early example, Alibaba's investments in the India-based mobile-payment platform, Paytm, dating from mid-2015 (Gong and Li 2019).

This points to two aspects of China's digital economy applications platform expansion thus far that differ from the approach used for digital infrastructure (Das 2017; Keane et al. 2021; Naughton 2020; Triolo et al. 2020; Tang 2020; Tritto, He, and Junaedi 2020; Yang 2022; Zhou and Xue 2020). Expansion has been marked by leading private companies investing in existing players (presumably with the approval of state actors) – Daraz in Pakistan; Ascend Money in Thailand; Flipkart in India; Lazada, Tokopedia, Gojek, and Grab across South-East Asia; multiple small fintech platforms in Indonesia – rather than direct expansion. And, as the examples illustrate, there has been a focus on South-East and South Asia more than other locations: by comparison, as shown in Figure 2,

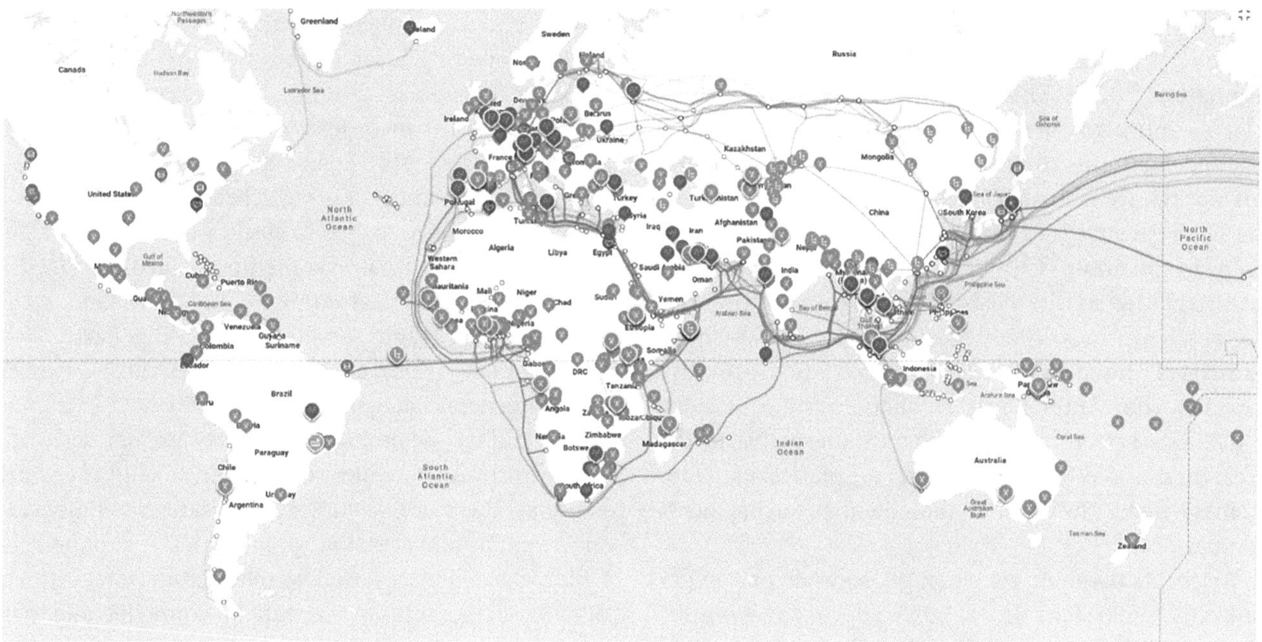

Figure 2. Chinese telecommunications infrastructure projects (ASPI 2023).

Figure 3. The Chinese technology stack.

digital infrastructure projects have focused in part on South-East Asia but also on China's borderlands and on Africa's coastal states. This has run in parallel with national and global institutional developments. e-Commerce figured more prominently in the 13th Five-Year Plan, which ran from 2016; within China's overall digital globalization plans, including Digital Silk Road; and in its 2016 submission to the World Trade Organization seeking to improve e-commerce for physical goods (Gao 2018; Huang 2019; Majcherczyk, and Shuqiang 2019; Wang 2020).

In a pattern seen in a number of more-recent digital initiatives, China's e-commerce expansion has often sought to follow the package approach noted above, for example, delivering a full e-commerce stack sufficient to create a "digital common market" (Naughton 2020). This has its technical elements – telecom infrastructure and platforms – but also financial and institutional components. For example, while not always welcomed by Global South governments, the Chinese state and leading digital firms have been keen to promote Chinese currency and financial infrastructure as the basis for cross-border transactions (Hemmings 2020; Shen 2018). Global South countries have been encouraged to join the Cross-Border Inter-Bank Payment System (CIPS), which was set up in 2015 to be an alternative to the West-based SWIFT. e-Commerce platforms from Chinese firms always offer the potential for payments in yuan.[5]

At the maximum, are attempts at what one might call an "ecosystem in a box" approach – multi-dimensional interventions that seek to develop e-commerce in Global South countries by simultaneously overcoming barriers of technological, physical, human, financial, and institutional infrastructure (Huang 2019; Luo 2019; Majcherczyk and Shuqiang 2019; Wang 2020). This is typified by Alibaba's Electronic World Trade Platform (eWTP). As well as being a lobbying initiative with a strong development rhetoric of helping small enterprise, eWTP is a trade facilitation initiative based on the company's own e-commerce platform but then building around that: physical transportation and logistics hubs, digital payment systems such as Alipay, digital and commercial training and advice for local entrepreneurs, and new digitized procedures and rules and norms for e-commerce-based trade (Hernandez 2019; Huang 2019; Johnston 2021; Triolo et al. 2020; Wang 2020; Yean 2018). Global South eWTP hubs were first set up in Malaysia's Digital Free Trade Zone in 2017 – with digital elements implemented particularly by Alibaba subsidiaries Cainiao (logistics) and Lazada (e-commerce) – and then in Rwanda and Ethiopia in succeeding years (Das 2017; Johnston 2021; Naughton 2020).

Of the other digital technologies shown in Figure 3, current literature only covers four in even limited detail: mobiles, use of satellite data, smart cities, and social media. Chinese mobile phone brands Xiaomi, Huawei, Oppo, Vivo, and Realme (the latter three all owned by BBK Electronics) occupy the third to seventh positions in the worldwide mobile phone market, and along with Transsion brands such as Tecno, Infinix, and Itel have roughly half the market in Africa (StatCounter 2023). They have been able to win this market share through low price, customization of phones to fit local market needs, and in a few cases by opening local assembly plants – for example, that of Transsion in Ethiopia, Huawei in Mexico, and ZTE in Brazil – in order to comply with local regulatory requirements (Djan and Owusu-Ansah 2020; Ellis 2013; Hernandez 2019; Micheli and Carrillo 2016).

Cutting across the tech stack, some parts of the literature discuss what is sometimes called the "Digital Belt and Road" Programme (Guo 2018; Guo et al. 2018; Jia 2017) and sometimes the "Big Earth Data Science Plan" (Kassenova and Duprey 2021). Part of a more general category of "digital science" (meaning use of digital technologies to foster greater scientific collaboration between China and Global South nations), these are scientific cooperation initiatives to share earth observation data, chiefly supplied by Chinese satellites as well as data from international organizations, among a group of countries and particularly those involved in the Belt and Road Initiative. While the initiatives have a relatively broad focus in seeking to use this data for achievement of the SDGs, there is a concentration on delivering environmental sustainability for the Global South countries involved. The small handful of papers discussing this are speculative; that is, reporting foreseen goals, success factors, and obstacles rather than actual development impacts.

Two application types receive some discussion; one being smart cities. Huawei and ZTE have more than 350 smart city projects in more than 60 countries, e.g., Manila Bay (Philippines), Lahore (Pakistan), Bentong (Malaysia), and Alibaba's City Brain (Malaysia) (Erie and Streinz 2021; Hemmings 2020; Hernandez 2019; Naughton 2020). These are starting to include e-government systems to improve public service delivery (Naughton 2020; Shen 2020) but to date these projects are mainly marketed and discussed as "safe cities" in relation to surveillance; an issue picked up separately below.

The other application area is social media and messaging; an element of overall expansion that especially gains attention from media and communications studies scholars (Keane and Wu 2018; Keane et al. 2021). Tencent has been active in this domain, pushing WeChat as a messaging app particularly in South-East Asia though with relatively limited success to date here, and even less so in other Global South markets (Triolo et al. 2020). TikTok has been more widely adopted, with particular success in India, at least until the 2020 ban following Indo-Chinese border clashes (Keane et al. 2021). Given the much greater adoption of these social media (as compared with Western services) by Chinese users, they provide a potential channel for learning and interaction between Chinese and Global South users (Li 2016), as well as a channel through which Chinese users based in the Global South seek to make sense of and share their experiences (Lu and Van Staden 2013).

Gaining even less research attention, the Chinese state and companies have also been active in development of human infrastructure, with actions ranging from donations of computers to schools, through scholarships for students to study digital-related topics in China and specific training programmes such as training for technicians to operate and maintain Chinese systems, to investments in local R&D centers (Gong and Li 2019; Huang 2019; Luo 2019; Wang 2020; Zhou and Xue 2020).

In all, the literature to date appears to be a partial reflection of the realities and trends of China's digital expansion in the Global South. This means, as discussed in the final section of this article, that there are lacunae that new research can usefully fill. Next, though, we review a number of issues that emerge within the literature reflecting commonalities across different types of digital activity.

Cross-cutting issues

Synergies and tensions

One Western stereotype of China's activities in the Global South is of "Team China" in which all Chinese actors – whether state, business or other – act in concert with a unified aim of advancing Chinese development and interests (Triolo et al. 2020; van der Lugt 2021). There is certainly evidence for joined-up activity.

First, between the Chinese state and Chinese tech firms. One aspect of this is finance, with Chinese government grants and state banking institution loans or lines of credit being used by Global South actors – typically national governments – to purchase goods and services from Chinese ICT companies (Tugendhat and Voo 2021). The sums are huge: by one estimate, state banks provided US$100bn of financing up to 2019 to support overseas expansion of Huawei alone (Hemmings 2020). Large specific examples include loans in 2006 and 2011 to Ethiopia totaling US$3.5bn, and in 2015 to India totaling US$2.5bn, all of which were used to pay for telecom infrastructure-related purchases from Huawei and ZTE (Gagliardone and Geall 2014; Lele and Roy 2019). These may not come with the neoliberal or social policy conditionalities of Western loans but they invariably come with the contractual conditionality that the money must be spent via Chinese contractors (Erie and Streinz 2021; Makundi, Huyse, and Develtere 2016).

While Chinese firms are generally happy to take on these contracts, sometimes the state has adopted "a combination of politics and business to encourage Chinese capital to participate" (Shen 2020, 44), leading Chinese tech firms to participate in state-initiated projects in the Global South in order to increase their chances of obtaining direct contracts from the state within China, and to obtain state support for other overseas ventures (Shen 2018). This highlights the second main connection between Chinese tech firms and the state, which is political. This relation is direct and overt in the case of state-owned enterprises such as China Mobile, China Unicom, and China Telecom. For others, "while Chinese corporations are not inherently instrumentalities of the Chinese state, they are still embedded within the party-state's systems of control" (Erie and Streinz 2021, 55). This is assisted by opaque ownership structures in the case of two key firms (Huawei, ZTE) that can allow for a measure of party control. That control is also exercised via the CCP cells within all companies, via legal requirements for data access, and via less formal mechanisms of pressure and inducement. As Kelly (2018) notes, these are not so much "private" but rather "less state" than state-owned enterprises (see also Tugendhat and Voo 2021).

There is also evidence for cooperation between Chinese companies, with state oversight. In formal terms, Chinese tech firms cooperate in funded projects; for example, Huawei and ZTE were both part of the US$1.6bn 3G infrastructure project in Ethiopia (Wen 2020), while Huawei and Hikvision provided complementary elements for a public security system in Brazil (Reis et al. 2021). Alongside this more formal and strategic collaboration, there has also been knowledge sharing. In Tanzania, the Chinese government encouraged more experienced firms to share knowledge with those which less experience; both technical expertise but also more informal "guidance on how to deal with local immigration, customs, taxation procedures and local labour laws as well as inter-cultural skills" (Makundi, Huyse, and Develtere 2016, 137). Looking more broadly, digital investments are used to facilitate non-digital investments; for instance, Alibaba's investment in cloud infrastructure in BRI countries "has served the purpose of 'paving the road and building the bridge' … for other Chinese companies in their overseas operations" (Shen 2018, 2689; see also Lele and Roy 2019). Mirroring this, investments in physical, e.g. transport infrastructure in BRI countries have been undertaken to enable movement of goods traded via Chinese e-commerce platforms (Das 2017).

On the other hand, there is some limited evidence of tensions between Chinese digital actors. This may be between companies, especially seen between Huawei and ZTE (Lin 2020), such as the public complaint by ZTE after Huawei won a data services contract in Ecuador despite ZTE being the lowest-cost bidder (Ellis 2013), or Huawei taking over contracts from ZTE in Africa including part of the Ethiopia 3G project (Wen 2020). Or it may be between state and business interests with geopolitical goals unable to completely override economic imperatives (Shen 2020; Wang, Bar, and Hong 2020). Shen (2020) instances this in the case of the Gilgit-Baltistan region of Pakistan. The Chinese state's desire for digital investments here stemmed from the region's adjacency to the politically-sensitive province of Xinjiang, but progress of digital projects stalled because the small, unstable local market did not justify the prioritization of these projects by China's tech firms. In general, though, evidence for these tensions and others – for example, between national and international digital policy with restrictions within the former hampering the latter, or between different agencies of the Chinese state[6] – remains largely "speculative" (Shen 2018; Shen 2021).

Strategy

Chinese state strategy

Publicity for bilateral and multilateral Digital Silk Road initiatives always emphasizes the mutual benefits for both China and the recipient countries (e.g. Huang 2019; Luo 2019) and that this "South-South cooperation" is doing development differently (Wen 2020). However, analysis of DSR-related policies and pronouncements within China – i.e., not intended for external consumption – finds little discourse relating to benefits for Global South countries (Shen 2018). Deriving from this, there is a literature that thus argues the rationale for DSR is: to deal with domestic over-capacity in production of digital goods; to help Chinese firms (digital and other) to expand overseas particularly into new markets and in competition with US firms; to assist internationalization of the renminbi; to provide a regional and then ultimately international digital ecosystem controlled by China not the US; to promote Internet-enabled inclusive globalization (a rather diffuse notion that could be related to greater inclusion of lower-income nations in globalization-based development); and more broadly to develop a positive image and political capital for China (Buckley 2020; Das 2017; He 2019; Hernandez 2019; Shen 2018; Triolo et al. 2020).

As one instance, specific analysis of China's ICT-related aid flows to Africa finds that these go to almost every country on the continent but are not correlated with size of the local telecom market; instead going particularly to smaller and poorer countries and to resource-rich countries (Wang, Bar, and Hong 2020). The explanation is that Chinese tech firms – at least the major players like Huawei and ZTE – need little help or guidance to themselves invest in large Global South markets. In these markets, the existence of Digital Silk Road facilitates but does not determine investment decisions (Vila Seoane 2020). In other markets, though, state-funded projects have been the "entry ticket" through which tech firms then obtain a cascade of further local contracts (Makundi, Huyse, and Develtere 2016). However, ICT aid such as DSR has not just been about opening up new digital markets, it is also linked to a transactional strategy in which funding has been used to build political links and support for China, particularly in countries with primary resources.

Notwithstanding the rhetoric of cooperation, this is largely a "tied aid"/"tied finance" approach (Gagliardone and Geall 2014; Malena 2021). Funding flows from China are used to implement ICT projects by Chinese tech firms and, at least based on the literature reviewed, the idea of helping develop local ICT firms or purchasing from non-Chinese sources is not notable (Luo 2019; Wang, Bar, and Hong 2020; Wen 2020). Claims of doing digital development differently to the West – "In contrast to the West, which rather stresses the commercial and enterprise-led side of development, China has been seeking a path that respects the national conditions and autonomy of African countries" (Huang 2019, 19) – may thus not at first sight appear correct. These elements of China's digital development strategy – primacy of domestic economic and political objectives and tied financing, plus others discussed below including asymmetrical trade, limited technology transfer, and retention of higher value-added elements of value chains – are familiar tropes from the West's approach to international development; particularly from the era of modernization but stretching well beyond that.

Having said this, even if not doing things particularly differently in terms of strategic purpose and methods, China is perceived as providing an alternative to the West. In financial terms, Western development programmes are seen as having "pulled out of infrastructure long ago, and started financing social [development] stuff instead" (Hellowell and Wakdok 2021, 51) including relatively limited emphasis on telecom infrastructure (Wang, Bar, and Hong 2020). China's approach is thus helping to address developmental priorities of Global South governments, particularly the specific favored plans of heads of state (Triolo et al. 2020). In perceptual terms, the Chinese narrative of "mutual benefit" is seen as "more reliable and … less insulting" than that of the West, given local politicians "like seeing their economies treated as business opportunities rather than places to run randomised trials for foreign aid" (Hellowell and Wakdok 2021, 50; see also The Economist 2022 and Wen 2020). At a geo-political level, some countries, such as the socialist regimes of Latin America, have willingly turned to China as an alternative to reliance on US digital infrastructure providers (Vila Seoane 2021; Wen 2020).

That willingness is also an indicator that Global South governments should not be cast as powerless dupes (van der Lugt 2021), with a few papers maintaining that decisions around Chinese digital development projects should be seen as more pull than push: driven more by recipient governments than by the Chinese state (Gagliardone 2020; Malena 2021; Neilson 2022). Additionally, while the process of discussions remains highly centralized to a very small group of high-level actors (Gong and Li 2019), in terms of content, there have been one or two recent signs of willingness of Chinese actors to consider more sourcing of local labor, technology transfer, and local data storage which may if realized get a bit closer to a reality of mutual benefits (Carrillo and Micheli 2020; Triolo et al. 2020). Such benefits, though, seem only likely to materialize if driven by specific policies of recipient governments: where they are absent, Chinese firms have fewer incentives to localize beyond the minimum necessary to serve local clients.

Chinese business strategy

The drivers to global expansion of Chinese tech firms reiterate the points just made: the pull of opportunity for profit, the push of competition, and saturation in the Chinese domestic market, alongside the encouragement and facilitation of government initiatives and policies (Lin 2020; Naughton 2020). In some instances, such as fintech, a further driver has been growing regulation of the Chinese market leading to migration of Chinese entrepreneurs to the digital "Wild West" of less-regulated Global South locations (Tritto et al. 2020).

A whole spectrum of positions within the literature offers explanations for the ability of Chinese tech firms to grow market share in the Global South that range from the straight illegality of collusion and corruption and theft of sensitive data, via use of state financing at below-market rates and sales of outdated surplus products, through to providing products that are cheaper and more suited to Global South markets, and to which competitors, particularly from the US, have paid insufficient attention (Djan and Owusu-Ansah 2020; Ellis 2013; Erie and Streinz 2021; Gagliardone and Geall 2014; Wen 2020). It is argued that Chinese tech firms are similar to Western counterparts in their capitalist business models but different in their strategic aims that, alongside profits, are politicized and nationalistic in seeking to help the Chinese state build its "political and economic influence" in the Global South (Wen 2020, 164). But the difference to Western firms may be overstated given, as one instance, the very tight historical links between economic interests of US multinationals and political interests of US state agencies in Latin America from the late nineteenth century onwards (Livingstone 2009).

Analysis of international business strategies looks at Huawei particularly and to a lesser degree, ZTE, and Alibaba. In Latin America, Huawei and ZTE adopted a "start-small" entry strategy that then progressed via development of local production and R&D facilities (Ellis 2013; Micheli and Carrillo 2016). That pattern has also been followed more broadly across the Global South, where these two firms have built on capabilities generated in the Chinese domestic market and focused first on smaller or less-developed overseas markets with relatively lower entry barriers before then moving to more competitive markets (Sun 2009 cited in Djan and Owusu-Ansah 2020; Micheli and Carrillo 2016; Wen 2020).

There are differences though between the state-aligned Huawei and the state-controlled ZTE: the latter brings prior state support and funding to its negotiations, focuses largely on government clients, and is tied more closely to the Chinese state's foreign policy priorities (Wen 2020). As noted above, the extent of state involvement in Huawei remains strong and a clearer contrast is made with Alibaba's relatively greater freedom from state control. For example, while Alibaba has undoubtedly benefited domestically from state support, its internationalization strategies seem to have been somewhat more driven by its own global priorities and/or by demand-pull from host country governments than is the case with Huawei (Lin 2020; Naughton 2020; Neilson 2022). The state clampdown on Chinese big tech – Alibaba particularly – from late 2020 may change this but had not yet appeared in the research reviewed here.

Design and implementation

With a tendency to focus on broad-brush issues and a dominance of social science disciplines that encompass more strategic and geo-political perspectives, there was relatively little focus within the literature on design and implementation of the Chinese technologies that are being diffused into the Global South. For instance, there is no clear evidence on whether Chinese tech firms design and implement differently to those of other countries, or on the proportion of products and projects that run into difficulties.

Positive arguments include the one noted above that Chinese firms may be better at designing for Global South markets. One strand argues these firms can transfer products and knowledge from serving lower-income (e.g. rural) markets in China, as Huawei did in its early days (Djan and Owusu-Ansah 2020; Wen 2020). Another strand argues for Chinese firms' ability to customize for local markets, though the only example given in the literature related to Chinese phones designed for the African market where, for example, Transsion's various brands, "include features that cater to the needs of local people including multiple SIM slots, long battery life, FM radio, anti-oil fingerprint (to withstand bad weather), camera exposures calibrated to darker skin tones, and … run in local languages such as Amharic and Swahili" (Hernandez 2019, 22).

On the other hand, there have been reports of implementation problems with Chinese digital projects including: the Bolivian government fining Huawei US$8m in 2010 for non-completion of a telecom infrastructure project (Ellis 2013); Huawei being fined in Costa Rica for collusion during bidding for a national 3G upgrade contract (Ellis 2013); Huawei and ZTE "ending up providing very poor-quality services that built a bad reputation for themselves" in Ethiopia (Gagliardone and Geall 2014; van der Lugt 2021); the China Unicom China-Myanmar international terrestrial cable launched in 2014 but not activated as of 2019 (Chan and Rawat 2019); the planned BRICS cable which "has not been successfully implemented" (Shen 2018, 2691); and the failure of some Baidu search products in Brazil, Egypt and Thailand (Keane et al. 2021).

In terms of approaches to implementation, there have been indications of mismatch between Chinese management practices and local norms and expectations (Neilson 2022), and one instance of Chinese actors taking a techno-centric and top-down approach that involved little beneficiary participation (Hernandez 2019). This would, for example, diverge significantly from the Principles for Digital Development created to guide good practice on digital projects in the Global South; a divergence that could explain some of the implementation failures (Heeks 2018). However, these implementation problems relate almost entirely only to telecom projects, and these have to be set alongside the many Chinese digital projects that are functioning as intended.

At the more strategic level of implementation, there is a perception among those in some Global South countries that Chinese digital firms adhere less closely to the law than Western counterparts (Erie and Streinz 2021); a finding that ties in with the wider estimate that, within BRI projects overall, more than one-third have encountered "major implementation problems—such as corruption scandals, labor violations, environmental hazards, and public protests" (Malik et al. 2021, 1). However, the prevalence and impact of these latter issues within digital projects is not known, nor how this compares with the implementation strategies of digital actors from other countries.

Impact

Despite reports of problems, there has been widespread implementation of Chinese digital systems in the Global South, and a final cross-cutting issue in some of the literature has been the impact of this activity. As noted above, China's digital expansion has brought economic benefits for Chinese digital companies, as demonstrated in their earnings from Global South markets but also in the knowledge and innovations derived from this engagement (Layton 2020). There are political benefits for the Chinese state though these tend to be assumed or asserted rather than empirically researched (Shen 2018; Wang, Bar, and Hong 2020).

Turning to the nations of the Global South, it should be at the core of the intended local impact but there is virtually no specific evidence as yet about the positive local economic impact of Digital Silk Road and other Chinese ICT investment. This, despite the huge size of these investments and the broader evidence of the positive socio-economic impact of both ICT infrastructure and overlying digital systems (Heeks 2018). Instead, the literature talks in generalized terms about China's investments having helped address digital infrastructural deficits and helped enhance the digitalization of local economies, or it gives very specific vignettes typically derived from news outlets (Das 2017; Djan and Owusu-Ansah 2020; Gong and Li 2019; Luo 2019; Wen 2020). In one of the few cases where more detailed analysis has been undertaken – of the China Telecom/Huawei-installed national ICT backbone in Tanzania – there was a mixed picture (Makundi, Huyse, and Develtere 2016; Pazi and Chatwin 2014). The backbone had enabled significant roll-out of e-banking, e-education, and e-government applications in the Tanzanian public sector. However, it was also heavily underutilized, leading to problems for the government in recouping its investment; a problem blamed on the government for pricing and policy constraints, and on the Chinese contractors for lack of local capacity building which "resulted in inadequate local operation and management of the infrastructure" (Agbebi, Xue, and Yu 2021, 9). Credible evidence of broader impacts of China's digital activity in the Global South – employment creation, technology transfer and local value-addition, local capability-building, and externalities such as price/quality improvements in local and Western competitors – is rarely found and, where provided, points so far to any benefits being at a level well below potential (Carrillo and Micheli 2020; Makundi, Huyse, and Develtere 2016; Rwehumbiza 2021).

Rather more has been written about negative impacts but the word "concerns" encapsulates the fact that these are often speculative worries rather than evidence-based. Two issues are technical constraints more than disbenefits: concerns about interoperability of Chinese digital systems with those from other countries which are already installed or in future could be, and sustainability in terms of ongoing maintenance and resilience of equipment (Djan and Owusu-Ansah 2020). The more disbenefit-related concerns relate to security, dependency, inequality, and environmental impact.

Discussion of cybersecurity includes issues of data sovereignty and surveillance by Chinese actors (Cheney 2019; Das 2017; Djan and Owusu-Ansah 2020; Ellis 2013; He 2019; Hemmings 2020; Shen 2020). Large datasets can be gathered about local populations with claims that they are being illicitly transferred to China though also with claims that weak local regulation means there is nothing illicit about such transfer (Erie and Streinz 2021; Kassenova and Duprey 2021). Perhaps best known was Huawei's provision of the digital infrastructure for the African Union (AU) headquarters in Addis Ababa, which was later found to have been transferring server contents to Shanghai every day for five years (Shahbaz 2018). Although the implications for Global South countries are yet to be really explored, the key concern is access to such data by the Chinese state. This arises in a general sense from an issue discussed above: the perceived close relationship between Chinese tech firms and the Chinese state or, at least, the extent of influence and control exercised by the state over Chinese firms. More specifically, this arises from China's National Intelligence Law that requires ICT companies to support the state in matters of intelligence, and which could enable Chinese authorities to access and use these datasets (Kassenova and Duprey 2021; Malena 2021; Peterson and Hoffman 2022).[7]

The extent to which concerns about data security are widespread in the Global South, though, is questionable (Malena 2021). The AU case, for example, seems to have aroused much more interest in the Global North than within Africa where the AU soon after signed new and expanded partnership agreements with Huawei (Triolo et al. 2020). More generally, US warnings about Huawei have been largely ignored in the Global South (Zhang, Alon, and Lattemann 2020). Perhaps more salient is the potential for Chinese state access to data to feed into the wider issue of the projection of "sharp power" – "manipulation of ideas, political perceptions and electoral processes" in order to further China's political interests (Nye 2018). This and even-sharper practices of cyber-espionage have characterized claimed activities including: use of Chinese-installed safe city projects to track those in neighboring countries such as Pakistan identified as terrorists by the Chinese government (Shen 2020); use of hacking and online misinformation to interfere in Global South elections to favor pro-Beijing candidates (Kliman 2019); and gathering intelligence on Asian geopolitical rivals (Insikt Group 2021).

Related to the security issue, China's digital expansion has been cast as a form of "digital colonization" (Shen 2020, 25) or "data colonialism" (Lele and Roy 2019, 49) in which China controls critical digital infrastructure, digital systems, and data flows and hence the foundations of countries' digital economies and broader digital society (Das 2017; Djan and Owusu-Ansah 2020; Ellis 2013; Gravett 2020; Kassenova and Duprey 2021). Global South countries are seen to therefore be technologically dependent on China for these key underpinnings of economic and social development, and to have enabled the Chinese state to use these as points of leverage or even vulnerability. These countries may also be moving into relations of financial dependency. While debt relating specifically to digital infrastructure was not discussed in the literature, China's international development finance overall runs at a "31-to-1 ratio of loans to grants … priced at relatively high interest rates" and directed primarily at "state-owned companies, state-owned banks, special purpose vehicles, joint ventures, and private sector institutions" which have debts – largely under-reported – of hundreds of billions of US dollars (Malik et al. 2021, 1). Accumulation and servicing of this debt represents a leverage point for China over these Global South entities.

Also echoing the notion that China's digital expansion represents a form of economic and political colonialism (Gravett 2020; Shen 2020) are concerns that it is fostering inequality between and within countries. e-Commerce may be something of an exception but, as noted above, in relation to Digital Silk Road and related digital infrastructure projects, it is Chinese firms which implement digital investments rather than their being used as the base to help develop local companies (e.g. Luo 2019; Wang 2020). Where local partnerships and joint ventures are involved, literature so far gives the sense that they are seen by Chinese actors as a necessary evil – e.g. to fit with local sourcing or financial regulations – with local value-addition and capacity-building being kept to a minimum (Carrillo and Micheli 2020; Ellis 2013; Makundi, Huyse, and Develtere 2016). The track record has been relatively poor on moving local staff into higher-level managerial or technical roles or on transferring technology and know-how to local firms (Makundi, Huyse, and Develtere 2016). So-called "R&D centers" are small and focus mainly on adapting Chinese software to local requirements, while 90% by value of components in assembly operations are from China (Carrillo and Micheli 2020; Micheli and Carrillo 2016).

Where data is captured from local consumers or citizens, it is the Chinese firms which extract the value from this rather than local data sources: data mining seen as akin to colonial and neo-colonial mining of physical resources (Gravett 2020; Vila Seoane 2020). Similarly, Chinese e-commerce platforms focus largely on exports from China (Ambalov and Heim 2020; Wang 2020). At most, if there is a more general increase in trade, it is an asymmetrical model: increasing trade in primary products from the Global South countries to China and manufactured goods moving in the opposite direction (Gagliardone and Geall 2014; Wang 2020). If primary products are successfully exported, then Chinese platforms often not only control sales and delivery in China but also take over the upstream in-country and cross-border supply chain, meaning limited value retention within the producer country (Yang 2022). Even where, as in the eWTP initiatives, there are concerted efforts to overcome local barriers to export, the very low level of export and digital capacities of local enterprises, the existence of non-tariff barriers, and asymmetrical import taxes mean exports from China to the country will probably exceed exports from the country (Hernandez 2019). There are thus fears that e-commerce platforms are a "Trojan Horse" for Chinese exports that enable Chinese exporters to drive local competitors out of business, enable Chinese e-commerce platforms to dominate local markets, and fail to enable a significant increase in export value-addition from the Global South (Gao 2018; Hemmings 2020; Neilson 2022; Yean 2018).

All of this – lack of development of the local digital economy, data extractivism, and growth in trade asymmetries – can therefore increase economic inequality between China and the recipient countries. As already noted, Chinese-led digital globalization has been promoted as an alternative to US-led neoliberal globalization; particularly sold as "inclusive globalization" that will reduce inequalities and be more recipient-centric than the approach of Western nations

(Hernandez 2019; Neilson 2022; Shen 2018). The evidence presented here suggests differences to Western models are questionable. Analysis of Alibaba/eWTP discourse, for example, shows it to promote a business-led, free-trade, small-state approach to development entirely congruent with the tenets of neoliberal globalization (Vila Seoane 2020). In a "meet the new boss, same as the old boss" scenario, Western digital oligopolies and monopolies and dependencies may simply be replaced by Chinese equivalents, and benefits may flow far more to their country rather than the Global South country (Vila Seoane 2020).

There may also be an increase in within-country inequalities. For example, Chinese e-commerce is likely to see a rise in inequality between the relatively few more-capable local enterprises that can make use of China's digitally-enabled trade, and the majority of local enterprises that cannot; and between those relatively-excluded groups that Chinese inclusivity favors (young people, women) and those which it does not ("ethnic minorities, indigenous communities, the LGBT community, and older people") (Vila Seoane 2020, 78). BRI more broadly is seen to have sometimes increased inequalities within recipient countries in part because it is negotiated only with local elites, to whom financial and political gains will flow, raising inequalities between them and non-elite groups in the country (Shen 2020). Direct evidence of this in relation to digital is not yet present but DSR is a state-centric model that makes little direct attempt to bring the benefits of digitalization to other stakeholders such as the private sector, let alone civil society (Gagliardone 2020).

Lastly in relation to concerns, China's digital expansion is seen to impact environmental sustainability through its carbon footprint and e-waste. In general terms, digital expansion of any kind is directly associated with growing pollution and with other indirect effects (Heeks 2018). For instance, growth in e-commerce will create a larger production- and transportation-related carbon footprint, and an increase in the waste and hazardous chemicals associated with packaging (Hernandez 2019). However, this is true generally of digital rather than being a particular feature of Chinese firms. China's ICT companies are reported as relatively poor or low-transparency performers in environmental terms but no empirical research was found on this topic (Hernandez 2019).

Does all of this matter to those in the Global South? Care must be taken to find some middle ground between the assumption that these concerns matter little to lower-income countries concerned to accelerate economic development, and the assumption that all countries and stakeholders value these concerns as much as some Global North stakeholders (Triolo et al. 2020). Equally, and as discussed already vis-a-vis strategy, care must be taken to avoid the trap of Chinese exceptionalism. Not just in relation to inequality, as already noted, but also in relation to security, dependency and environmental damage, all of these types of impacts have also been associated with the digital activities of Western states and companies (e.g. Kshetri 2015; Kwet 2019).

Domain-specific issues

Exporting digital authoritarianism?

Chinese firms have sold surveillance-related digital systems either explicitly, e.g. video surveillance systems, or implicitly, e.g. telecommunications management software that can be used to monitor calls and messages (Gravett 2022; van der Lugt 2021). A key vehicle for the explicit route has been various "safe city" projects around the world utilizing digital technologies developed in China including – and particularly – in Xinjiang province (Erie and Streinz 2021; Layton 2020; Shen 2020; van der Lugt 2021). For example, the Lahore safe city system installed by Huawei has a command center storing big data from sensors around the city and analyzing it using artificial intelligence, with the city-wide system involving "some 8000 high-grade CCTV cameras, 4G wireless connectivity, facial recognition, automated vehicle number plate recognition, multiple tracking options, integrated communication platforms, geographic information systems and specialized apps on security personnel's smartphones" (Layton 2020, 880-881). These can be understood as part of a more general digital surveillance stack for which China is seen as both role model and supplier: firewalls and other technologies to control and block information flows, identification devices including video cameras and fingerprint scanners, surveillance software (including growing use of artificial intelligence) to recognize and analyze populations' physical and digital actions, with cloud/telecom infrastructure and legal frameworks to underpin this (Cheney 2019; Peterson and Hoffman 2022). Locations of projects using Chinese surveillance technologies are shown in Figure 4.

While the explicit surveillance technologies are promoted as systems to support local authorities in fighting crime, there are concerns about more political applications of the technology; for example, the Pakistan government potentially using Chinese-supplied digital infrastructure and systems to strengthen its control including over marginalized groups within the country such as ethnic minorities (Shen 2020). Such potential has been seen in practice with instances of use of these systems in Zimbabwe and Zambia and Uganda to block or surveil the communications of political opponents (Gagliardone and Geall 2014; Parkinson, Bariyo, and Chin 2019; Woodhams 2020).

Put together this all crystallizes in the concern that China is exporting a "digital authoritarianism" model that threatens rights and freedoms across the Global South. This sees China's digital actions entrenching authoritarian and illiberal regimes, nudging more democratic regimes toward the authoritarian end of the spectrum and, more generally, creating a new undemocratic world order (Gravett 2022; Hemmings 2020; Kliman 2019; Lele and Roy 2019; Polyakova and Meserole 2019):

> "A central pillar of China's Digital Silk Road is using technology to further its model of political illiberalism, which undermines democracy and human rights (11). … Through the Digital Silk Road, China aims to export digital authoritarianism to alter the current international order (16)" (Cheney 2019, 11, 16)

Three cautions are required. First, there are a lot of "coulds," "mays," and "mights" in the writing. As with other aspects of China's digital expansion, the concerns of Western writers sometimes run ahead of hard evidence, with many assumptions being made about China and political use of ICT in the Global South and with claims that: "the perception of Chinese surveillance tech as particularly effective and sophisticated is not matched by the actuality of its chaotic implementation" (Gagliardone 2020, 2; see also Feldstein 2019). In part, this may arise from design-reality gaps: that features of, say, the "Xinjiang model" may not be readily replicable outside China (Layton 2020). Evidence on causal links may also be weak. Looking at just one country, van der Lugt (2021) performs a rare forensic analysis of the potential causal mechanisms that could link sale of Chinese ICT in Ethiopia to greater use of digital systems by the Ethiopian government to control its population. A number of the links – that China is training local officials in surveillance techniques, that the Ethiopian government is requesting surveillance tools specifically from China, that the government is turning to China because other countries will not supply surveillance systems – find little or no evidence. Absence of evidence is not evidence of absence but this work is reminder that it is too easy to fill in gaps in a causal chain without proper evidence.

Second, as elsewhere, it is important to avoid the trap of Chinese exceptionalism – in this case, assuming the Chinese state and Chinese firms are the only ones supporting use of surveillance technology in the Global South. They are of course not. Rather than a one-to-few picture of China supplying technology to a few dictatorial regimes, the reality is many-to-many with

Figure 4. Chinese surveillance-related digital projects (ASPI 2023).

Chinese and Western firms supplying regimes across the political spectrum (Feldstein 2019; Gagliardone 2020; see Figure 5). There are examples of firms and agencies from the US, UK, Canada, France, Germany, Italy, Switzerland, Israel, and other Western nations providing surveillance technology, including use for surveillance of political opponents in Ethiopia, Rwanda, and other countries (Erie and Streinz 2021; Feldstein 2019; Marczak et al. 2018; Peterson and Hoffman 2022; van der Lugt 2021; Woodhams 2020). Hence, for example in Ethiopia, it is likely that "the outcome would not be so different if the Ethiopian government did not use Chinese ICT" (van der Lugt 2021, 338). Some Western surveillance companies do also have connections to their national states which gather, analyze, and utilize data in their own interests: think of the revelations of Edward Snowden or of the main encryption provider to Global South states having been a CIA front for decades during the twentieth century (Gagliardone 2020; Miller 2020).

Third, even though there may be benefits for the Chinese state, it may not always be the main actor: "It appears that on the Chinese side it is the commercial interests of Chinese firms, rather than the geopolitical interests of the Chinese government, that is driving involvement in Ethiopia ... the main Chinese actor involved in the digitization of Ethiopia does not seem to be the Chinese Communist Party (CCP) or the central state, but commercial and state-owned enterprises. This does not preclude 'Chinese influence' (i.e., state influence) but points to the complexity of the reality on the ground" (van der Lugt 2021, 339; see also Gagliardone 2020). Support for innovation is one commercial interest for Chinese tech companies as technologies such as artificial intelligence can be tested and innovated in a broader range of environments and datasets than available within China (Cheney 2019; Layton 2020; Vila Seoane 2021). As a specific example, Chinese artificial intelligence (AI) firm, CloudWalk Technology, is seen as a main beneficiary of its installation of facial recognition systems at key entry/exit points and transport hubs in Zimbabwe; building an ability to recognize darker skin tones that could then be exported to other countries (Hernandez 2019, Reddy 2021).

Local actors and agency must also be recognized: "The focus in Western media on China's export of surveillance technology to Ethiopia attributes most of the agency to Chinese firms and the Chinese state. However, this study has found that the Ethiopian government has the agency to independently choose what technology it acquires and from where" (van der Lugt

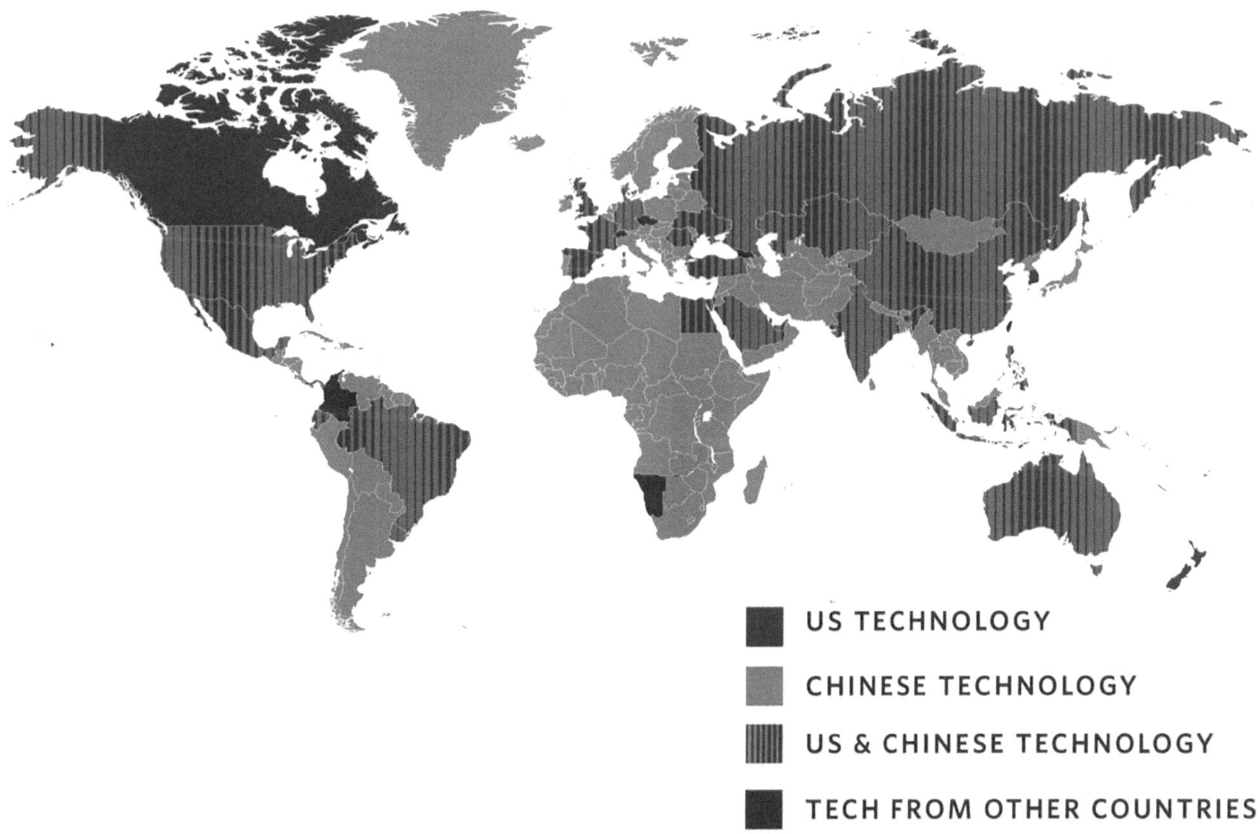

Figure 5. Surveillance technology origin (Feldstein 2019).

2021, 339). Others too, see the pull of demand from Global South governments having as much or more influence than some concerted attempt to export China's model of digital authoritarianism (Erie and Streinz 2021; Feldstein 2019; Triolo et al. 2020). The same recognition of agency should also apply to use of the technology: Chinese firms may have installed systems and shown how to use them, but local agents should be seen as largely responsible for determining how the systems are actually put to use (Gagliardone 2020).

One should not swing too far the other way. Assisted by concessionary state finance, Chinese firms are now far and away the biggest suppliers of surveillance technology in the Global South, with Hikvision and Dahua producing around 40% of the world's surveillance cameras, while "Huawei alone is responsible for providing AI surveillance technology to at least fifty countries worldwide" including dozens of BRI countries (Feldstein 2019, 8; see also Hillman 2021a; Peterson and Hoffman 2022). Chinese firms also differ from Western counterparts in more often implementing and managing systems rather than just selling them, in their greater proximity to the state, and in facing no domestic pressures from state or public to limit who they do business with (Gravett 2022; Malena 2021). Nonetheless, overall, the simple formulation that actions and interests of the Chinese state are fomenting a growth in digital authoritarianism in the Global South – and certainly the idea that this would not happen in China's absence – is questionable and remains to be further investigated.

Global division in digital governance and standards?

As illustrated by the foundational layer of the technology stack (Figure 3), China's digital expansion is not merely technological but also institutional. Digital infrastructure and systems come bound up with at least three institutional components (Erie and Streinz 2021; Hemmings 2020). There are informal norms, for example, relating to everything from management culture to views on human rights. There are more formal norms that constitute mechanisms and processes, such as choice of currency for e-commerce transactions. And there are formal institutions in the form of laws, policies, regulations, and standards.

It is the latter that are the main focus here and Global South countries are impacted by three main and overlapping domains of Chinese digital governance. Control of the physical foundation of digital infrastructure is undertaken by cyber/Internet governance and digital standards. Control over the data flows that move over these physical foundations is covered by data governance. Lastly, service and application layers require their own governance such as digital trade/e-commerce governance or governance of digital surveillance.

As a generalization, China has increasingly adopted its own position that is different from that of the earlier-dominant West, and has sought allies for its position from the Global South (Tugendhat and Voo 2021). It has sought to balance control and connection by advocating sovereign national control rather than laissez-faire or solely-international regulation, and locates this within a global system governed by a regime of inter-governmental institutions in which only states are represented rather than a regime of multi-stakeholder institutions that give voice to civil society (Arsene 2012; Gao 2018; Kassenova and Duprey 2021; Shen 2016). Hence, for example, its attempt to have control over Internet resource allocation transferred from the multi-stakeholder Internet Corporation for Assigned Names and Numbers, ICANN, to the inter-governmental International Telecommunication Union.

A key digital governance statement of relevance is "the International Strategy of Cooperation on Cyberspace jointly issued by the Chinese Ministry of Foreign Affairs and the Cyberspace Administration of China in March 2017" (Luo 2019, 56). While containing what could appear to be generic formulations about openness, fairness, and cooperation, it also has a particular Chinese perspective on cyber and data sovereignty (van der Lugt 2021). This restricts control of digital governance to the state, asserts the right of individual nation-states to control over the Internet within their own borders, and is quite restrictive in relation to cross-border data transfers (Cheney 2019; Kassenova and Duprey 2021). Some literature has therefore differentiated this from – and even seen it as in conflict with – more open digital policies in the West, while noting that the Chinese position may contain its own tensions. The version of digital sovereignty being promoted by the Chinese state is seen as antipathetic to cross-border data flows at the same time as it supports extraction of value from local data by Chinese companies and, potentially, by the Chinese state (Liu 2021; Triolo et al. 2020). A vision advocating national digital control at the same time as growing reliance on Chinese digital infrastructure could mean Global South governments are ceding control to China (Erie and Streinz 2021).

Notwithstanding any contradictions, this approach to digital governance is something that China is promoting in global digital advisory forums such the Internet Governance Forum or the UN's Group of Government Experts on digital development, in digital resource allocation bodies such as ICANN, and in discussions about digital trade and e-commerce in the World Trade Organization (Erie and Streinz 2021 Gao 2018,; Liu 2012; Shen 2016). Alongside these global forums, Chinese officials and official channels offer bilateral training and advice to Global South countries on development of local laws and policies based on China's experience (Huang 2019; Luo 2019). While it is debatable whether this advice seeks to directly promote replication of China's own national model (Gagliardone 2020), China is using relational, discursive and technological power to promote its approach to digital governance and to generate a support base for that approach within the Global South.

In building a network of support for its views across the Global South, the Chinese state continues to refer to China as a "developing country" and uses this as the basis for the claim that it can play the lead role to "vigorously represent the opinions of developing countries" in the development of a new regime of global digital governance; one which – not without some validity – it casts as having been shaped to date in the interests of the Global North, and the US in particular (Huang 2019; Luo 2019). The narrative of a self-determined alternative to Western domination or even neocolonialism, and of national governmental control and stability combined with economic growth through Chinese delivery of digital development infrastructure and services is seen as a means to gain support among Global South countries for China's particular views on Internet governance (Kliman 2019; van der Lugt 2021). With China presenting itself as a role model for digital sovereignty with digitally-enabled growth, this narrative does indeed find an appeal, even among democratic governments, and despite the potential costs of more limited global connection, of greater dependency on China, and of the growing opportunity for China to leverage its "infrastructural power" (Erie and Streinz 2021, 86; see also Tugendhat and Voo 2021).

Related to this global digital governance agenda has been China's promotion of its own technical standards, typically in competition with those set by Western actors, following "a popular saying in China … that third-tier companies make products, second-tier companies make technology, first-tier companies make standards" (Seaman 2020, 3). The literature has focused on this – albeit outside the scope of the search undertaken for this article – including the process of standards development within China (Gao, Gao, and Liu 2021; Murphree and Breznitz 2018) and China's actions in global bodies such as the ITU to promote its standards (Hoffmann, Lazanski, and Taylor 2020; Kim, Lee, and Kwak 2020). This sees China as having first sought to catch-up with standards and standards-setting, for example on 3 G and 4 G, and now being intent on taking a lead, for example on 5 G, artificial intelligence, Internet of Things, and blockchain.

This and the literature identified in the course of the search for this article makes reference to the perceived role of Global South countries, as allies to be enrolled by China into support for its standards (Triolo et al. 2020; Tugendhat and Voo 2021). Growing adoption of Chinese standards is seen as occurring almost by stealth through the spread of all elements of the Chinese digital stack which embed those standards; something the Chinese state has facilitated (Erie and Streinz 2021; Kliman 2019; Naughton 2020). But the state has also taken a more direct and proactive role in promotion of Chinese standards, with the Belt and Road Initiative being a key vehicle. In 2015, the Chinese state created a small group of officials to promote Chinese standards in BRI countries and, in 2017, laid out the BRI Connectivity and Standards Action Plan (Lele and Roy 2019; Malena 2021). Dozens of Global South countries have now signed standards recognition agreements with China, and information provision and translation facilities about Chinese standards have been a formal part of wider BRI since 2019 (Seaman 2020).

The rapid rise in participation of Chinese actors in standards-setting or -advocating bodies such as the ITU, International Organization for Standardization, Institute of Electrical and Electronics Engineers, and the Internet Engineering Task Force has led to some pushback from the US (Erie and Streinz 2021; Liu 2012; Shen 2016). In parallel, and partly in response to institutional resistance it finds in its bid to shape global standards, China has been creating its own digital governance groups, and there are suggestions of China creating its own Asian regional standards outwith the global bodies; something which might create another dimension for conflict between China and the West within the Global South (Lele and Roy 2019; Triolo et al. 2020).

In positing this potential – or actual – conflict with the West over digital governance, the literature typically seeks to differentiate China's stance from that of the West along dimensions of market vs. state, civil society vs. state, and the simplistic formulation of freedom vs. sovereignty. Yet, while the content of China's approach may be different, the underlying driving forces – to promote its own national interests, to promote its own digital multinationals, and to partly remake the Global South in its own digital image – are not that different from those seen with Western countries; the US particularly (Gao 2018; McCarthy 2015). Western attempts to point out the contradictions, even hypocrisy, of China's stance on digital governance may find their critiques ring a little hollow in the wake of the Snowden revelations or the Cambridge Analytica scandal (Erie and Streinz 2021).

Digital policy implications

Echoing the perspectives just outlined, the main narrative running through the literature in relation to digital policy implications is that of the "new digital Cold War." This and similar terminologies posit the Global South as a site of digital competition or even conflict between China and Western powers, with China particularly seen to challenge US digital hegemony; a challenge that extends earlier contention in the material sphere of territory and physical resources into the immaterial sphere of data, governance, and standards (Cheney 2019; Das 2017; Hemmings 2020; Kliman 2019; Malena 2021; Shen 2020; Triolo et al. 2020; Zhao 2020). While the Cold War narrative is criticized, Global South countries do increasingly perceive themselves to be the battleground for superpower conflict (Mukherjee 2020; Namingit and Haddad 2020).

However, to date in the literature, the focus remains the superpowers and where policies are discussed, they are those of China and the West. China's policies are as outlined previously and are seen as challenged by competing initiatives from the US, EU, and Japan (Wang 2020; Zhao 2020). These include the G7's Build Back Better World and the EU's Global Gateway, though the scope, actuality, and digital content of these remains unclear – responses have sometimes been limited or, in the case of the EU, fractured (Triolo et al. 2020). Discussions about global digital governance in the sampled literature focus on the actions of China and, to a lesser degree, the reactions of the US and other Western powers (Liu 2012; Negro 2020; Peterson and Hoffman 2022; Polyakova and Meserole 2019; Shen 2016). Barring one exception that analyses an instance of African country support within ITU for Chinese "new Internet protocol" proposals (Tugendhat and Voo, 2021), these discussions cast Global South countries, if mentioned at all, in a reactive role that is subservient to Chinese or Western interests. Other accounts treat the Global South as something akin to a blank, undifferentiated *terra nullius* on which the new digital Great Game will be played out: "in developing nations where digital connectivity is essentially absent" (Cheney 2019, 12), "Several underdeveloped states ... are in the pre-steam period" (Ly 2020, 12). Such views are quite wrong given the majority of the world's Internet users are now in the Global South, and given the role – acknowledged above – of local agency.

Yet recommendations for programmes and policies in light of China's digital expansion, at least in the English-language literature surveyed here, also give limited consideration to the Global South; instead mainly addressing policy of the Western powers even though this may mean the Global South is thereby under represented or marginalized (Naughton 2020; Peterson and Hoffman 2022; Zhao 2020). An example, in relation to digital surveillance exports from China, is recommendations for the US-led Western powers to counteract China's global plan for change: through much greater financing for digital infrastructure in the Global South, controls on exports of surveillance technologies, and a competing democratic model for use of surveillance technology (Polyakova and Meserole 2019; Woodhams 2020).

There were three limited exceptions to this side-lining of Global South policy recommendations. Two papers discuss the policy implications for India's own digital expansion of China's Global South activities (Lele and Roy 2019; Rawat and Chan 2018). These recommend that India should go deeper rather than broader: building a digital cooperation model that focuses on regional neighbors rather than all of the Global South, concentrating on technological niches where it can have an advantage, and adopting a transparent approach of mutual benefit in order to distinguish itself from China's approach. Three papers from pro-China writers took a paternalistic approach that called for DSR-recipient countries to simply align their digital policies with those of China especially on issues such as data/digital security and technical standards (Luo 2019; Wang 2020; Zhou and Xue 2020). Three papers, and without specifics, advocate Global South countries should adopt an approach of balance: balancing the benefits of low-cost technologies against security and other risks by seeking to minimize the latter; balancing the benefits of immediate access to technology against longer-term benefits of building local capacity; setting Western and Chinese firms to compete against each other to offer the best deal; developing EU links and regional and multilateral digital governance institutions as a bulwark against Sino-US techno-nationalism; and, more generally, "hedging" to avoid a one-sided pro-China or pro-US position that would risk antagonizing the other side (Lele and Roy 2019; Mukherjee 2020; Vila Seoane 2021).

As yet, though, all of the needed governance elements identified here that arise with China's growing digital presence – the geopolitical steer between major digital powers, the formation of digital policy, the passage of digital/data laws, etc. – remain under-developed in the Global South, as do related recommendations in the literature (Erie and Streinz 2021; Gravett 2020).

The future research agenda

Given the limited extent of systematic research so far undertaken on China's digital expansion in the Global South, below, six specific directions for future research are drawn out from the literature review. These specifics, though, sit within a general requirement for more research on this topic (Gagliardone and Geall 2014; Hillman 2021a). Calls in the literature for additional research are most-pronounced in relation to the Digital Silk Road component of the Belt and Road Initiative. Even foundational details of DSR – investments, companies, timescale, geographical scope, mapping of projects and countries involved – are incomplete (Hernandez 2019; Tugendhat and Voo 2021); something hampered by the fact that "The DSR ... shows a flurry of discourse production that can often obscure the actual operative mechanisms and reality on the ground" (Erie and Streinz 2021, 48) which "make it difficult to assess on its own terms how successfully the Chinese government's program has been implemented" (Tugendhat and Voo 2021, 4-5).

More Southern voices

Our above analysis of the literature showed an absence of Southern voices in a number of ways that future research will need to address. Authors from the Global South need to form a greater presence within the literature. This, in turn, may help address two other necessities: more primary research that draws evidence directly from Global South stakeholders, and more research on individual countries, particularly those in Africa. The local stakeholders who need to be heard from include the government policy-makers seeking to regulate digital, the officials signing deals with Chinese actors, those working for Chinese digital companies and for local firms competing or collaborating with Chinese digital companies, those consuming Chinese digital goods and services, and contextual stakeholders including local universities and NGOs. Within these groups, those who traditionally benefit less from digital and who so far do not figure in the literature particularly need to be heard from: women, older people, those with disabilities, ethnic minorities, etc. While the principal focus will be on policy, practice, and impact within individual Global South countries, growth in China's digital-related activity in international organizations and forums means Global South representatives in these milieu will also need to be included in research. There can also be an investigation of Chinese-heritage diaspora in the Global South. While sometimes a target market for Chinese platforms, there remains a gap around understanding the role of the diaspora not just as consumers but also as producers, investors and/or facilitators in relation to China's digital expansion.

Updating the scope of research

Looking at the layers of the Chinese technology stack (Figure 3), there has been – reflecting the historical focus of investment – a significant concentration of research to date on national telecommunications infrastructure. The layer below this had received limited attention in the literature surveyed, thus leaving a gap for more work on international telecommunications: submarine, terrestrial, and satellite. However, the main gap relates to research to catch up with the higher levels of the stack which in many cases have been the locus for relatively more-recent investments and projects. This applies to all devices, though perhaps particularly to those other than phones – tablets, PCs, modems, etc. – which were not discussed at all in the reviewed literature. And it applies to all types of web-based data services: cloud, server farms, and data centers.

In relation to applications, e-commerce has been investigated to some extent but fintech and social media much less so. The surveillance aspects of smart or safe cities have attracted some attention but other application areas need to be researched such as traffic and pollution management, and e-governance systems. This overlaps with a requirement for research on what can be called Chinese ICT4D projects – application of information and communication technologies for development goals including health, education, public service delivery, and agricultural development which themselves represent an under-developed opportunity area for China to make a clear and positive contribution to development of lower-income nations.

Research will also be needed to address emerging technologies that have been prioritized by the Chinese state (Naughton 2020; Triolo et al. 2020) but which are not yet adequately represented in the literature including artificial intelligence, blockchain, Internet of Things, and autonomous vehicles. The same applies to the non-technological elements that are integral to formation of the Chinese tech stack. The role of data in China's digital expansion must be studied further given its much greater salience within all digital systems in recent years, particularly analyzing issues of ownership, sovereignty and value extraction from data gathered in Global South countries. Other elements warranting further work are the development of human infrastructure in the form of skills and other capabilities, and the financial and institutional foundations for the tech stack.

Finally, there are broader trends that warrant research given they have more-recently started to impact China's digital expansion in the Global South. These include the impetus to digitalization arising from Covid and any outrun from this as the world moves toward post-Covid; the impact on Global South activities of Chinese tech firms following the Chinese government clampdown on big tech that began in late 2020; the implications for Global South countries of the responses to China's digital activities from the US, Europe, Japan, and others; the collective impact of the tech stack, from the realities of technical interoperability through to the exact nature of any lock-in that occurs for Global South users; and growing tensions around underlying digital technologies not yet explicitly discussed within the tech stack such as semiconductors and operating systems.

Beyond the "team China" monolith

There are calls for research to move beyond speculation to understand the actual coherence, collaboration, competition, and conflict between different Chinese state agencies, between Chinese state agencies and tech firms, between Chinese tech firms, and between Chinese ICT and non-ICT businesses (Gagliardone 2020; Hong and Harwit 2020; Wang, Bar, and Hong 2020). This can include the political economy and coherence of vision for China's digital expansion and digital governance/standards over time given this has been "a contingent historically unfolding process" (Shen 2016, 307) involving different state agencies, Chinese big tech, and a fluctuating relation between state and capital.

The "usual suspects" recur in the literature in terms of tech firms and projects: Huawei, Alibaba and to a lesser extent ZTE as firms; CloudWalk in Zimbabwe and Huawei in the African Union headquarters as projects. There is a strong need to broaden the empirical base to a wider range of examples including state-owned firms like China Telecom and China Mobile, and other large tech firms like Tencent, Baidu, Xiaomi, Transsion, and BBK. At least these firms receive a mention in the current literature but there is a wide range of smaller Chinese ICT firms operating in Global South countries whose activities have yet to be studied. The focus of literature has also been on the legitimate digital economy, leaving a research gap in relation to a penumbra of activity that is either quasi- or actually illegal – such as unethical peer-to-peer lending platforms in Indonesia (Tritto et al. 2020) or illicit online gambling and money laundering in Pacific Island states (Hayakawa and Anson 2021) – often set up by those escaping tighter regulation within China.

Steering between Chinese exceptionalism and identicalism

Future research needs to steer between the extreme positions that China is unique in its digital interactions with Global South countries, and that China is no different; in particular, no different to Western nations. Rather than a specific research topic, this would be more of a thread that runs through the other topics identified here, asking especially to what extent China is similar or different to the West – the US above all. Focal points for this arising from the literature review would include: whether aid and funding strategies for digital development differ from those of Western counterparts; comparative analysis of Chinese tech firms' internationalization strategies; whether Chinese digital design and implementation is better able to match Global South realities and the extent to which its approach adopts the Principles for Digital Development; relative success and failure rates of Chinese and Western digital projects; and similarities and differences in relation to development-related impacts across the whole range of technology stack applications including the four key concerns of security, dependency, inequality, and environmental impact.

A main interest would be the implications of any similarities and differences for Global South actors in planning their response. However, evidence-based advice also seems lacking for Chinese actors in relation to good practice for policy, strategy, design, and implementation for digital development in the Global South that learns from these similarities and differences.

Evaluating development impact

Moving beyond the positive and negative hypothesizing and speculation that has tended to dominate the literature to date, the broadest question in relation to China's digital expansion in the Global South is *cui bono* – who benefits from it? In more detail, what is the distribution of benefits and disbenefits from China's digital expansion? Reflecting the previous research gap, it would be especially valuable to assess this in comparison with Global South digitalization supported by other countries.

This can be approached via more systematic analysis of the costs and benefits of engagement with China in the digital sphere, either generically, or considering the parallel spheres of economic, social, and political development, or addressing particular Sustainable Development Goals. Such evaluation could focus on different levels – at the micro-level of the business and individual consumers of Chinese digital products and services, at the midi-level of individual systems (data centers, e-commerce platforms, smart city systems, etc.), at the meso-level of sectors, and at the macro-level of nations and regions. Evaluation could also address particular research gaps. One is the delivery of Chinese tech firms against emerging environmental, social and governance agendas in the Global South given some recent signs of responsiveness. Another is employment: both the broad impacts in terms of the quantum and quality of jobs created or destroyed by China's digital expansion, and the micro-level of pay, conditions, and management of local workers employed by Chinese stakeholders. Another is the formation and geography of new economic and political digital value chains; particularly the implications of growing China—local bilateral links for internal, regional, and West—local connections. Lastly, spillover effects must be better understood given the potential for significant positive impact in relation to upgrading skills, knowledge and technology, and demonstrator effects; but also negative impacts of crowding out local firms.

At both individual project and aggregate level, more empirical research is required in relation to the four concerns raised in the literature. How is cyber security including data sovereignty and locus of control and storage of data strengthened or weakened by involvement of Chinese tech firms? How dependent are Global South countries becoming on Chinese digital technologies and capabilities? Are between-country and within-country inequalities being reduced or exacerbated by China's digital expansion; especially dimensions of inequality on which the literature has so far been silent – gender, ethnicity, age, disability, etc.? What positive and negative impacts on environmental sustainability are Chinese digital systems having? Across all of these, how concerned should Global South governments be about this, and how concerned are they?

At the overall macro-level, we need to know what the broader implications are of Global South engagement with Chinese state and private digital actors: especially political and geo-political and macro-financial impacts around contested issues such as realignments in regional and national markets and polities.

Local agency in a "digital Cold War"

Future research can interrogate the notion of China's digital imperialism and of a digital Cold War. To what extent does China's use of telecommunications and related technologies echo that of the British Empire during the nineteenth century, and US neoimperialism during the twentieth century? To what extent does the relationship between the US and China in the Global South echo earlier imperial confrontations in the same locations, from the UK-Russia Great Game of the nineteenth century to the US-USSR Cold War of the twentieth century? What lessons can be learned from similarities and differences? Beyond the rhetoric of conflict, what evidence is there of collaborations between Chinese and Western stakeholders in Global South markets?

Whatever the terminology ultimately used, the current superpower focus tends to assume that they are the locus of agency, with some parts of the literature appearing neocolonial, marginalizing and even disrespectful in characterizing the Global South merely as the background landscape for conflict and Global South stakeholders as passive ciphers or pawns in the game between the US and China. Research is therefore required that puts local actors and agency center stage and understands the balance of demand-pull vs. supply-push in procurement of Chinese technology. Such research would analyze the role of local officials in negotiating deals, for example, the extent of their ability to play off and select between Western and Chinese actors, and their ability through negotiation and policy to improve the outcomes of China's digital projects including the impact of recipient government policies on the decisions of Chinese companies and the Chinese state. It can also: analyze the role in US-China tensions of Global South members within international forums from the ITU to ICANN to the Internet Governance Forum; investigate the role and strategy of local digital companies when Chinese big tech rolls into town; and understand the balance of operational responsibilities and control between local and Chinese staff for implemented digital systems.

From this should come some practice and policy lessons, perhaps including role model examples that can be shared across the Global South, to provide guidance on how best to maximize the benefits and minimize the risks of interactions with China's digital expansion, e.g. via local participation in digital design and implementation; development and localization of digital skills and control and value; cyber-security and cyber-sustainability and digital inclusion plans; national policies on other aspects of digital governance; etc. This would also look at the role of international agencies (UN, other multilateral and bilateral, INGOs) in supporting policy/strategy design and implementation, and at the role of Chinese state and business actors in influencing local policies and strategies.

While the main focus of this will be national policy, there will be three other domains of implication. One is strategy for other local stakeholders, particularly local digital firms seeking to either compete or collaborate with Chinese big tech, and other firms seeking to respond to growth of import threats and export opportunities via Chinese e-commerce platforms. The second is the regional interests of many Global South countries – India, Indonesia, Pakistan, South Africa, Mexico, Brazil to name but a few, which host digital companies that export into their regions. Research can investigate the implications of China's digital expansion on these countries' regional political and economic policy. The third is the provision of guidance for Global South countries on both strategy and content in navigating US-China tensions in global digital governance and standards forums, and in formulating and promoting their own position.

Finally, local agency involves recognition of Global South countries as repositories of knowledge or, at least, as sites of knowledge creation. In the literature, Chinese actors appear to make little explicit provision for learning from the Global South. However, this may not be the case in practice, and research can usefully analyze: whether and what Chinese policy-makers are learning from China's digital expansion; what Chinese tech firms are learning from their engagement in the Global South including any signs of reverse innovation from the South into China; and whether learning from experience is creating any move among Chinese implementers toward a more locally-customized approach that includes genuine inputs from local stakeholders or at least advances beyond a one-size-fits-all approach to digital system design and implementation.

Notes

1. Global South here refers to the low- and middle-income countries of Asia, Africa, Oceania, Central/South America, and the Caribbean.
2. Of these, just over one quarter were in journals ranked in the first quartile by the Scimago ranking system; meaning less than 15% of papers in total were refereed in highest-quality journals.
3. As an example, the first paper mentioning platforms in its title was published in 2018.
4. Noting that Digital Silk Road investments are primarily but not exclusively focused on Global South countries, with investments also in, for example, higher-income countries of Eastern Europe and the Middle East.
5. More nascent is the Digital Currency Electronic Payment (DCEP) system, based on a digital version of China's own currency, which is currently being rolled out only within China.
6. For the Digital Silk Road, these agencies include: the BRI lead agency, the National Development and Reform Commission; the lead digital governance agency, the Cyberspace Administration of China; and key BRI actors, the Ministries of Science and Technology, and of Industry and Information Technology plus finance-related agencies such as the Ministry of Commerce, Ministry of Finance, Export-Import Bank, and China Development Bank (Triolo et al. 2020; Tugendhat and Voo 2021; Wang, Bar, and Hong 2020). This dispersed responsibility creates the potential for tensions, fragmentation and even incoherence that some have characterised within the wider Belt and Road Initiative (Jones and Zeng 2019).
7. It is argued that this could face Chinese tech firms with a "deep versus broad" challenge: the deeper their relation to the Chinese state either out of self-interest or necessity, the greater the jeopardy to breadth of their international expansion (Liu 2021).

Acknowledgements

The literature review reported in this paper was funded by the School of Environment, Education and Development, University of Manchester, UK.

Disclosure statement

No potential conflict of interest was reported by the author(s).

ORCID

Richard Heeks http://orcid.org/0000-0002-4551-2208
Christopher Foster http://orcid.org/0000-0001-7827-2485
Nicholas Jepson http://orcid.org/0000-0003-0163-3179
Seth Schindler http://orcid.org/0000-0003-2233-0628
Qingna Zhou http://orcid.org/0000-0002-7516-884X

References

* - Denotes items from the systematic literature review.

*Agbebi, M., G. Xue, and Z. Yu. 2021. China-powered ICT infrastructure: Lessons from Tanzania and Cambodia (Policy Briefing 252). Johannesburg: South African Institute of International Affairs.

*Ambalov, V., and I. Heim. 2020. Investments in the Digital Silk Road. In *Kazakhstan's diversification from the natural resources sector: Strategic and economic opportunities*, ed. I. Heim, 111–49. Cham: Palgrave Macmillan.

*Arsene, S. 2012. The impact of China on global Internet governance in an era of privatized control. Paper presented at the Tenth Annual Chinese Internet Research Conference, Los Angeles, CA, May 21-22.

ASPI. 2023. 2023. Mapping China's tech giants. Barton, Australia: International Cyber Policy Centre, Australian Strategic Policy Institute. Accessed December 19 https://chinatechmap.aspi.org.au/

Bu, L., V. Chung, N. Leung, K. W. Wang, B. Xia, and C. Xia. 2021. The future of digital innovation in China: Megatrends shaping one of the world's fastest evolving digital ecosystems. Shanghai: McKinsey.

*Buckley, P. J. 2020. China's Belt and Road Initiative and the COVID-19 crisis. *Journal of International Business Policy* 3 (3):311–4. doi:10.1057/s42214-020-00063-9.

*Carrillo, J., and J. Micheli. 2020. Huawei Mexico: Between the construction of upgrading and the uncertainty caused. In *Huawei goes global, Vol II: Regional, geopolitical perspectives, and crisis management*, eds. W. Zhang, I. Alon, and C. Lattemann, 165–85. Cham: Palgrave Macmillan.

Chalk, W. 2019. China's digital imperialism: Shaping the global Internet. Accessed December 19, 2023. https://supchina.com/2019/07/02/chinas-digital-imperialism-shaping-the-global-internet/

*Chan, J. H., and D. Rawat. 2019. China's Digital Silk Road: The integration of Myanmar (RSIS Commentary). Accessed December 19, 2023. https://www.rsis.edu.sg/wp-content/uploads/2019/04/CO19084.pdf

Chaudhury, D. R. 2021. China reportedly investing $ 8.43 bn in Africa as part of Digital Silk Road initiative. *The Economic Times,* October 15. https://economictimes.indiatimes.com/news/international/world-news/china-reportedly-investing-8-43-bn-in-africa-as-part-of-digital-silk-road-initiative/articleshow/87039334.cms

*Cheney, C. 2019. China's Digital Silk Road: Strategic technological competition and exporting political illiberalism (Working Paper WP8). Honolulu, HI: Pacific Forum.

Clement, J. 2022. Market capitalization of the largest Internet companies worldwide as of June 2022. Accessed July 27, 2023. https://www.statista.com/statistics/277483/market-value-of-the-largest-internet-companies-worldwide

Clémençot, J. 2019. Chinese tech giant Huawei wins support in Africa. *The Africa Report*, June 11. Accessed December 19, 2023. https://www.theafricareport.com/13764/chinese-tech-giant-huawei-wins-support-in-africa/

*Das, S. B. 2017. OBOR's digital connectivity offers both benefits and risks (Perspective). Singapore: ISEAS Yusof Ishak Institute. Accessed December 19, 2023. https://www.iseas.edu.sg/images/pdf/ISEAS_Perspective_2017_60.pdf

Deeks, R. 2018. The Digital Silk Road: China's $200 billion project. *BBC Science Focus*, December 8. Accessed December 19, 2023. https://www.sciencefocus.com/future-technology/the-digital-silk-road-chinas-200-billion-project/

*Djan, K. O., and W. A. Owusu-Ansah. 2020. Assessing the impact of the Huawei brand on the information communication technology infrastructure of Ghana. In *Huawei goes global, Vol II: Regional, geopolitical perspectives, and crisis management*, eds. W. Zhang, I. Alon and C. Lattemann, 187–205. Cham: Palgrave Macmillan.

Eder, T. S., R. Arecesati, and J. Mardell. 2019. Networking the "Belt and Road": The future is digital. Accessed December 19, 2023. https://merics.org/en/tracker/networking-belt-and-road-future-digital

*Ellis, R. E. 2013. The strategic dimension of Chinese activities in the Latin American telecommunications sector. *Revista Científica General José María Córdova* 11 (11):121–40.

*Erie, M. S., and T. Streinz. 2021. The Beijing effect: China's Digital Silk Road as transnational data governance. *New York University Journal of International Law and Politics* 54 (1):1–92.

*Feldstein, S. 2019. The global expansion of AI surveillance (Working paper). Washington, DC: Carnegie Endowment for International Peace. Accessed December 19, 2023. chrome- https://carnegieendowment.org/files/WP-Feldstein-AISurveillance_final1.pdf

Field, M., and N. Smith. 2021. Stop using Chinese smartphones over hidden censorship software, consumers warned. *The Telegraph*, September 22. Accessed December 19, 2023. https://www.telegraph.co.uk/technology/2021/09/22/stop-using-chinese-smartphones-hidden-censorship-software-consumers/

*Gao, H. 2018. Digital or trade? The contrasting approaches of China and US to digital trade. *Journal of International Economic Law* 21 (2):297–321. doi:10.1093/jiel/jgy015.

Gao, P., X. Gao, and G. Liu. 2021. Government-controlled enterprises in standardization in the catching-up context: Case of TD-SCDMA in China. *IEEE Transactions on Engineering Management* 68 (1):45–58. doi:10.1109/TEM.2020.3005274.

*Gagliardone, I. 2020. The impact of Chinese tech provision on civil liberties in Africa (Policy Insights 99). Johannesburg: South African Institute of International Affairs. Accessed December 19, 2023. https://www.jstor.org/stable/resrep29588?seq=1

*Gagliardone, I., and S. Geall. 2014. China in Africa's media and telecommunications: Cooperation, connectivity and control (Expert analysis). Accessed December 19, 2023. https://www.files.ethz.ch/isn/179376/7880fd6b12b93bdd18eddcbd4f4e207f.pdf

Garcia, A. 2019. China embarks on Digital Silk Road. Accessed December 19, 2023. https://www.invesco.com/apac/en/institutional/insights/china/china-embarks-on-digital-silk-road.html

*Gong, S., and B. Li. 2019. The Digital Silk Road and the Sustainable Development Goals. *IDS Bulletin* 50 (4):23–45.

*Gong, S., J. Gu, and F. Teng. 2019. The impact of the Belt and Road Initiative investment in digital connectivity and information and communication technologies on achieving the SDGs (K4K Emerging Issues Report). Brighton, UK: Institute of Development Studies. Accessed December 19, 2023. https://assets.publishing.service.gov.uk/

media/5c86628940f0b6369b76a372/K4D_Emerging_Issues_-_BRI_Investment_Part_A_-_final.pdf

*Gravett, W. H. 2020. Digital coloniser? China and artificial intelligence in Africa. *Survival* 62 (6):153–78. doi:10.1080/00396338.2020.1851098.

*Gravett, W. H. 2022. Digital neocolonialism: The Chinese surveillance state in Africa. *African Journal of International and Comparative Law* 30 (1):39–58. doi:10.3366/ajicl.2022.0393.

*Guo, H. 2018. Steps to the Digital Silk Road (Comment). *Nature* 554:25–7.

*Guo, H., J. Liu, Y. Qiu, M. Menenti, F. Chen, P. F. Uhlir, L. Zhang, J. van Genderen, D. Liang, I. Natarajan, L. Zhu, and J. Liu. 2018. The Digital Belt and Road program in support of regional sustainability. *International Journal of Digital Earth* 11 (7):657–69. doi:10.1080/17538947.2018.1471790.

Hayakawa, R., and J. Anson. 2021. ICT4D turns to ICT4CCC (Chinese cyber crimes). Paper presented at the UK Development Studies Association 2021 Conference, July 2

*He, Y. 2019. Connecting the emerging markets: China's growing role in global digital infrastructure (Thought Leadership Brief 26). Hong Kong: Institute for Emerging Market Studies, Hong Kong University of Science and Technology.

Heeks, R. 2018. *Information and Communication Technology for Development (ICT4D).* London: Routledge.

Hellowell, M., and S. Wakdok. 2021. Disaster relief. *Prospect,* March, 48–51.

*Hemmings, J. 2020. Reconstructing order: The geopolitical risks in China's Digital Silk Road. *Asia Policy* 15 (1):5–21. doi:10.1353/asp.2020.0002.

*Hernandez, K. 2019. Achieving complex development goals along China's digital Silk Road (K4D Emerging Issues Report). Brighton, UK: Institute of Development Studies. Accessed December 19, 2023. https://assets.publishing.service.gov.uk/media/5c866463e5274a2a51ac0b67/Hernandez_Chinese_Belt_and_Road_Digital_-_final.pdf

*Hillman, J. E. 2021a. *The digital Silk Road: China's quest to wire the world and win the future.* London: Profile Books.

Hillman, J. E. 2021b. Techno-authoritarianism: Platform for repression in China and abroad (Statement before the Congressional-Executive Committee on China). Washington, DC: Centre for Strategic and International Studies.

Hoffmann, S., D. Lazanski, and E. Taylor. 2020. Standardising the splinternet: How China's technical standards could fragment the internet. *Journal of Cyber Policy* 5 (2):239–64. doi:10.1080/23738871.2020.1805482.

*Hong, Y., and E. Harwit. 2020. China's globalizing Internet: History, power, and governance. *Chinese Journal of Communication* 13 (1):1–7. doi:10.1080/17544750.2020.1722903.

*Huang, Y. 2019. China-Africa joint endeavor on the Digital Silk Road: Opportunities, challenges and approaches. *China International Studies* 78:13–28.

Insikt Group. 2021. Chinese state-sponsored cyber espionage activity supports expansion of regional power and influence in Southeast Asia. Accessed December 19, 2023. https://go.recordedfuture.com/hubfs/reports/cta-2021-1208.pdf

*Jia, H. 2017. Scientific collaborations shine on Belt and Road. *National Science Review* 4 (4):652–7. doi:10.1093/nsr/nwx096.

Jiang, Y., A. Tonami, and A. M. Fejerskov. 2016. China's overseas investment in critical infrastructure: Nuclear power and telecommunications (DIIS Report 2016: 08). Copenhagen: Danish Institute for International Studies. Accessed December 19, 2023. https://www.econstor.eu/bitstream/10419/197634/1/875113524.pdf

*Johnston, L. A. 2021. World trade, e-commerce, and COVID-19: Role of and implications for China's Electronic World Trade Platform (eWTP). *China Review* 21 (2):65–86.

Jones, L., and J. Zeng. 2019. Understanding China's "Belt and Road Initiative": Beyond "grand strategy" to a state transformation analysis. *Third World Quarterly* 40 (8):1415–39. doi:10.1080/01436597.2018.1559046.

*Kassenova, N., and B. Duprey. 2021. *Digital Silk Road in Central Asia: Present and future.* Cambridge, MA: Harvard University.

Keane, M., and H. Wu. 2018. Lofty ambitions, new territories and turf battles: China's platforms 'go out'. *Media Industries* 5 (1):51–68.

*Keane, M., and H. Yu. 2019. A digital empire in the making: China's outbound digital platforms. *International Journal of Communication* 13:4624–41.

*Keane, M., H. Yu, E. J. Zhao, and S. Leong. 2021. *China's digital presence in the Asia-Pacific: Culture, technology and platforms.* London: Anthem Press.

Kelly, D. 2018. Reining in red entrepreneurs. Accessed December 20, 2023. https://www.eastasiaforum.org/2018/01/26/reining-in-red-entrepreneurs/

Kim, M. J., H. Lee, and J. Kwak. 2020. The changing patterns of China's international standardization in ICT under techno-nationalism: A reflection through 5G standardization. *International Journal of Information Management* 54:102145. doi:10.1016/j.ijinfomgt.2020.102145.

*Kliman, D. 2019. Addressing China's influence in Southeast Asia: America's approach and the role of Congress. Accessed December 20, 2023. https://www.cnas.org/publications/congressional-testimony/addressing-chinas-influence-in-southeast-asia-americas-approach-and-the-role-of-congress

Kshetri, N. 2015. Cybercrime and cybersecurity issues in the BRICS economies. *Journal of Global Information Technology Management* 18 (4):245–9. doi:10.1080/1097198X.2015.1108093.

Kwet, M. 2019. Digital colonialism: US empire and the new imperialism in the Global South. *Race & Class* 60 (4):3–26. doi:10.1177/0306396818823172.

*Layton, P. 2020. Artificial intelligence, big data and autonomous systems along the belt and road: Towards private security companies with Chinese characteristics? *Small Wars & Insurgencies* 31 (4):874–97. doi:10.1080/09592318.2020.1743483.

*Lele, A., and K. Roy. 2019. Analysing China's digital and space Belt And Road Initiative (IDSA Occasional Paper No. 54). New Delhi: Institute for Defence Studies and Analyses.

*Li, L. 2016. The image of Africa in China: The emerging role of Chinese social media. *African Studies Quarterly* 16 (3-4):149–60.

*Li, Y. 2019. Influence of the Internet on the economic growth of the Belt and Road Region. *Global Journal of Emerging Market Economies* 11 (3):248–59. doi:10.1177/0974910119887054.

*Lin, J. 2020. Exemplar partner or controversial outsider? Huawei's strategic engagement in Oceania. In *Huawei goes global, Vol II: Regional, geopolitical perspectives, and crisis management*, eds. W. Zhang, I. Alon, and C. Lattemann, 249–68. Cham: Palgrave Macmillan.

*Liu, L. 2021. The rise of data politics: Digital China and the world. *Studies in Comparative International Development* 56 (1):45–67. doi:10.1007/s12116-021-09319-8.

*Liu, Y. 2012. The rise of China and global Internet governance. *China Media Research* 8 (2):46–55.

Livingstone, G. 2009. *America's backyard: The United States and Latin America from the Monroe Doctrine to the War on Terror*. London: Zed Books.

*Lu, J., and C. Van Staden. 2013. Lonely nights online: How does social networking channel Chinese migration and business to Africa? *African East-Asian Affairs* 0 (1):94–116. doi:10.7552/0-1-5.

*Luo, X. 2019. Building China-Latin America Digital Silk Road: Challenges and roadmap. *China International Studies* 77:48–63.

*Ly, B. 2020. Challenge and perspective for Digital Silk Road. *Cogent Business & Management* 7 (1):1804180. doi:10.1080/23311975.2020.1804180.

*Majcherczyk, M., and B. Shuqiang. 2019. Digital Silk Road: The role of cross-border e-commerce in facilitating trade. *Journal of WTO and China* 9 (2):106–28.

*Makundi, H., H. Huyse, and P. Develtere. 2016. Cooperation between China and Tanzania on ICT: Fish, fishing tackle or fishing skills? *Journal of Chinese Economic and Business Studies* 14 (2):129–49. doi:10.1080/14765284.2016.1174459.

*Malena, J. 2021. The extension of the Digital Silk Road to Latin America: Advantages and potential risks. Accessed December 20, 2023. https://www.cfr.org/blog/extension-digital-silk-road-latin-america-advantages-and-potential-risks

Malik, A. A., B. Parks, B. Russell, J. J. Lin, K. Walsh, K. Solomon, S. Zhang, T.-B. Elston, and S. Goodman. 2021. *Banking on the Belt and Road: Insights from a new global dataset of 13,427 Chinese development projects*. Williamsburg, VA: AidData, Global Research Institute, William and Mary.

Marczak, B., J. Scott-Railton, S. McKune, B. Abdul Razzak, and R. Deibert. 2018. Hide and seek: Tracking NSO Group's Pegasus spyware to operations in 45 countries (Citizen Lab Research Report No. 113). Toronto, ON: Munk School of Global Affairs and Public Policy, University of Toronto. Accessed December 20, 2023. https://tspace.library.utoronto.ca/bitstream/1807/95391/1/Report%23113–hide%20and%20seek.pdf

McCarthy, D. R. 2015. *Power, information technology, and international relations theory: The power and politics of US foreign policy and the Internet*. Basingstoke, UK: Palgrave Macmillan.

Meserole, C. 2022. Digital authoritarianism and religious repression in China (Testimony before the Congressional Executive Commission on China. Hearing on "Control of Religion in China through Digital Authoritarianism). Accessed December 20, 2023. https://www.cecc.gov/sites/chinacommission.house.gov/files/documents/Meserole%20CECC%20Testimony%20v090922_0.pdf

*Micheli, J., and J. Carrillo. 2016. The globalization strategy of a Chinese multinational: Huawei in Mexico. *Frontera Norte* 28 (56):35–58.

Miller, G. 2020. "The intelligence coup of the century": For decades, the CIA read the encrypted communications of allies and adversaries. *The Washington Post*, February 11. Accessed December 20, 2023. https://www.washingtonpost.com/graphics/2020/world/national-security/cia-crypto-encryption-machines-espionage/

Minority Staff, US Senate Committee on Foreign Relations. 2020. The new big brother: China and digital authoritarianism (A minority staff report). Accessed December 17, 2023. https://www.govinfo.gov/content/pkg/CPRT-116SPRT42356/pdf/CPRT-116SPRT42356.pdf

*Mukherjee, D. 2020. Huawei goes to India: Can the dragon and the elephant marry? In *Huawei goes global, Vol II: Regional, geopolitical perspectives, and crisis management*, eds. W. Zhang, I. Alon and C. Lattemann, 231–48. Cham: Palgrave Macmillan.

Murphree, M., and D. Breznitz. 2018. Indigenous digital technology standards for development: The case of China. *Journal of International Business Policy* 1 (3-4):234–52. doi:10.1057/s42214-018-0010-3.

*Namingit, S., and S. Al Haddad. 2020. Huawei's carrier business in Southeast Asia. In *Huawei goes global, Vol II: Regional, geopolitical perspectives, and crisis management*, eds. W. Zhang, I. Alon and C. Lattemann, 207–30. Cham: Palgrave Macmillan.

*Naughton, B. 2020. Chinese industrial policy and the Digital Silk Road: The case of Alibaba in Malaysia. *Asia Policy* 15 (1):23–39. doi:10.1353/asp.2020.0006.

*Negro, G. 2020. A history of Chinese global Internet governance and its relations with ITU and ICANN. *Chinese Journal of Communication* 13 (1):104–21. doi:10.1080/17544750.2019.1650789.

*Neilson, B. 2022. Working the Digital Silk Road: Alibaba's Digital free trade zone in Malaysia. In *Digital work in the planetary market*, eds. M. Graham and F. Ferrari, 117–36. Cambridge, MA: MIT Press.

Nye, J. S. 2018. How sharp power threatens soft power: The right and wrong ways to respond to authoritarian influence. *Foreign Affairs*, January 24. Accessed December 20, 2023. https://www.foreignaffairs.com/articles/china/2018-01-24/how-sharp-power-threatens-soft-power

Parkinson, J., N. Bariyo, and J. Chin. 2019. Huawei technicians helped African governments spy on political opponents. *Wall Street Journal*, August 15. Accessed December 20, 2023. https://www.wsj.com/articles/huawei-technicians-helped-african-governments-spy-on-political-opponents-11565793017

Pazi, S., and C. Chatwin. 2014. The impact of NICTBB in facilitating the e-services and m-services in Tanzania. *International Journal of Social, Human Science and Engineering* 8 (3):186–92.

*Peterson, D., and S. Hoffman. 2022. Geopolitical implications of AI and digital surveillance adoption (Brookings policy brief). Accessed December 20, 2023. https://www.brookings.edu/wp-content/uploads/2022/06/FP_20220621_surveillance_exports_peterson_hoffman_v2.pdf

*Polyakova, A., and C. Meserole. 2019. Exporting digital authoritarianism: The Russian and Chinese models (Brookings policy brief). Accessed December 20, 2023. https://www.brookings.edu/wp-content/uploads/2019/08/FP_20190827_digital_authoritarianism_polyakova_meserole.pdf

PRC. 2015. *Vision and actions on jointly building Silk Road Economic Belt and 21st Century Maritime Silk Road*. Beijing: National Development and Reform Commission, Ministry of Foreign Affairs, and Ministry of Commerce of the Government of the People's Republic of China.

*Rawat, D., and J. H. Chan. 2018. China's Digital Silk Road: Implications for India. *Institute of South Asian Studies Insights* 521 (18):1–6.

Reddy, R. K. 2021. Mapping China's presence in Africa's digital economy. *Eurasia Review*, July 16. Accessed January 4, 2024. https://www.thedispatch.in/mapping-chinas-presence-in-africas-digital-economy/

Reis, C., E. C. Almedia, F. F. Dourado, and F. R. da Silva. 2021. *Vigilância automatizada*. Brasilia, Brazil: Laboratório de Políticas Públicas e Internet.

Ren, X. 2019. Digital Silk Road helping developing countries. *China Daily*, April 27. Accessed December 20, 2023. https://www.chinadaily.com.cn/a/201904/27/WS5cc3a6e7a3104842260b8add.html

*Rwehumbiza, D. A. 2021. Huawei's linkages with local firms in Tanzania: Idiosyncratic benefits and risks. *Global Business and Organizational Excellence* 40 (3):20–35. doi:10.1002/joe.22076.

Seaman, J. 2020. China and the new geopolitics of technical standardization. Paris: French Institute of International Relations. Accessed December 20, 2023. https://www.ifri.org/sites/default/files/atoms/files/seaman_china_standardization_2020.pdf

Shahbaz, A. 2018. The rise of digital authoritarianism: Fake news, data collection, and the challenge to democracy. Accessed December 20, 2023. https://freedomhouse.org/report/freedom-net/2018/rise-digital-authoritarianism

*Shen, H. 2016. China and global Internet governance: Toward an alternative analytical framework. *Chinese Journal of Communication* 9 (3):304–24. doi:10.1080/17544750.2016.1206028.

*Shen, H. 2018. Building a digital Silk Road? Situating the Internet in China's Belt and Road Initiative. *International Journal of Communication* 12 (19):2683–701.

*Shen, X. Y. 2020. Chinese ICT on the Digital Silk Road: A case study of infrastructure building in Pakistan., Master's thesis., School of Communication, Simon Fraser University.

Shen, X. 2021. China to pursue digital trade expansion under new five-year plan as cross-border data flow restrictions remain in place. *South China Morning Post,* October 21. https://www.scmp.com/tech/policy/article/3153196/china-pursue-digital-trade-expansion-under-new-five-year-plan-cross

StatCounter. 2023. Mobile vendor market share worldwide Jan 2022 – Jan 2023. Accessed February 12, 2023. https://gs.statcounter.com/vendor-market-share/mobile/worldwide

Sun, S. L. 2009. Internationalization strategy of MNEs from emerging economies: The case of Huawei. *Multinational Business Review* 17 (2):133–59.

Tang, M. 2020. From "bringing-in" to "going-out": Transnationalizing China's Internet capital through state policies. *Chinese Journal of Communication* 13 (1):27–46. doi:10.1080/17544750.2019.1657474.

Tanjangco, B., Y. Cao, R. Nadin, L. Calabrese, and O. Borodyna. 2020. *Pulse 1: Covid-19 and economic crisis – China's recovery and international response*. London: ODI. Accessed December 20, 2023. https://odi.cdn.ngo/media/documents/odi_economic_pulse_1_v6.pdf

*Teng, K. 2020. Economic impact of Internet and information development on countries along the Belt and Road Route. *Journal of Physics Conference Series* 1533 (2):022107.

The Economist. 2022. Countering China in Africa. *The Economist*, May 20. Accessed December 20, 2023. https://www.economist.com/special-report/2022/05/20/countering-china-in-africa

*Triolo, P., L. Allison, C. Brown, and K. Broderick. 2020. *The Digital Silk Road: Expanding China's digital footprint*. New York: Eurasia Group.

*Tritto, A., Y. He, and V. A. Junaedi. 2020. Governing the gold rush into emerging markets: A case study of Indonesia's regulatory responses to the expansion of Chinese-backed online P2P lending. *Financial Innovation* 6 (1):1–24. doi:10.1186/s40854-020-00202-4.

*Tugendhat, H., and J. Voo. 2021. China's Digital Silk Road in Africa and the future of Internet governance (Policy brief No. 60). Washington, DC: School of Advanced International Studies, Johns Hopkins University. Accessed December 20, 2023. https://www.econstor.eu/bitstream/10419/248239/1/sais-cari-pb60.pdf

*van der Lugt, S. 2021. Exploring the political, economic, and social implications of the Digital Silk Road into East Africa. In *Global perspectives on China's Belt and Road Initiative: Asserting agency through regional connectivity*, ed., F. Schneider, 315–46. Amsterdam: Amsterdam University Press.

*Vila Seoane, M. F. 2020. Alibaba's discourse for the digital Silk Road: The electronic World Trade Platform and "inclusive globalization. *Chinese Journal of Communication* 13 (1):68–83. doi:10.1080/17544750.2019.1606838.

*Vila Seoane, M. F. 2021. Chinese and US AI and cloud multinational corporations in Latin America. In *Towards an international political economy of artificial intelligence*, eds., T. Keskin and R. D. Kiggins, 85–111. Cham: Palgrave Macmillan.

*Wang, H. 2020. China and Central Asian countries jointly building the Digital Silk Road: Foundations, challenges and paths. *China International Studies* 82:141–76.

Wang, Y. 2022. Jointly advancing the Global Development Initiative and writing a new chapter for common development. (Keynote address by State Councilor and Foreign Minister Wang Yi at the Ministerial Meeting of the Group of Friends of the Global Development Initiative, New York, September 21). Accessed December 20, 2023. https://www.mfa.gov.cn/eng/topics_665678/GDI/xw/202209/t20220922_10769721.html

*Wang, R., F. Bar, and Y. Hong. 2020. ICT aid flows from China to African countries: A communication network perspective. *International Journal of Communication* 14:1498–523.

*Wen, Y. 2020. Huawei's expansion into the Global South: A path toward alternative globalization?. In *Huawei goes global, Vol I: Made in China for the world*, eds. W. Zhang, I. Alon and C. Lattemann, 147–69. Cham: Palgrave Macmillan.

*Woodhams, S. 2020. China, Africa, and the private surveillance industry. *Georgetown Journal of International Affairs* 21 (1):158–65. doi:10.1353/gia.2020.0002.

Xi, J. 2017. Work together to build the Silk Road Economic Belt and The 21st Century Maritime Silk Road. (Speech at Belt and Road Forum for International Cooperation, Beijing, May 14.) Accessed December 20, 2023. https://

www.fmprc.gov.cn/mfa_eng/wjdt_665385/zyjh_665391/201705/t20170527_678618.html

*Yang, C. 2022. Cross-border expansion of digital platforms and transformation of the trade and distribution networks of imported fresh fruits from Southeast Asia to China. *Global Networks* 22 (4):716–34. doi:10.1111/glob.12352.

*Yean, T. S. 2018. The Digital Free Trade Zone (DFTZ): Putting Malaysia's SMEs onto the Digital Silk Road (ISEAS Yusof Ishak Institute Perspective No. 17). Accessed December 20, 2023. https://www.iseas.edu.sg/images/pdf/ISEAS_Perspective_2018_17@50.pdf

*Zhang, W., I. Alon, and C. Lattemann. eds. 2020. *Huawei goes global*, Vol I andII. Cham: Palgrave Macmillan.

*Zhao, M. 2020. US perception of and response to the Digital Silk Road. *China International Studies* 84:84–106.

*Zhou, T., and Q. Xue. 2020. 2023. The Digital Silk Road and Southeast Asian countries. In *The Fourth Industrial Revolution and the future of work: Implications for Asian development cooperation*, ed. A. Mulakala, 132–63. Seoul: KDI School of Public Policy and Management. Accessed December 20 https://asiafoundation.org/wp-content/uploads/2021/01/Korea_The-Fourth-Industrial-Revolution-and-the-Future-of-Work_EN.pdf.

Chinese digital platform companies' expansion in the Belt and Road countries

Yujia He

ABSTRACT

The emergence of digital platforms is shifting the digital economy toward a platform economy, and Chinese platform-based businesses like Alibaba, Tencent, and JD are increasingly expanding in the Global South. Alongside this, the Chinese government has been promoting digital economy collaboration with emerging markets through high-level engagement under the banner of the Belt and Road Initiative (BRI) and its digital economy component the Digital Silk Road (DSR). Despite significant market interest and policy attention, grounded empirical analysis of Chinese digital platforms' expansion within Belt and Road Initiative countries is scarce. This study employs a mixed-methods approach, drawing on both quantitative data of Chinese platform companies' overseas foreign direct investment and qualitative data obtained from fieldwork interviews in Southeast Asia and from secondary sources to conduct a case study of Chinese platforms in Indonesia. It finds that Chinese digital platforms largely undertook their overseas expansion based on commercial interests, and Beijing's high-level policy framework BRI has had a limited direct impact on the expansion of the privately-owned Chinese platforms and their local business operations within host countries. The vagueness of BRI/DSR has also given platform companies investing in Indonesia room to choose how they engage with Chinese BRI/DSR rhetoric depending on the local context. Furthermore, local contextual factors, including Indonesian policy, policy implementation, and labor market, have shaped the platforms' business expansion. Firms have been pushed to adapt to local policy priorities and socioeconomic context, seek local partners and invest in local capacity building. The findings suggest a more complicated state-firm relationship in Chinese digital platforms' expansion than that which is often perceived, and the importance of host country contexts in shaping Chinese digital platforms' local business strategies.

Introduction

The digital economy is now equivalent to 15.5% of global GDP, growing two and a half times faster than global GDP over the past 15 years (World Bank 2020). Chinese firms are key players in this growth: from 2005 to 2019, China's digital economy value-added increased from RMB 2.6 trillion to RMB 35.8 trillion (USD 0.41 trillion to USD 5.63 trillion) (CAICT 2020). Chinese ICT (information and communications technology) firms have also embarked on ambitious global expansion: in 2020, in terms of deal value, the technology, media and entertainment, and telecommunications sector was the top sector for overseas mergers and acquisitions of Chinese firms (EY 2021). Southeast Asian countries, some of the world's fastest-growing digital markets, are among the major areas of interest of Chinese firms and investors. For instance, Chinese venture capital firms quadrupled their investments in Southeast Asian startups in 2019 alone (Zinser 2021).

The Chinese government promotes digital economy collaboration through high-level engagement under the banner of the "Digital Silk Road" (DSR), part of the Belt and Road Initiative (BRI) to promote connectivity with other emerging markets. Chinese State Councilor Wang Yi remarked in 2020 that the "Digital Silk Road is a priority area for BRI cooperation in the next stage" (PRC Ministry of Foreign Affairs 2020). China and the Association of Southeast Asian Nations (ASEAN) states designated the Year 2020 as the ASEAN-China Year of Digital Economy Cooperation (Xinhua 2020). On the other hand,

Beijing's rhetoric of "win-win" digital economy collaboration with emerging economies has garnered suspicions. For instance, former US Attorney General William P. Barr criticized the DSR as "PRC's plans to dominate the world's digital infrastructure" (US Department of Justice 2020).

Despite the significant market interest and policy attention, scholarly analysis of Chinese ICT companies' and especially digital platform companies' expansion in the Belt and Road countries is still limited (Keane and Wu 2018; Shen 2018, 2021; Su and Flew 2021; Vila Seoane 2020).[1] In discussing China's presence in the BRI countries and in the Global South more broadly, the dominant narratives focus on the interests and actions of the Chinese state (Rolland 2017). Such state-centric perspectives, while important, can neglect the role of private firms and the influence of host country environments in shaping Chinese firms' expansion and business operations. Therefore, scholars have called for more empirical inquiries "from the ground" (Oliveira et al. 2020) to understand the complex realities of Chinese overseas investments (Lai, Lin, and Sidaway 2020) in the BRI countries. This article contributes to this nascent area of inquiry with a mixed-methods study, using both quantitative data on Chinese overseas investment, and qualitative data gathered from fieldwork interviews and secondary sources. It seeks to answer the following research questions: How do Chinese digital platforms engage with the BRI in their overseas investment in emerging markets? How do host country contexts influence the expansion of Chinese digital platforms within the BRI countries?

This study's findings overall suggest a more complicated state-firm relationship in Chinese digital platform companies' overseas expansion than what is often perceived, with the host country context, including policies, policy implementation, and the labor market as important factors shaping the firms' business strategies. Chinese platform companies, as private-sector firms backed by transnational capital, largely conducted their overseas expansion based on commercial interests. BRI/DSR, Beijing's high-level policy framework, remained a vague slogan, offering few direct incentives and thereby having limited impact on the firms' expansion on the ground. Considering local sentiment toward the BRI, firms cautiously engaged with Chinese state rhetoric such as the DSR/BRI in local business operations. At the same time, host country governments and market players are not passive actors in their engagement with Chinese platforms, but play vital roles in shaping the trajectory of Chinese platforms' expansion. Platforms were pushed to align with host country government's digital economy development aspirations, while also adapting to the realities of policy implementation, seeking local partners, and investing in local capacity building.

This article is structured as follows. The next two sections situate the study's contribution within two main bodies of scholarship – state-firm relationships in Chinese ICT firms' overseas expansion and host country contexts in Chinese ICT firms' overseas expansion – and outline the research methods. The subsequent section presents an overview of the scope and the country destinations of Chinese digital platform companies' overseas investments. The penultimate section focuses on Chinese platforms' expansion in Indonesia, the country receiving the largest volume of platform investments among the BRI countries. Drawing on interview-based fieldwork data and secondary documents, it analyzes Chinese platform companies' engagement with the BRI/DSR in their expansion in Indonesia, and importantly, how Indonesia's particular policy and market context shaped their expansion. The final section concludes the study and reflects on the importance of shifting away from a Beijing-centric lens to studying firms' interests and behaviors and the host country's development context in understanding Chinese digital expansion in the Global South.

Chinese digital platforms' expansion in the Belt and Road countries

Beijing launched the Belt and Road Initiative in 2013 to promote "policy coordination, facilities connectivity, unimpeded trade, financial integration, and people-to-people bonds" (Jenkins 2022, 15) with developing economies in Asia, Europe, and later added Latin America and the Caribbean countries in 2018 (PRC NDRC 2015). The Digital Silk Road was conceived as its digital economy component. According to Shen (2018), the Chinese state aims to achieve five policy objectives through DSR: cutting industrial overcapacity in both the ICT sector and the broader economy, enabling Chinese firms' global expansion, supporting the internationalization of the Chinese currency (RMB), constructing a China-centered transnational network infrastructure, and promoting its vision of Internet-enabled inclusive globalization.

Existing literature on the political economy of Chinese ICT firms' overseas expansion in the BRI countries largely focuses on traditional large-scale telecommunications infrastructures such as fiber-optic cable construction, network equipment, 5G, and satellite networks[2] (Aboul-Dahab 2021; Blanchard and Hooijmaaijers 2021; Brown and Burjanadze 2020; Cheney 2019; Erie and Streinz 2021; Hemmings 2020; Mochinaga 2020; van der Lugt 2021). With a few exceptions (Hernandez 2019; Keane and Yu 2019; Logan, Molloy, and Smith 2018; Shen 2017, 2021; Su and Flew 2021; Vila Seoane 2020), digital platform companies have largely not received scholarly attention. On the other hand, Chinese government documents and state media articles indicate that investments promoted under the DSR/BRI banner cover wide-ranging areas in the digital economy beyond the telecommunications infrastructure. They include e-commerce, artificial intelligence, cloud computing, smart cities, the Internet of Things, financial technologies (Fintech), social networking, blockchain, online entertainment, animation, online games, science and technology parks, technology transfer centers, innovation hubs, startup incubators, student scholarships and exchange programs (CAICT 2016; PRC MOST 2016, 2017; PRC NDRC 2015; Xinhua 2017a, 2017b, 2017c, 2018, 2019). In other words, all kinds of investments and partnership projects involving Chinese ICT firms in the Belt and Road countries could fall under the BRI/DSR umbrella. Considering the important role that platforms play in today's digital economy, the expansion of Chinese digital platforms into the BRI countries calls for further analysis.

State-firm relations

The international affairs literature on Chinese digital expansion in emerging markets has a predominant focus on the strategic interests of the Chinese state. Chinese scholarly works tend to portray an idealistic vision of ICT expansion as a beneficial and "win-win collaboration" for both China and the host countries (Woon 2021). On the other hand, Western scholarly works tend to view Chinese digital expansion as a means for the Chinese state to project its power abroad amid growing US-China competition. For instance, scholars in several prominent Western think tanks argue that the rising power of Chinese players could challenge the US-centric Internet and cyber-governance model and threaten American security interests (Hemmings 2020; IISS 2021; Mochinaga 2020). Cheney (2019) argues that the Chinese government perceives "technological advancement as the sphere in which it can most adequately challenge the United States' global power without creating direct confrontation" (1), and through DSR Beijing could "maintain economic components of the (liberal) order that have facilitated its economic rise, while spreading a politically illiberal model of governance" (2). Thomas-Noone (2018) argues that China is in a growing struggle against the US over "who will lead in new technologies and set the rules for how they are used and built, as well as how and where they are deployed", and developing countries accepting Chinese investment should avoid entering "another colonial period, this time in the digital age".

Analyses through the lens of Chinese state interests in the US-China great power rivalry certainly bring forth important policy concerns. However, such state-centric analyses are primarily based on traditional telecommunications infrastructure projects – not digital platform companies. They also tend to utilize secondary policy documents instead of first-hand empirical data from emerging markets.

To be sure, Chinese platforms' rise to prominence poses a challenge to the dominant position enjoyed so far by only a handful of US tech platforms companies like Facebook, Amazon and Google on the global Internet (Gray 2021; Shen and He 2022). Still from a scholarly standpoint, it is critical to move beyond the interests of the Chinese state and great power rivalry, and direct more attention to the interests and behavior of other players including the privately-owned platforms and the various host country players. The existing literature on Chinese firms' overseas expansion in other industries has shown differences in the motivations and behaviors of state-owned enterprises (SOEs) and privately-owned enterprises (POEs). Compared to most SOEs that have large resource bases and enjoy high-levels of government financial support and a protectionist policy environment, most Chinese POEs face an unfavorable domestic institutional environment, operate in highly competitive markets, and expand overseas with the intention to seek new markets or strategic assets like technology and brands (Huang and Chi 2014). Unlike SOEs that have access to preferential financing from Chinese banks, POEs tend to expand overseas using their own capital and profit, raise capital through international markets, or with private equity funds (Sutherland and Ning 2011). Studies have documented how Chinese private business elites relate to and interact with international corporate networks while simultaneously being linked to domestic state-business networks (De Graaff 2020). As private firms in sectors like agriculture, textiles and electronics follow their own paths overseas, tensions can also arise between their commercial interests and Chinese state interests in private firms' expansion in developing countries (Gu 2009).

Rejecting the state-centric view that would treat the Chinese digital platform companies as mere extensions of the state, a small but growing body of literature in media and communications highlights their complex relationships with the state and international capital (Keane and Wu 2018; Keane and Yu 2019; Shen 2017 2021; Su and Flew 2021). Platform companies certainly benefited from "China's state-led digital capitalism" in their domestic market expansion (Hong 2017, 145). Yet in domestic markets, there are "tensions and potential contradictions arising from the reliance of the Chinese state on the BAT [Baidu, Alibaba, Tencent] to build digital infrastructure" (Su and Flew 2021, 67), as firms seek to minimize direct state regulation for their business models. Chinese firms may also engage in fierce battles with each other, instead of acting in concert under state demands as some would assume, e.g., ByteDance's lawsuit alleging that Tencent's WeChat and QQ messaging apps ban their users from sharing content from Douyin, the Chinese version of short-form video app TikTok owned by ByteDance (He 2021).

As this study will show, the tension between the digital platform companies' profit-seeking logic and the state's political interests also exists in overseas expansion. On the one hand, high-tech firms' overseas merger and acquisition activities can exhibit a certain degree of rhetorical alignment with policies like the BRI (Oh and No 2020). For instance, Alibaba has promoted its Electronic World Trade Platform by employing the BRI discourse of "inclusive globalization" benefiting developing countries and disenfranchized groups such as small enterprises, youth, and women (Du 2017; Vila Seoane 2020). However, firms also seek profits in overseas markets, and profit-seeking inevitably prioritizes tangible commercial interests and incentives and seeks to minimize any possible negative impacts on their business operations. Chinese private digital platforms companies have relied on their own capital and international capital to fund business expansion, making them subject to the profit-driven interests of shareholders, global funds, and international markets. For instance, as Shen (2021) pointed out, different units of domestic and international capital, and state agencies both inside and outside of China, have interacted with Alibaba's developmental strategies and influenced the company's global expansion.

Moreover, from the side of the Chinese government, contrary to popular perceptions, the BRI or its digital economy component the DSR is far from a top-down plan carefully orchestrated by Beijing and imposed effectively upon platform companies. In the ICT sector more broadly, Greene and Triolo (2020) critically examining the implementation of the DSR, note that it "did not occur with the degree of coordination that Beijing has projected, and foreign observers have feared". Analyses of Chinese telecommunications firms' expansion show that they provide low-cost products and localized services that appeal to price-conscious vendors and consumers in emerging markets (Harwit 2013; Namingit and Al Haddad 2020; Wen 2020), and firm-initiated expansion can be merely rebranded by Beijing as part of the DSR (Greene and Triolo 2020). More broadly, various stakeholders in China, including local governments and firms, employ the BRI as a broad policy slogan that is open to interpretation, competition, and contestation (Jones and Zeng 2019; Zeng 2019). Survey research of Chinese firms across all industries and their attitudes toward investment in the BRI countries shows that unlike SOEs, Chinese private firms' perceptions of investment opportunities and decisions around overseas expansion are more driven by commercial interests rather than BRI policy (Li and Zeng 2019).

Therefore, treating Chinese firms monolithically, and their overseas business expansion as a direct outcome of policies like the BRI would be an oversimplification, giving much credit to the Chinese state, while underestimating the role of commercial interests and other factors shaping Chinese firms' expansion. As this study will show, for platform companies, because the DSR/BRI as a high-level policy framework lacks clear definitions of participation, the vagueness of the state narrative also allows the firms to choose whether, and how to engage with the initiative in substance or rhetorically, without jeopardizing their business interests in the host country.

Host countries' contexts

While the scholarship on Chinese digital platform companies' engagement with host country players is limited, a growing body of literature on Chinese firms' overseas projects examines how the host countries' development agendas overlap with Chinese firms' commercial interests. For instance, on Chinese firms' overseas projects in areas such as e-commerce, 5G, broadband, cable networks, and smart city development, scholars highlight the host countries' rationale for bringing in Chinese players, including fulfilling unmet infrastructure, financing, or technology needs (Aboul-Dahab 2021; Blanchard and Hooijmaaijers 2021; Chen 2020; Das 2017; Gagliardone 2019; He 2019; He and Tritto 2022; Martinus 2020a; Naughton

2020; Paulo 2018; UNESCAP 2017; Yean 2018, 2020; Zhu, Lan, and Zhang 2021).

Host countries' governments and political elites may also have other political calculations for welcoming Chinese technologies. For instance, the Pakistani government's need for data infrastructure motivated it to seek out collaboration with Chinese tech firms (Erie and Streinz 2021). Security concerns, such as preventing the interception of critical financial and security information by Western intelligence agencies, also motivated projects like the proposed BRICS cable network (Lee 2016; Shen 2018). As Gagliardone (2019) show, both authoritarian and democratic states in Africa have partnered with Chinese ICT firms for development projects, and contrary to the depiction of China's influence as spreading authoritarianism, leaders in authoritarian states in Africa justify their measures for improving surveillance as their emulation of the West rather than China.

Depending on host countries' policies, collaboration with Chinese players may not preclude them from seeking other partners. For instance, in Ethiopia, the government "has the agency to independently choose which technology to acquire and from where" and cooperates with both Chinese and European firms (van der Lugt 2021, 339). Countries in Southeast Asia have sought diverse partners from multiple countries for smart city and 5G partnerships (Martinus 2020b, 2020c; Namingit and Al Haddad 2020). More broadly, studies of BRI implementation in host countries across various industries also show that local and national political elites even in much smaller and relatively weaker states such as Cambodia, Malaysia, Vietnam and Myanmar, are adept in engaging Chinese and other foreign actors and to further their own political or development agendas (Alves, Gong, and Li 2023; Calabrese and Cao 2021; He and Tritto, 2022; Liu and Lim, 2019; Loughlin and Grimsditch 2021; Tritto 2019).

As with other types of Chinese firms' overseas expansion, local context inevitably shapes the outcomes of Chinese ICT firms' expansion and the partnerships they form with other players. For instance, AliExpress' expansion in Central Asia shows high flexibility and adaptability to local circumstances, as the firm collaborates and competes with all existing players, regardless of whether they are Russian, Chinese, American, or local, and leverages whichever social media networks and payment methods are popular in a specific host country to grow its business (Oreglia, Ren, and Liao 2021). Host countries' governments and politicians, firms and other stakeholders may have specific interests and leverage which they can apply to influence Chinese tech businesses. For instance, Chinese-invested smart city projects in Malaysia, such as the KL City Brain and the Forest City in Johor, have suffered delays due to Malaysia's domestic political contentions (He and Tritto 2022; Naughton 2020). Baidu's expansion into Vietnam was hampered by false local media reports about its business practices, playing on Vietnamese users' anger against China in the South China Sea dispute (Logan 2015). New technologies and business practices brought by Chinese firms may also incur socioeconomic issues, prompting the host country government to respond with new regulations. For instance, the influx of Chinese capital into Indonesia's Fintech lending sector led to a rapid expansion of the industry, but also escalating socioeconomic risks such as privacy violations. In response, Indonesia imposed new regulations to curb risks and promote financial inclusion (Tritto, He, and Junaedi 2020).

In effect, treating host countries as merely pawns of Beijing leads to overlooking of their roles in engaging Chinese players in ICT development. Since considerable differences exist between the political, economic, and social contexts of China and emerging markets that firms expand to, their expansion in the host country needs to be highly contextualized.

Methodology

To understand the scope of Chinese platforms' overseas expansion and more specifically the primary locations of investments in the BRI vs. non-BRI countries, first a quantitative analysis was conducted using data on Chinese outward foreign direct investment (OFDI). The official bilateral FDI data published by the Chinese Ministry of Commerce is incomplete, due to missing information on the final destination: about 75% of Chinese OFDI goes *via* Hong Kong SAR or tax havens (e.g., the British Virgin Islands and the Cayman Islands), with destination unknown (Diao and Park 2021). Therefore project-level investment data from the China Global Investment Tracker (CGIT) database of the American Enterprise Institute[3] was used.

The CGIT database tracks published corporation reports and official documents for investment transactions of at least USD 100 million, providing a more accurate description of the final destinations of investments. The drawback of using CGIT database is that small investments, such as venture capital financing for early-stage startups that are typically less than USD 100 million, are excluded. Nevertheless, descriptive statistical analysis using this dataset can illustrate the trend of major investments by platform companies across time, and the geographical distribution of their final destinations. To determine which destination countries are the BRI countries, the study follows the Council of Foreign Relations data of 139 countries which were participants in the initiative as of March 2021[4].

The original CGIT database includes "Technology" as a specific category, however many investments made by Chinese platform companies are categorized as "Other" or specific services (for instance, Alibaba's investment in the Indonesian ride-hailing platform Gojek was categorized as "Transport"). Therefore, the author manually went through the entire database to re-identify and include all investments recorded in the database by digital platform companies (including Alibaba, Baidu, ByteDance, Didi Chuxing, JD.com, Jumei, Meituan Dianping, NetEase, Qihoo, Renren, Shanda, Tencent, Trip.com, YY). This also narrowed the time frame, from 2010 until the end of 2021, as the first recorded investment was Tencent's investment in Digital Sky Technologies in 2010.

To further examine the platform companies' local operations in the BRI-participating countries, a case study of Chinese digital platforms' expansion in Indonesia was conducted. As the quantitative data shows, Indonesia was the largest recipient of OFDI from Chinese platform companies among all the 139 BRI-participating, therefore it is a "critical case" in Yin's (2003) terminology.

The analysis draws on data from two main sources: (1) semi-structured interviews conducted with key informants in Indonesia, Singapore, and China either in person or mediated (phone, Skype or Zoom) to obtain both retrospective and real-time accounts of their experience with Chinese platforms' expansion; (2) secondary documents about Chinese platforms' expansion in Indonesia, including press releases, industry and news reports. Summary information of the 50 interviewees including their organizations, job titles and acronyms, and a description of the interviews can be found in Table 1. Interviewees represented a range of government officials, Chinese and local businesses, industry associations, consulting firms, startup founders, venture capitalists, lawyers, NGOs, and university and think tank researchers. The selection of interviewees followed a mix of purposeful sampling (selecting interviewees based on their knowledge and work experience with Chinese firms) and snowball sampling (identifying additional interviewees from the networks of existing interviewees).[5]

Interviews were semi-structured, generally divided into five parts: background information about the Indonesian digital market, the industry, and the interviewee's organization; relationships with the Chinese players; perceptions of Chinese government policies like the BRI/DSR; Indonesian government policies and other socioeconomic factors important for Chinese platform investments; and local business strategies. To enable triangulation across different interviews, a pattern thematic analysis was conducted by grouping interview data under themes initially derived from the earlier review of literature such as the drivers of Chinese platforms' expansion, engagement with the BRI and other Chinese government initiatives, policy for foreign investment in the digital sectors, Chinese platforms' relations with local players and regulators, and business practices. Data analysis was performed to compare the findings of the case against the initial statements and concepts identified in the literature review and against the quantitative evidence, to develop further insights into how Chinese digital platforms engage with the BRI in their overseas expansion and how host countries' context impacts the platforms' local operations.

Chinese digital platforms' overseas investment: Statistical analysis

This section presents the results from the descriptive statistical analysis of major overseas investments made by Chinese digital platforms, including the trend across time before and after the BRI announcement, and the geographical distribution of the investments across both BRI-participating and nonparticipating countries. As the data shows (see Figure 1), Chinese digital platforms have significantly expanded their global footprint since the first major investment in 2010. The volume of yearly overseas foreign direct investment began to increase significantly after the 2013 BRI announcement, and despite the decline in recent years, investment has been consistently higher than the pre-2013 level. The decline in investment since 2016 was due to several factors. The 2016 peak value was likely an anomaly, due to a one-time USD 8.6 billion deal involving Tencent's acquisition of the majority stake in Finnish mobile game company Supercell. The domestic market al.so experienced a downturn, as China's real GDP growth rate fell to a 28-year low of 6.6% in 2018, creating pressure for Chinese tech firms to conserve cash flow (Kawakami 2019). Growing scrutiny of Chinese high-tech investments in the US since the start of the Trump administration in 2017 also led to some troubled transactions, such as Alibaba's failed attempt to acquire MoneyGram (Roumeliotis 2018). Consequently, Chinese platforms' major investments in the US plunged from USD 4220

Table 1. List of interviewees.

Interview no.	*Organization (anonymized when requested)*	*Role*	*Topics discussed*
1	Indonesian FinTech Lending Association	Vice chairman	Chinese and other foreign investments; Fintech development and regulation
2	An Indonesian Fintech firm	Founder	Relationship with Chinese players
3	Indonesian Institute of Sciences	Researcher	Chinese investment in Indonesia
4–5	An Indonesian think tank	Program officers	Chinese investment in Indonesia
6	Indonesian Fintech Lending Association	Executive	Relationship with Chinese players
7	A Chinese-Indonesian joint venture firm	Executive	Local business strategies; relationship with BRI and Chinese authorities; Indonesian regulation
8–10	An Indonesian law firm	Attorney, associate attorney, associate	Chinese investment in Indonesia; Indonesian regulation
11–12	Indonesian Institute of Sciences	Researcher, research assistant	Indonesia's digital economy; e-commerce development; Fintech
13	China Council for the Promotion of International Trade Indonesia	Official	Chinese investment in Indonesia; BRI; local response
14–15	An Indonesian Fintech firm	Co-founders	Relationship with Chinese players
16	Indonesian Chamber of Commerce and Industry	Advisor	Chinese investment in Indonesia; Indonesian policy on ICT development
17	Indonesian subsidiary of a Chinese firm	Director	Local business strategies; relationship with BRI and Chinese authorities; Indonesian regulation
18	PwC Indonesia	Senior associate	Indonesia's digital economy; mergers and acquisitions activities and regulations
19–20	Economic Research Institute for ASEAN and East Asia	Senior economist; research associate	Chinese investment in Indonesia; Indonesian policy on ICT development, e-commerce
21–22	UN Pulse Lab Jakarta	Officers	ICT for sustainable development
23	An Indonesian research institute	Research head	Indonesia's digital economy
24	A Chinese-Indonesian joint venture firm	CEO	Local business strategies; relationship with BRI and Chinese authorities; Indonesian regulation
25–27	An Indonesian law firm	Partners	Chinese investment in Indonesia; Indonesian regulation
28	JD.id	Executive	Local business strategies; relationship with BRI and Chinese authorities; Indonesian regulation; e-commerce
29	Indonesian subsidiary of a Chinese firm	Vice head	Local business strategies; relationship with BRI and Chinese authorities; Indonesian regulation
30–31	Indonesian Consumer Protection Foundation	Directors	Chinese business in Indonesia; consumer complaints; Indonesian regulation
32	Indonesia Investment Coordinating Board	Consultant	Chinese investment in Indonesia; Indonesian ICT development policy
33–34	Nanyang Technological University	Researchers	Chinese investment in Southeast Asia
35–37	National University of Singapore	Researchers	Chinese investment in Southeast Asia
38	A Singaporean venture capital firm	Founder	Digital economy in Southeast Asia; early-stage investment for startups; Chinese investments
39	An Indonesian venture capital firm	Partner	Indonesia's digital economy; early-stage investment for startups; Indonesian policy for entrepreneurship
40	Gadjah Mada University	Program officer	Early-stage investment for startups; university training
41	Nanyang Technological University	Researcher	Technology policy in Southeast Asia
42–43	National University of Singapore	Researchers	China-Southeast Asia relations
44–45	Nanyang Technological University	Researchers	Chinese investment in Southeast Asia
46	Monash University Malaysia	Researcher	Chinese investment in Southeast Asia
47–48	ISEAS–Yusof Ishak Institute	Researchers	Digital economy in Southeast Asia; Chinese investment
49–50	UNSW Sydney	Researchers	Digital economy in Southeast Asia

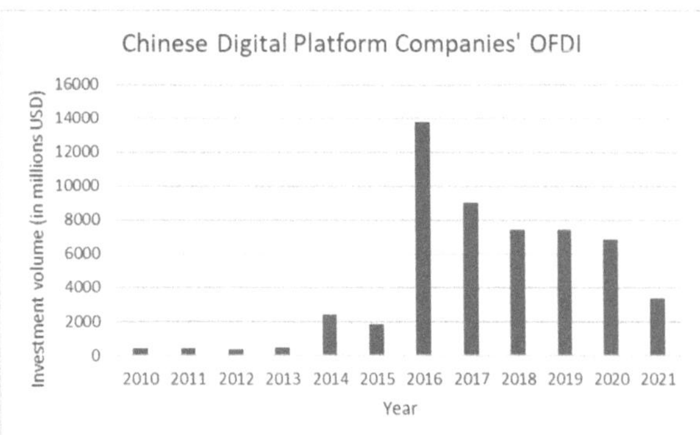

Figure 1. The total volume of major overseas foreign direct investments (no less than USD 100 million) by Chinese digital platform companies in 2010–2021.
Note: OFDI (outward foreign direct investment)

million in 2016 to USD 250 million in 2017. Similar calls for screening Chinese high-tech investments in the EU may have also deterred some investments (Kirkegaard 2019).

In terms of the geographic distribution of investment destinations, the data shows that Chinese platform companies' investments in the BRI countries have grown compared to pre-BRI levels, but their investments in the non-BRI countries, including most developed economies and some large developing economies not participating in the BRI had much stronger growth. As shown in Figure 2, total OFDI in the 139 BRI-participating countries increased after the 2013 BRI announcement, suggesting increased investment interest. In comparison, however, OFDI in non-BRI countries grew much more significantly. Despite the decline since 2017, investment in non-BRI countries has been consistently higher than in BRI countries. A breakdown of the major investment destinations by country, including the top-20 destination countries by OFDI volume (shown in Figure 3), shows that Chinese platform companies' investments have concentrated in major non-BRI countries, notably the advanced Western economies like the US and various European countries which could offer strong market demand and innovative technology assets, and nonparticipating large developing economies like India and Brazil.

The case of India in particular challenges the notion that a country's participation in the BRI can be the primary motivator for Chinese platform companies' investments. The Indian government has refused to participate in the BRI since its inception, citing issues such as the China-Pakistan Economic Corridor's (CPEC) infringement of its territorial sovereignty (Indian Ministry of External Affairs 2017). India also has a highly uncertain domestic policy environment targeting foreign tech firms, such as an "e-commerce policy that prohibits foreign firms from selling their own products on their platforms" (World Bank 2021, 235). Nevertheless, India has held the top spot among developing country recipients of Chinese platform companies' OFDI, as Figure 3 shows. Chinese companies are drawn by India's vibrant ICT sector and its large population coming online: among India's 30 unicorns (startups valued at over USD 1 billion) in 2020, 18 were Chinese-funded (Kharpal 2020). India's attractiveness as an overseas expansion destination, however, declined following the India-China border clash in 2020. India banned scores of Chinese apps and the Indian public started boycotting Chinese tech products (McMorrow and Findlay 2020). Reflecting this changed host country context, the CGIT data does not show any major investments (of more than USD 100 million) from Chinese platform companies in India since 2020.

Among emerging markets that do participate in the BRI, notable investment destinations for Chinese digital platform companies include Indonesia, Russia, Thailand, Turkey, and Pakistan. Chinese state initiatives for promoting trade, investments and connectivity like the BRI/DSR certainly can play a role in facilitating the engagement between relevant players in China and the host countries. Yet host country factors, including market size and geographic proximity to China, have also been shown to be key factors in Chinese platforms' business expansion (Jia,

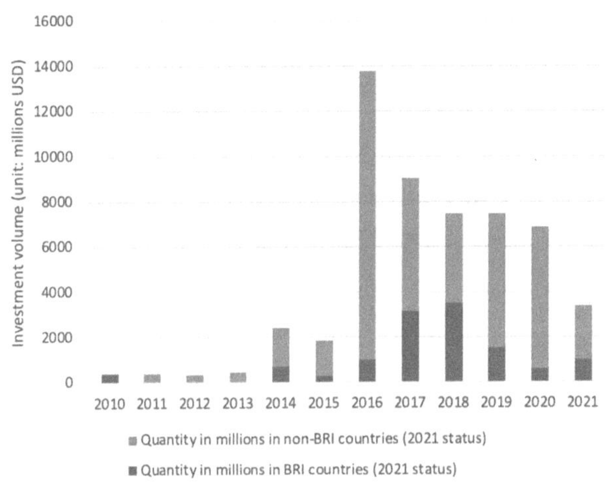

Figure 2. Chinese digital platform companies' major overseas foreign direct investments in BRI vs. non-BRI countries in 2010–2021.

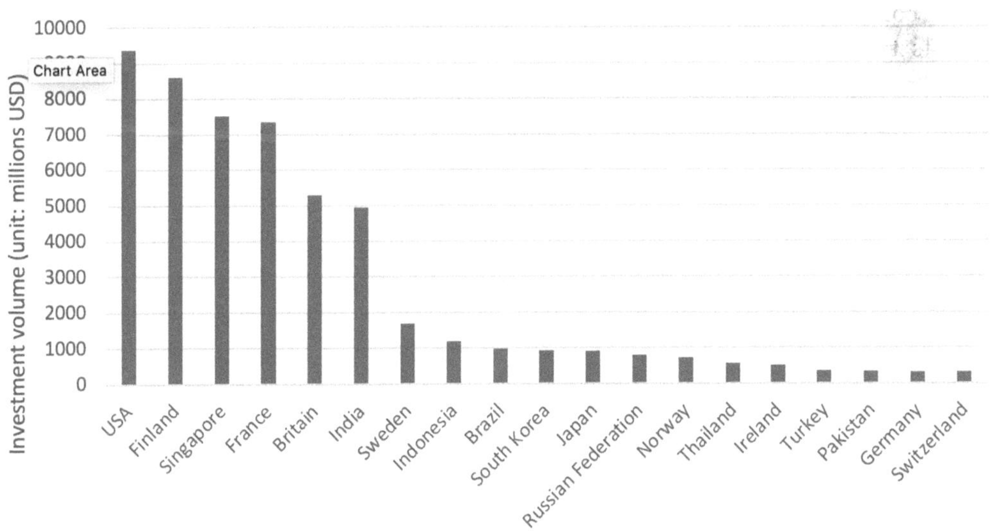

Figure 3. Top-20 destination countries of Chinese digital platform companies' major overseas foreign direct investments in 2010–2021.

Kenney, and Zysman 2018; Tritto, He, and Junaedi 2020; Zhu, Lan, and Zhang 2021). Like India, these emerging markets have a large population with growing spending power, creating strong market potential that draws Chinese firms (Tritto, He, and Junaedi 2020). Geographical proximity to China also makes them more desirable destinations for overseas expansion for companies new to international expansion, compared to populous countries further away in Africa or Latin America. For instance, some digital platforms employ the strategy of "following Chinese users abroad", expanding to proximate countries and regions in Asia where Chinese tourists visit frequently, and where a large local Chinese diaspora with business and cultural ties to China also drives demand (Jia, Kenney, and Zysman 2018; Zhao 2018).

National digital economy development policies can also help attract foreign tech firms to the country, not just the Chinese ones. For example, Thailand launched its Thailand 4.0 national strategy in 2016, devoting business-friendly industry regulations, tax incentives, and investment policies to attracting tech firms from Japan, China, the US, and elsewhere (Kohpaiboon 2020). As the next section will show, in the case of Indonesia, the largest recipient of Chinese digital platforms' OFDI among all the 139 BRI-participating countries, commercial interests largely prevailed in firms' expansion, and host country environments are influential in shaping their engagement with the BRI discourse, their expansion and localization strategies.

Case study: Indonesia

Major investments (above USD 100 million) by Chinese platform companies in Indonesia have primarily been in its two tech unicorns, ride-hailing company Gojek and e-commerce company Tokopedia, now merged as GoTo (see Table 2). For instance, Alibaba Cloud's promotional materials tout that Tokopedia uses its "cloud infrastructure as a service, big data solutions, AI capabilities, and security features to provide more intelligence and better user experience to their end customers". In addition, Chinese-invested platforms headquartered in Singapore, such as Tencent-invested gaming and e-commerce firm SEA (also the parent company of e-commerce platform Shopee), and Alibaba-invested e-commerce firm Lazada, are also active in Indonesia.

Table 2. Major investments by Chinese platform companies in Indonesia.

Year	Chinese Investor	Indonesian Investee	Amount in USD
2017	Tencent	Gojek	$ 150 m
2017	JD.com	Gojek	$ 100 m
2017	Alibaba	Tokopedia	$ 500 m
2019	Tencent, JD.com	Gojek	$ 340 m
2021	Primavera Capital, Tencent	GoTo (formed after the merger of Gojek and Tokopedia)	$ 100 m

Data source: China Global Investment Tracker (CGIT) database of the American Enterprise Institute.

Among the top ten e-commerce platforms by monthly web visits in Indonesia in the third quarter of 2021, five were linked to Chinese platforms, including the top four, Tokopedia, Shopee, Bukalapak (backed by foreign investors including Ant Financial, Alibaba's Fintech affiliate) and Lazada, plus JD.com's local subsidiary JD.id ranking ninth (iPriceInsights 2021). Among the three most widely used mobile payment platforms in Indonesia, Chinese platform companies hold minority shares in two: Gojek's Tencent- and JD-backed payment platform GoPay, and Ant Financial-backed DANA.

The next section analyzes these investments, focusing on how Chinese platform companies engaged with the BRI/DSR initiative in Indonesia and how the host country's contextual factors shaped their investments and local business operations.

Drivers of Chinese platforms' investments in Indonesia

As will be seen below, in Indonesia commercial interests, rather than the Chinese government's foreign policy initiatives such as the BRI/DSR, have largely driven the influx of Chinese platforms and their investments. With a large market, a young population with growing spending power, and geographic proximity to China, Indonesia appeals to Chinese digital platforms looking to expand overseas. It also has the largest digital economy in Southeast Asia, with gross merchandise value reaching USD 70 billion in 2021 and projected to reach USD 146 billion in 2025, at a 20% compound annual growth rate (Google, Temasek, and Bain & Company 2021). Around half of its population is under 30 years old, the prime market for tech products and services. In contrast, the Chinese market has undergone a slowdown since 2017 and its population is aging, making the growth potential of Indonesia even more attractive.

Interviewees highlighted the appeal of Indonesian market growth for Chinese platforms looking to expand overseas. For instance, a venture capitalist (VC) remarked:

> In recent years, it [Chinese investment] has gravitated towards technology, partly because Internet penetration in Southeast Asia is where China was in 2014,

> but Southeast Asia is growing twice as fast. So we see a lot of activity coming here to tap on the growth in Internet penetration, and also the demographic dividend of the growing middle class … growth in some areas in China is slowing down, and this is particularly true for asset-light investors … it's not [just] the Chinese coming, but also Korean and Japanese investors flocking to Southeast Asia. (Interview 38)

Similarly, a JD.id executive explained the decision to set up the local subsidiary:

> Indonesia is the biggest country in ASEAN, and that's why this is our biggest investment outside China. Indonesia has one of the youngest populations in the world, growing middle class so we see a lot of potential here. (Interview 28)

The Vice-Chairman of the Indonesian FinTech Lending Association, a self-regulatory organization set up by the Indonesian Financial Services Authority to regulate Fintech lending platforms, concurred that "Chinese tech VCs follow what the market wants" (Interview 1).

The influx of Chinese tourists and businesses to Indonesia has also helped facilitate Chinese platforms' expansion. For instance, research has shown that because Chinese tourists are accustomed to using e-wallets at home and prefer not to carry large amounts of cash, Chinese digital payment services, such as WeChat Pay, have expanded to popular destinations like Bali by partnering with local startups developing point-of-sales devices for local merchants to cater to their demand (Pranata 2019). Chinese business people using platform services within China have also helped drive the local demand when their businesses expanded to Indonesia. As one interviewee observed, "for AliCloud, people that are using Ali in China would use it in Indonesia too, because they are very familiar with the management of the cloud, the dashboard and the support team." (Interview 7)

Indonesia is home to a large ethnically Chinese population, constituting about two percent of its entire population (Fossati 2019). It has helped facilitate partnerships with Chinese platforms. Despite deep-rooted anti-Chinese sentiments, the top listed Indonesian conglomerates with the highest market capitalization have all been founded by ethnic Chinese businessmen. The growing economic power of China has led to Chinese-Indonesian business moguls being more open to using their ethnic identity to promote business partnerships with Chinese firms (Liu and Zhou 2019). Major conglomerates, including Sinar Mas Group, Salim Group, Lippo Group, and Astra Group, accounting for 17.5% of total market capitalization in Indonesia altogether, all have business lines in media, information, and communications (Liu and Zhou 2019). Some have partnered with Chinese platforms to enhance the conglomerates' incumbent positions and tap into the digital market boom. For instance, Astra International established a joint venture with the Chinese Fintech platform WeLab to launch an online lending firm for unsecured consumer loans (Freischlad 2018). Lippo Group invested IDR 628 billion (USD 44.35 million) in Chinese Internet giant Tencent through shares and equity-linked notes to promote the group's digitalization (Reuters 2018). However, the desire for partnership should not only be associated with Chinese Indonesian-owned businesses; it has also come from other Indonesian conglomerates. For instance, MNC Group, an Indonesian media conglomerate became the local partner for Tencent's WeChat messaging service, because the company was interested in expanding into social media, and Tencent could provide the platform for promoting MNC's media and user-generated content (Tapsell 2017).

In comparison, the BRI and its digital component the DSR, have been perceived by interviewees as a vague policy framework, yielding very limited direct influence on the platforms' expansion into Indonesia. Interviewees viewed BRI as a high-level policy primarily promoting large-scale government-funded infrastructure projects in sectors like mining and energy, or a vague policy discourse with largely symbolic value promoting exchanges between Indonesian firms and Chinese firms. Unlike Chinese state-owned telecommunications equipment providers like ZTE or mobile service providers like China Mobile, Chinese digital platform companies are predominantly private-sector firms, whose business decisions are dominated by profit-seeking interests. The BRI/DSR as a high-level framework provided few direct commercial incentives for them on the ground. For instance, as one interviewee remarked:

> Most of those preferential policies … like the loans from the [Chinese] state, from CDB [China Development Bank], preferential bank loans, any kind of loans … most go to the state-owned companies, so many private companies or SMEs [small and medium enterprises] cannot access those benefits. (Interview 13)

The vagueness of the BRI/DSR as a high-level initiative also allowed firms to choose to engage with the initiative in ways deemed suitable for their business interests, leading to different strategies when dealing with stakeholders in Indonesia. Some firms linked their expansion in Indonesia to the broader discourse of the BRI such as BRI's espoused win-win collaboration for both China and Indonesia, while still recognizing that commercial interests instead of Chinese foreign policy were the primary driver of expansion for private-sector collaborations. For instance, a JD.id executive remarked:

> I'm a big advocate of BRI. I think it's a fantastic idea. But under that umbrella, it's more about the people. BRI is more visionary, Chinese companies have invested in a lot of infrastructure projects through government to government agreements. But for us [JD], this is purely private sector driven … the BRI idea is pretty good in bridging China and Indonesia. I see more and more strategic partnership, but it's more on the macro atmosphere that allows private sector to engage in. (Interview 28)

For some firms, associating their expansion rhetorically with BRI seems to be part of a public relations strategy to promote their businesses to domestic regulators and players within China, instead of in Indonesia. For example, a Fintech platform operating in Hong Kong and mainland China expanded into Indonesia *via* a partnership with an Indonesian conglomerate. Its expansion was recognized with an award for innovation during the Belt and Road International Innovation Forum in Beijing, where the firm's chief executive attended and shared their insights on the expansion. Yet when asked about BRI and its impact on the company's expansion, the firm's executive in charge of international markets in Indonesia was unfamiliar with the BRI or the award, concluding that there was "no incentive (from BRI) or government support" (Interview 7). The executive speculated:

> this [BRI] is one of the China initiatives as well, right? Wherever we are, we want to do what we can to help the government. Like, in Indonesia, if we have the chance to meet with the OJK [Financial Services Authority], we also say the same thing – if you need anything, you want to see how China does business or technology, we are more than happy, you can come to visit us anytime … So I think the impact is not felt in Indonesia on this BRI thing, but it's helpful for our colleagues in [mainland] China and Hong Kong … So this is helpful attention. We welcome these recognitions. (Interview 7)

In some cases, the local executives of Chinese-invested joint ventures showed hesitancy to associate their business expansion even rhetorically with the BRI. They cautioned that unintended negative consequences may occur when engaging local players critical of the BRI. For instance, one local executive of the subsidiary of a Chinese firm who preferred to be off the record remarked:

> One Belt One Road initiative is quite sensitive, especially in Southeast Asia. So for us, we don't mention the One Belt, One Road initiative so much here, especially to Indonesian companies. Maybe we mentioned a lot to Chinese companies [at home] …The world situation is changing a lot recently and hard to predict … for us, we don't have any expectations from [Chinese] government to give us support or whatever. (Interview 29)

It should be noted that Indonesia's history of anti-Chinese ethnic prejudices has long stirred negative sentiments toward Chinese presence, and anti-Chinese rhetoric is frequently employed by politicians in political campaigns (Freedman 2003). Indonesia is a Muslim-majority society, and Chinese Indonesians, both as an ethnic and religious minority, display a high-level of cultural distance from the other Indonesians, despite having long played a key role in domestic and international business (Fossati 2019). Survey research shows that cues to the ethnicity of Chinese investors substantially lower public support for foreign investment (Fossati 2019). While there has been growing admiration among the public of China's economic power, criticisms of the economic consequences of Chinese investments, such as the influx of Chinese workers perceived as negatively impacting local employment, have also grown, along with socio-cultural concerns of growing Chinese influence (Damuri et al. 2019). Furthermore, opposition politicians employed anti-BRI messaging in the lead-up to the presidential election in 2019 (Priyandita 2018), creating a more hostile environment for Chinese firms at the time of the interviews. Such factors could be influential in some firms' decisions to distance themselves from the BRI or any Chinese government incentives in Indonesia, in comparison to countries with a more friendly environment. Nevertheless, this shows the importance of the host country context in shaping the Chinese platforms' expansion and business strategies.

Interestingly, while Chinese foreign policy such as the BRI seemed to have a very limited direct effect on the Chinese platforms' expansion, China's domestic regulatory shift toward stringent regulations over its ICT industries played a role in pushing some firms' expansion. For instance, the Chinese government clamped down on the Fintech lending sector in 2015–18 to address growing financial and socioeconomic risks. Many Chinese platforms as a result shifted their business overseas, including to Indonesia (Tritto, He, and Junaedi 2020). As regulations tightened within China, coupled with intense competition for a saturating market, the option of expanding overseas grew more attractive for some Chinese platforms. As a consultant for the Indonesian Investment Coordinating Board remarked:

> I think it all boils down to policies. In promoting investment Chinese government can push firms to go out without forcing them ... you have two choices, you can just stay here [in China], but the cost of doing business is rising. (Interview 32)

Since mid-2021, Beijing has initiated a new round of crackdowns on tech platforms in numerous sectors such as ride-hailing, cloud computing, online education, Fintech, e-sports, e-commerce, social media, online home rentals, virtual reality, live streaming, and entertainment, for issues such as data security risks, market monopoly, financial risks, tax evasion, marketing deception, failure to protect workers' rights, failure in content moderation, or perceived negative influence on minors (China Project 2021). It will be interesting to see whether this expedites the growing interest of Chinese platforms in expanding to emerging markets like Indonesia.

Indonesian context: Chinese platforms' local business strategies

As will be seen below, in the case of Indonesia, the host country's context, including its policy environment for foreign investment in the digital economy, the gaps between the stated policies and the policy implementation in practice, and its labor market and policy have further shaped Chinese platforms' expansion and their localization business strategies.

The policy environment for foreign investment in the digital economy: Local partnership expectations and preferential treatment

The Indonesian government has vowed to make the digital economy a key engine of its economic growth, using the nation's strength as the fourth most populous country in the world and the largest market in Southeast Asia (BeritaSatu 2020). In a speech to Parliament in 2019, President Joko "Jokowi" Widodo remarked that "data is the new type of wealth for our nation, it is now more valuable than oil" (Reuters 2019). The government is keen to support innovation and local tech firms. For example, Nadiem Makarim, the co-founder of Gojek, was appointed by Jokowi as the Education, Culture, Research, and Technology Minister in the current Jokowi administration.

Similar to other developing countries with large markets such as China (Huang and Sharif 2015), to develop its national innovation capabilities, Indonesia must rely on foreign investment to bring much-needed technology and capital to the country. Accordingly, the policy environment actively promotes foreign direct investments in the digital economy (Indonesia Investment Coordinating Board 2021). This promotion is actively supported by a variety of digital economy stakeholders, as the following interviewees' responses show:

> The fact that we are very technology-dependent [on foreign technologies] makes it easier for everybody to come in, not just from China ... China is in the position to provide that technology, the ecosystem. Indonesia's demographic circumstance, it's almost like a perfect combination. (Interview 16: Indonesian digital/investment advisor)

> The foreign investment's role is very, very influential for our country ... because local investors are quite afraid to do early investment. Early investments are mostly taken by foreign investors ... without the capital from the foreign investor, it is hard to achieve what we achieved. (Interview 12: Indonesian digital economy researcher)

> Government doesn't care who invested in technology. There's no citizenship in money. Money can come from the US, come from China, we don't worry about where the money is from. (Interview 6: Indonesian digital startup founder)

In order to attract foreign investments to the digital economy, the government provides incentives such as tax breaks. Under the Ministry of Finance Regulation No. 150/PMK.010/2018, the "Digital Economy Sector" has been included among a list of 18 "pioneer industries" for a tax holiday (exemption of tax) since 2018. Investments of IDR 100–500 billion (USD 7–35 million) are eligible for a 50% tax holiday for five years; IDR 500 billion-1 trillion (USD 35–70 million) qualify for a 100% tax holiday for five years; larger investments can secure a 100% tax holiday for even longer periods depending on the size of the investment, with investments of IDR 30 trillion (USD 2 billion) or more qualifying for 100% exemption for 20 years. Once the tax holiday expires, an additional two-year tax holiday is provided with a 25% exemption for investments of IDR 100–500 billion (USD 7–35 million) and a 50% exemption for larger investments.

On the other hand, similar to other sectors in Indonesia, most foreign investments in the digital economy were still subject to foreign ownership restrictions, requiring Indonesian firms as local partners. This suggests that the government wanted local firms to retain some or majority control of business operations, while receiving the benefits of partnering with foreign firms to access capital, technology or other resources. The Indonesia "Negative Investment List" (effective until 2021 under *Presidential Regulation No. 76 of 2007* and *Presidential Regulation No. 44 of 2016*), and now the "Priority List" (effective under

Presidential Regulation No. 10 of 2021) provide sector- and industry-specific guidance on foreign ownership. For example, web portals and digital platforms in the information and communications sector allowed 100% foreign ownership for investments involving at least IDR 100 billion (USD 7 million), while investments smaller than IDR 100 billion were restricted to 49% foreign ownership under the 2016 Negative Investment List (HSF 2021). For businesses such as e-commerce, 100% foreign ownership was allowed only if the retailer sold a specific list of goods and had entered into partnerships with local cooperatives and micro, small and medium enterprises (HSF 2021). These restrictions appeared to have been scrapped under the "Priority List" since March 2021, but legal experts caution that the new investment policy is still at an early stage and that investments may be scrutinized on a case-by-case basis (HSF 2021).

Regulators responsible for specific digital sectors have also imposed requirements of Indonesian shareholdership, regardless of the scale of investment. For instance, for Fintech lending, under regulation *POJK No. 77* effective since 2016, the regulating Financial Services Authority requires platforms to have at least 15% Indonesian ownership. This low-level suggests that the government is eager for foreign investment to help propel the industry's growth to promote the underbanked populations' access to credit. For payment platforms, the regulating Bank Indonesia requires non-bank payment services to have at least 15% Indonesian ownership, but at least 51% of shares with voting rights must be owned by Indonesian individuals or entities (Reuters 2021). Bank Indonesia requires non-bank payment infrastructure companies providing clearing and settlement services to be at least 80% Indonesian-owned, with at least 80% of the voting rights held by Indonesian investors (Reuters 2021). This suggests that the government sees these payment platforms to be crucial to financial security and seeks to avoid significant influence of foreign platforms.

In addition, Indonesia's data governance policy has been cited for requiring data localization to promote investments in local industry development, such as investments in data centers and digital infrastructure (Foster and Azmeh 2020). In 2012 Indonesia imposed *Government Regulation No. 82 on the Management of Electronic Systems and Transactions* to require websites and applications that provide public services (which was interpreted to cover almost all websites and applications) to establish local data centers for storage. The blanket data localization requirement was in place for seven years. In 2019, facing pressure from the western corporate lobby and US digital trade agenda (Basu 2020; Diela 2019), Indonesia rolled back its data localization mandates with the implementation of *Government Regulation No. 71 on Organization of Electronic Systems and Transactions* allowing private firms to store commercial data abroad. This shift suggests that Indonesia has become more receptive to foreign platform companies' demand for cross-border data flows.[6]

How have these policies shaped the Chinese platforms' investments and expansion? As the quantitative data showed earlier, Indonesia is the largest recipient of Chinese platforms' OFDI among all 139 BRI-participating countries. Interviewees also generally agreed that the policy environment for large-scale foreign investments in the digital economy was supportive, and combined with Indonesia's market potential, drew many Chinese and other foreign platforms to Indonesia. The favorable investment policies for the digital economy even led to some pushback from other sectors. For instance, one local think tank researcher observed:

> Most big VCs come from the US, Singapore, and Japan, for the Chinese, capital mostly comes from tech firms ... the [investment] policy is quite supporting and wonderful, very open compared to the other sectors ... Indonesian government is very supportive for the digital [sectors] even compared to other sectors, the other sectors have been complaining that the government has a special [treatment] for the digital economy, very open and they provide quite a lot of incentives and easy procedures for the foreign investor, that's also become the problem for the other sectors because they feel that their sector does not get the same regulatory ease for foreign investment. (Interview 3)

Interviewees also highlighted the importance of seeking local partners for Chinese players. This was often required by the regulations but could also be motivated by business considerations such as tapping into the local user base. In general, Chinese firms' expansion can take several forms, including establishing or acquiring a local subsidiary in which the parent company holds a controlling interest, establishing a joint venture with one or more local firms (with more balanced interest arrangements and control over corporate affairs), or investing in local firms as a minority shareholder with limited voting rights (such as VC investments). Chinese firms seeking predominant control over their local business operations would often seek close to 100% ownership or at least a majority ownership stake (Interview 8), yet this might not be possible for certain sectors and smaller investments due to the foreign ownership restrictions outlined above. As one lawyer explained:

> The key for an international investor is to have majority stake ... the logic [for Indonesia's foreign ownership restrictions] is, foreigners are only here for big projects, that Indonesians do not have the capital or the expertise. (Interview 8)

The process of finding a good local partner could certainly take time and effort. As one interviewee remarked, "the problem is not that Chinese firms don't want a local partner, but [sometimes] there is no local partner. But the law says you must have a local, even if it's 5%." (Interview 9). Chinese platforms often found local partners through mutual business contacts or employees with overseas experiences. For example, one joint venture executive explained how a Chinese platform XX approached its Indonesian partner:

> from a mutual friend ... XX and ourselves, we do our research. Based on our research, we felt it might be a good match. Early on, what's important, is that I wouldn't say it's easy, but it's to be upfront with the Chinese companies, this is what we want, what do you guys think, then put it in writing in the JV [joint venture] agreement, and then set up the company. There are some cultural frictions, but that's natural. In my experience, what bridges that was that in XX these top managers had some experiences overseas. They've gone to schools overseas like Northwestern, Babson, they've worked overseas, so those guys know the overseas market. (Interview 24)

As noted earlier, Indonesia is home to a large ethnic Chinese population with strong business interests. This also allowed some platforms to enter Indonesia through partnerships with local ethnic Chinese businesses. As one interviewee remarked:

> Here there are many Chinese companies, Chinese people from the mainland, but also here, there are many Chinese Indonesians, so more natural and easier to use them, like "Laoxiang" ["fellow townsmen" in Chinese], to help them ... some of the successful companies, they only do business internally within [ethnic] Chinese business circles, they can survive here. (Interview 13)

Gaps between policy and implementation: Leeway for Chinese platforms' local partnerships and business practices

As in most developing countries, in Indonesia, policies were not always implemented as they were stated. Although the digital economy sectors enjoyed preferential treatment and less regulation compared to other sectors, the process of securing incentives and regulatory approvals for business expansion could still be cumbersome for Chinese platforms. While some (Interview 28; Interview 32) said implementation was improving, interviewees generally concurred that regulations applicable to digital economy sectors remained scattered across different laws and different government agencies. Also, there were other issues such as the lack of qualified personnel, bureaucratic red tape, and inter-agency infighting within the government. For instance, one interviewee compared Indonesia with nearby Singapore, another hub of Chinese tech investment, "you go to Singapore, everything just works so perfectly, and then we have the same technology here, it [gaining approval] just doesn't seem to work" (Interview 9). Another interviewee highlighted the limited governing capacity at the Financial Services Authority, where a small team of "only about 8 to 10 people" were responsible for supervising all Fintech platforms in Indonesia (Interview 11).

As many Chinese platform companies and investors were new to Indonesia, the gaps between the policies and their implementation prompted them to rely on local partners, consultants, and lawyers for dealing with government agencies in business registration and expansion. For instance, one joint venture executive remarked:

> I see some Chinese investors probably have a cultural gap, especially on the regulation, they are not really prudent ... if Chinese investors would like to invest in Indonesia, they need to have a strong partner that really understands the market and be vocal. We [Indonesian partner] need to be bold, you cannot have a local partner that would only say yes as long as your money is coming in ... I always tell them [Chinese partner] good corporate governance and always everything by the law, let's do this. If you are thinking of doing otherwise, maybe you are meeting up with the wrong person. I know regulations can sometimes be troublesome ... once you read and you follow the guidelines you will believe you can make a good business. (Interview 24)

One local law firm working with Chinese firms remarked:

> For lawyers, it's a good business opportunity ... sometimes one government agency issues this regulation and then the other [agency] issues [another one], and then they clash, so which one you should follow? And even the lawyers can only mention [to the Chinese firm], these two are contradicting, and how will it be enforced, we don't really know, but then we could do this and this. (Interview 25)

Another consultant working with Chinese firms and the Indonesian Investment Coordinating Board also remarked that Chinese firms typically used local consulting services:

> The policy is constantly changing, the government does not have a good reputation of keeping to its words ... whenever a new policy comes out, we ask which agencies will be taking part, then we ask all these agencies, and when they give us more or less the same answers, we can respond [to Chinese firms] ... that's why they [Chinese firms] typically use local agents like us because you cannot do it alone, but it is getting better. (Interview 32)

The government's uneven capacity to implement policies also resulted in some Chinese platforms, especially smaller players in sectors where the regulatory capacity was limited, to attempt to circumvent the regulations for investment. For instance, some Chinese Fintech platforms simply ran their local operations without registration (Interview 2), leading to unfavorable perceptions of Chinese investments among some local competing businesses and consumer rights groups (Interview 2; Interview 30). Some used pseudo-Indonesian partners with potentially serious legal ramifications. As one local business association leader observed:

> The regulation says 85%, they are actually owned 100% by the Chinese, they'll have a nominee, an Indonesian, who they'll just identify through mostly their employees. They'll say, "look, I'll just use your name because you are Indonesian. You own 15%, but actually it's ours." That's not an ideal model ... customers come and complain, then we [industry association] pass the complaint down, we cannot call the Chinese national, usually the director is Indonesian because it is required, so we call the Indonesian, and they'll say, "OK, I told these guys already but they are not listening." But you are the director, you have a judicial responsibility, the company is under you, if you are under violation, they are going after you, not the Chinese guy because he is not on the board. (Interview 16)

As another example of the gap between the stated policies and their implementation shaping firm practices, interviewees reported different practices with respect to the requirement for firms to invest in local data centers for storage. Some firms reported strict compliance by storing all their data on local servers, or using cloud services with local servers in Indonesia like AliCloud (Interview 17; Interview 24). Yet some tried to circumvent the rule, as the enforcement was weak before it was rolled back in 2019. As one lawyer working with Chinese firms remarked:

> No one cares about the data center and all this ... they [the government] are playing checkers, but everyone is playing chess ... the data center requirement is antiquated really, because it doesn't address the reality on the ground ... how can they [the government] tell the difference between the mirroring or a data center? ... [the firms] have a data center in Singapore, or in Hong Kong, which they built for hundreds of millions of dollars for the region, so it's secure. Then the government says you must build your data center here in Indonesia. Why? You'll just build something which is cheap, but not secure. So actually it will not fulfill the purpose ... my friend said for the data center, he just once put a box with some Christmas lights on it, saying "that's our server", will they [the government] know? (Interview 8)

Talent shortage and pro-local labor policy: Chinese platforms investing in local capacity building

Indonesia has a severe human capital shortage, as 58% of the population has an education of junior high school or below (Jakarta Post 2020). In terms of tech talents, the country produces only 278 engineers per 1 million people each year, far behind regional peers such as Malaysia or Thailand (Tani 2019). On the other hand, Indonesian regulations on employment prioritize the employment of the local workforce in foreign-invested tech firms operating in Indonesia, with the hope of building up the talent pool for indigenous innovation over the long term. For firms, hiring foreign workers from overseas could be a solution but one that is time-consuming and costly: a number of interviewees commented on the lengthy work permit process, the requirement for the foreign worker to learn Bahasa Indonesia, and for the firm to show that no local workers can qualify for the job (e.g., Interview 10; Interview 29). There is an exemption to the Foreign Manpower Utilization Plan approval (by the Ministry of Manpower) for Indonesian tech-based startups, yet this exemption only lasts for three months, and the startups must apply for a work visa afterward for any staff hired this way.

Importantly, Indonesia requires that each foreign worker must have a parallel Tenaga Kerja Pendamping (Indonesian companion employee) appointment for the transfer of technology and skills from the foreign worker, and that firms must provide training for the Indonesian companion employees, per the *Ministry of Manpower Regulation No. 10 of 2018*. The policy's goal is that "this apprentice he [the foreign worker] must teach [so as] to replace him, and transfer his knowledge" (Interview 9). Foreign nationals also cannot serve in human resources positions, per the Ministry of Manpower regulations, on the grounds that Indonesian nationals are more adept in dealing with local employees in a manner consistent with local cultural norms.

On the incentives side, the Jokowi administration unveiled tax incentives for training local workers. Under the Super Deductible Tax Scheme, companies can receive a reduction of taxable income as high as 200% of the cost of vocational education activities, such as working with local vocational and polytechnic schools to provide vocational training, industrial equipment, and apprenticeship activities, and deduction of up to 300% for the cost of R&D activities conducted within Indonesia (Jakarta Post 2019). Interviewees cautioned, however, that due to the talent shortage, Chinese platforms would likely still consider nearby countries with stronger talent pools such as Singapore or Malaysia as primary location choices for R&D activities in Southeast Asia (e.g., Interview 32; Interview 33; Interview 35).

As a result of the policies promoting the hiring of local workers, Chinese-invested platforms have devoted significant attention and resources to local workforce hiring and retention (at least rhetorically). Chinese firms, being relatively new players in the market, are still not as highly regarded among local tech workers as Western businesses like Google (Interview 39; Interview 40). Thus, the competition for the limited pool of local talent is fierce, and talent with specialized skills in high demand, such as product managers, senior developers and software engineers have strong bargaining power. Some Chinese firms and Chinese-invested startups have reportedly offered 30%-50% above-market rates of compensation to attract talent from other firms (36kr 2021; Timmerman 2022). Some firms reportedly engaged in intense competition with Western firms, even writing blank checks for high performers (Monk's Hill Ventures & Glints 2021)[7]. As one interviewee vividly described:

> Everybody would complain the same thing. We hired this guy, six months later he's gone. So we keep on paying expensive money to get people in ... These local tech talents are like San Francisco 49ers. their grade is actually 4, but for us, the pay is 9 ... once we have our own Technology Center here, then the challenge would be, can we retain these talents. (Interview 7)

Aligning with the government's priority of local workforce development, businesses also highlight talent training and education activities as key parts of their localization and corporate social responsibility efforts. For instance, Alibaba Cloud Indonesia promotes its Digital Talent Empowerment Program providing workshops on cloud services to lecturers at Bina Nusantara University and Prasetya Mulya Business School, and training for local developers through partnering with startup incubator BLOCK71 and IT providers Trinocate and Inovasi Informatika (Jakarta Post 2020). JD.id runs its own management training programs, sending selected local students to work in the JD.com headquarters in Beijing and then back to Indonesia; an initiative that had helped the company grow its local Indonesian workforce to about 3000 people by 2018 (Interview 28). In 2020 JD's core e-commerce platform operations employed about 1200 people in Indonesia, 95% of whom were Indonesians, and only 5% were foreign employees including Chinese; in addition, its warehousing and logistics business in Indonesia, which served to fulfill orders for not only its own platform but also other corporate clients like IKEA, employed about 2000 people, predominantly local Indonesians (Xinhua 2020).[8] Interviewees also highlighted initiatives such as developing training programs with their local partners, offering paid student internships to local schools, free open seminars, and business competitions with prizes (Interview 7; Interview 24; Interview 40). These are not just public relations exercises but business-oriented initiatives aiming to attract future employees in a challenging local labor market. As one joint venture executive explained:

> We go to the campus directly sometimes, what else can we do? Because all the best qualified are already hijacked the minute they leave the campus. We try to prepay them first before they graduate, in return we give them some knowledge. At the end of the day, when it's so difficult, then we bring in our expertise, the Chinese team that are working in Jakarta ... I've been dealing with IT talent for many years, it's so difficult to find the right IT talent because 100% of our IT talents are not ready to work, what they have been taught in schools are completely different from the real world ... but the good thing is that Indonesian IT students are super smart ... they can adjust pretty quickly ... once they have a good mentor. (Interview 24)

Admittedly, the evidence of such efforts' impacts on developing Indonesian talents' capability for learning is still limited. A consensus among business leaders and venture capitalists is that the limited local talent pool hinders significant technology transfer (Interview 6; Interview 39). In addition, some Chinese firms opted to use tourist visas to bring in Chinese or other foreign workers for short-term assignments to circumvent the regulations, a controversial practice with potentially serious legal ramifications (Interview 10). Some poached employees from local firms, leading to acrimonious relationships (Interview 14). Nevertheless, the local talent shortage and the labor policies to promote local workforce participation have resulted in the Chinese platforms investing in local capacity building, building more local partnerships, and further localization of their business operations.

Conclusion

Existing literature on China's digital expansion in the Global South has focused primarily on the role of the Chinese state, with analyses based on Chinese policy documents and/or documents related to Chinese telecommunications infrastructure projects and firms. By contrast, this article relies on empirically-grounded research to investigate a much less studied phenomenon: expansion of Chinese digital platforms in overseas emerging markets, focusing especially on Belt and Road countries. It highlights the nuanced engagement Chinese platform companies have with Chinese government's policies like the BRI/DSR. It also highlights the role of host country development aspirations, policies and their implementation in practice, and socioeconomic context in shaping platforms' operations in the host countries.

This study finds limited impact of the BRI/DSR, Beijing's high-level policy framework, on Chinese platform companies' overseas investments. Commercial interests, shaped by local market opportunities and host countries' socioeconomic and policy environments, largely influence these private-sector companies' decision-making. In some cases, China's domestic regulatory crackdown and the resultant rising costs of doing business at home also motivated their expansion overseas. In this regard, the findings of this study accord with survey findings of Chinese firms across different sectors that report the predominance of commercial interests, rather than the BRI, motivating the private firms' decisions regarding overseas expansion (Li and Zeng 2019). They lend support to scholarly calls for understanding Chinese platform companies and their global expansion not merely as an extension of the Chinese state, but as a dynamic process involving different units of domestic and international capital, and state agencies both in China and in the destination countries (Shen 2021).

With the case study of Indonesia, recipient of Chinese platform companies' largest overseas investment among the 139 BRI countries, this study further contextualizes the platform companies' engagement with the initiative in a BRI-participating host country. The Chinese government has advanced BRI as its overarching policy framework to promote investments, trade, and connectivity between China and emerging markets, and the DSR as its digital economy component. This has played at least some role in directing Global South investments of Chinese state-owned and state-affiliated telecommunications companies (Vila Seoane 2020). However, the evidence presented here from Indonesia at least suggests that, for platform companies, BRI/DSR has become a policy slogan with enough vagueness that allows them to choose whether and how to engage with it based on specific local circumstances. At home in China, the BRI/DSR may be used by platforms as a beneficial branding tool to liaise with regulators and other actors and to promote the firms' internationalization efforts. In the expansion in the host country, the BRI/DSR's impact appears more limited and dependent on the context of the host country. In the case of Indonesia, Chinese platform companies perceived the BRI/DSR as lacking an economic payoff for private firms, therefore they engaged cautiously with the BRI/DSR in their local operations. Indonesia's history of anti-Chinese sentiments and its political environment has led to some platform companies distancing themselves from not just the policy but also any discourses of the BRI/DSR in their local operations and business partnerships.

The findings of study accord with other research showing that the BRI is far from "a monolithic program designed in Beijing and imposed upon others", but "a bundle of intertwined discourses, policies and projects that sometimes align but that are sometimes contradictory" (Oliveira et al. 2020, 1). Beijing's loose branding of all Chinese ICT-related overseas projects as falling under the "BRI/DSR" umbrella, regardless of the firms' varied level of alignment or even non-engagement with the state policy framework on the ground as shown in this study, also prompts critical reflections on such narratives and possible varied interests behind their usage, a topic suitable for future research. For scholars, this study also suggests rethinking the rather singular focus on the Chinese state – its policies and rhetoric and US-China great power rivalry – in much of the literature on the expansion of China's technology footprint. More attention needs to be devoted to studying the interests and the behaviors of the firms, and the circumstances and the perspectives of the affected host countries. The impact of Beijing's BRI/DSR may thus also not be as far-reaching as popular perceptions – both positive and negative – assume, with China's digital expansion depending more on the preferences of Chinese firms and host countries' stakeholders.

The power dynamics that Chinese platforms face both at home and abroad are constantly shifting, which may impact the firms' calculations of their commercial interests and their business strategies. Domestically, amidst economic downturn, Beijing recently softened its regulatory crackdown on dominant tech platforms, instead national and local state agencies moved to acquire "golden shares", tiny minority stakes with special rights, in the domestic subsidiaries of platforms like Alibaba and Tencent (McMorrow et al. 2023a). Internationally, broader market and political dynamics, such as the retreat of some US venture capital funds from China due to rising geopolitical tensions (McMorrow et al. 2023b), also signal fast-changing relationships between Chinese platforms and their overseas partners and global investors. Chinese platform companies are in the process of recalibrating their business units (Horwitz 2023), while investing in overseas assets and possibly seeking diversification away from China or distancing their China operations from global operations and product branding (McMorrow et al. 2023a; Olcott and Liu 2023; Reuhl and Lewis 2022). An in-depth analysis of these recent developments is beyond the scope of this article. Future research moving beyond the state-centric lens could further examine Chinese platforms' dynamic linkages with different domestic and international capital, and state agencies and other stakeholders in China and overseas.

Moving beyond a narrow focus on the interests and actions of the Chinese state, this study centers on the context of the host country shaping Chinese platform companies' overseas expansion. In the case of Indonesia, the host country's aspirations to develop its digital economy led to the use of favorable but also selective foreign investment policies and regulations attracting Chinese platform companies to bring much-needed capital, technology and services to help propel Indonesia's growing digital economy, while also prompting the Chinese platforms to partner with local businesses.

The capacity of the government to implement the policies and streamline the regulatory environment for business registration and expansion was however constrained, leading to a gap between the policies and their implementation. This prompted Chinese firms to rely on local partners and consultants to engage the regulators, but also led to some firms exploiting the limited enforcement on the ground. The local labor market context characterized by talent shortage and labor policies prioritizing the local workforce in foreign-invested businesses also prompted the platforms to invest in local workforce development. The Indonesian government under the pro-business Jokowi administration is keen to develop the capacity of local firms and talents to learn from Chinese partners and build indigenous capability for innovation over the long term. While the impact of the Chinese platforms on the local innovation system is limited without substantial evidence of technology or knowledge transfer, and the host country's governing capacity needs to be strengthened, the analysis shows that companies have been prompted to localize their business operations, seek local partners and talents, and adapt to local circumstances.

The response of Chinese platforms to Indonesian policies has often imposed higher costs: in identifying, evaluating, and engaging local partners; in retaining the services of local legal and consultancy advisors; and in the recruitment and retention of both foreign and local workers. Where the platforms have sought ways around local policy – using sleeping partners to nominally meet ownership rules; evading local data ownership regulations; using tourist visas for foreign workers; or poaching staff from local competitors – this imposes additional risk and, potentially, further costs. In all cases, though, it is local policy and local context that has determined these behaviors.

Care must, of course, be taken in generalizing from the particular circumstances of Indonesia, even given its preeminent role as a platform investment location. Nonetheless, this study adds credence to a small but growing body of literature highlighting how the political, socioeconomic, and regulatory contexts of host countries shape the localization of Chinese technology firms, with case studies drawn from other parts of the world such as Africa, Europe and Central Asia (e.g. Drahokoupil et al. 2017; Gagliardone 2019; Oreglia, Ren, and Liao 2021). The study also adds to our understanding of Chinese platforms' flexible and tailored localization strategies in response to host country environments, leveraging and accommodating the preexisting host country conditions and market players in each country (Oreglia, Ren, and Liao 2021). Furthermore, as this study shows, the host country policymakers and local firms are not passive players: they have their own interests which vary based on local circumstances, driving their interactions with both Chinese and other foreign (including the US) technology players and capital. Therefore, Chinese tech expansion in Southeast Asia and broadly in the BRI countries in Global South is not a one-way street, nor is there a single business model, strategy, or policy template to be used by the host country. It is a two-way street where the interactions between businesses and the institutional and socioeconomic contexts on both sides can shape deals and outcomes.

For scholars and strategists, then, this study highlights the importance of understanding host country-specific policy, policy implementation, and labor market contexts shaping Chinese digital expansion in the Global South on the ground. The way in which local policy shapes behavior also suggests that opportunities exist for governments within emerging markets to foster development gains from the expansion of Chinese platform companies. Future research may seek to expand the focus beyond Indonesia to other BRI countries, and to add a comparative dimension that helps understand the developmental gains to be obtained from different host country policy instruments.

Notes

1. More broadly, given that the existing research on digital platforms focuses on business models in the Global North, there is a need for studies on the expansion of platforms in developing country settings (Nicholson, Nielsen, and Saebø 2021).
2. The Chinese state exerts considerable influence over Chinese firms' overseas telecommunications infrastructure projects by taking ownership stakes and its term for financing (Hsueh 2011). Also, state-owned enterprises are major players in the telecommunications sector, e. g., all major telecommunications network operators are state-owned. In the same vein, telecommunications equipment providers like ZTE are state-financed, and Chinese state-backed policy-directed banks such as the Export-Import Bank of China and China Development Bank, and funds like the China-Africa Development Fund, have financed major telecommunications infrastructure projects, mandating the use of Chinese suppliers and equipment (Agbebi, Gong, and Zheng 2021). Furthermore, private companies like Huawei piggyback on diplomatic missions and state financing for overseas deals, building strategic alliances with state-owned telecom firms and party officials (Hawes 2021). In contrast, digital platform companies like Alibaba, Tencent, and ByteDance are private firms that have amassed significant revenue and capital from the Chinese market, domestic and international stock exchanges, and global investors for their overseas expansion (Jia and Liang 2021; Jia and Winseck 2018; Shen 2017, 2021), and they are embedded in different state-business relationships and power dynamics in their overseas expansion.
3. Available at http://www.aei.org/china-global-investment-tracker/.
4. Available at https://www.cfr.org/blog/countries-china s-belt-and-road-initiative-whos-and-whos-out
5. In selecting key informants in developing country settings, efforts were made to seek out interviewees within divergent organizations and holding divergent perspectives (Kumar 1989). This included first identifying the relevant groups from which the interviewees can be drawn, as already noted in the text; then selecting a few informants from each group based on the consideration that informants possess an intimate knowledge of the Chinese platforms' expansion and local business practices or relevant work experiences, and reaching out to possible informants through networks and colleagues, and attending conferences like the Indonesia Development Forum, industry and startup community events, and academic seminars on relevant topics (purposeful sampling). The author also asked interviewees to suggest names of other persons who in their opinion are knowledgeable experts (snowball sampling).
6. As Foster and Azmeh (2020) pointed out, in latecomer economies including China and Indonesia, industrial policy objectives are important drivers of national digital strategies. Both countries also share similar policy preferences in maintaining the domestic policy autonomy for imposing data localization requirements. Yet, the Indonesian legislation mandating data localization was first implemented in 2012, prior to the significant inflow of Chinese capital. So in this sense, Chinese capital's influence on Indonesian national digital policy in this area was fairly limited. In fact, Indonesia's roll-back of its data localization requirement in 2019 was mainly because of pressure from the US government's digital trade agenda and US tech firms (Basu 2020; Diela 2019).
7. It is possible that such intense competition for talent using compensation packages may experience some cooling, as the mass tech layoffs at tech firms in both the US and China starting in 2022 also affected the tech sector in Indonesia (Timmerman 2022).
8. It should be noted that companies like JD did not disclose the ratio of local to foreign employees at senior management level, so the extent of workforce localization at the senior level is unknown. The post-pandemic bear market and the mass tech layoffs also affected JD's operations in Indonesia. As part of overseas business restructuring, JD shut down its JD.id e-commerce platform that was having difficulty sustaining revenues in 2023 and chose to focus on expanding the logistics business in Indonesia. So, it is possible that the local to foreign ratio now has changed.

Disclosure statement

No potential conflict of interest was reported by the author(s).

Funding

This research project was partly funded by the Strategic Public Policy Research Funding Scheme from the Central Policy Unit of the Hong Kong Special Administrative Region Government, China (Project Number: S2016.A7.003).

ORCID

Yujia He http://orcid.org/0000-0002-0931-2698

References

36kr. 2021. Chinese going-out businesses return to Indonesia (in Chinese). Accessed August 13, 2023. https://letschuhai.com/go-overseas-indonesia-southeast-asia

Aboul-Dahab, K. M. 2021. The virtual silk road between China and the Arab States. *Asian Journal of Middle Eastern and Islamic Studies* 15 (1):51–65. doi:10.1080/25765949.2021.1898813.

Agbebi, M., X. Gong, and Y. Zheng. 2021. China-powered ICT infrastructure: Lessons from Tanzania and Cambodia (Policy Brief 252). Johannesburg: South African Institute of International Affairs. Accessed September 13, 2023.

https://saiia.org.za/wp-content/uploads/2021/12/Policy-Briefing-252-agbebi-xue-yu.pdf.

Alves, A. C., X. Gong, and M. Li. 2023. The BRI: A new development cooperation paradigm in the making? Unpacking China's infrastructure cooperation along the Maritime Silk Road. *World Development* 169:106280. doi:10.1016/j.worlddev.2023.106280.

ASEAN-China Center. 2020. The 2020 ASEAN-China Digital Economy Cooperation Conference successfully held in Chengdu. Accessed August 13, 2023. http://www.asean-china-center.org/english/2020-11/5474.html.

Basu, A. 2020. The retreat of the data localization brigade: India, Indonesia and Vietnam. *The Diplomat,* January 10. Accessed August 13, 2023. https://thediplomat.com/2020/01/the-retreat-of-the-data-localization-brigade-india-indonesia-and-vietnam/

BeritaSatu. 2020. Jokowi claims Indonesia among world's biggest digital economies. Accessed August 20, 2023. https://jakartaglobe.id/business/jokowi-claims-indonesia-among-worlds-biggest-digital-economies/.

Blanchard, J. M. F., and B. Hooijmaaijers. 2021. Connecting into the social sustainability effects of infrastructure through China's Digital Silk Road: Issues, indices, and indications. *Sustainability* 13 (22):12739. doi:10.3390/su132212739.

Brown, K., and A. Burjanadze. 2020. The Digital Silk Road: Upgrading the "16+1 cooperation? In *China and the New Silk Road*, ed. H. Pechlaner, G. Erschbamer, H. Thees, and M. Gruber, 137–45. Cham, Switzerland: Springer.

CAICT. 2016. White paper on China-ASEAN information technology development and cooperation (in Chinese). Beijing: China Academy of Information and Communications Technology. August 13, 2023. http://www.caict.ac.cn/kxyj/qwfb/bps/201804/P020160911662398099416.pdf.

CAICT. 2020. Digital economy development in China. Beijing: China Academy of Information and Communications Technology. Accessed August 13, 2023. http://www.caict.ac.cn/english/research/whitepapers/202007/P020200728343679920779.pdf.

Calabrese, L., and Y. Cao. 2021. Managing the Belt and Road: Agency and development in Cambodia and Myanmar. *World Development* 141:105297. doi:10.1016/j.worlddev.2020.105297.

Chen, L. 2020. Improving digital connectivity for e-commerce: A policy framework and empirical note for ASEAN (ERIA Discussion Paper Series No. 327). Jakarta: Research Institute for ASEAN and Southeast Asia (ERIA). Accessed August 13, 2023. https://www.eria.org/uploads/media/discussion-papers/Improving-Digital-Connectivity-for-E-commerce.pdf.

Cheney, C. 2019. China's Digital Silk Road: Strategic technological competition and exporting political illiberalism (Issues & Insights Working Paper Vol. 19 WP8). Honolulu, HI: Pacific Forum. Accessed August 13, 2023. https://pacforum.org/wp-content/uploads/2019/08/issuesinsights_Vol19-WP8FINAL.pdf.

China Project. 2021. China's Red New Deal: Tracking all the different crackdowns on companies going on right now. Accessed August 25, 2023. https://supchina.com/2021/09/09/chinas-red-new-deal-a-guide-to-all-the-different-crackdowns-on-companies-going-on-right-now/

Damuri, Y. R., V. Perkasa, R. Atje, and F. Hirawan. 2019. Perceptions and readiness of Indonesia towards the Belt and Road Initiative (Working paper). Center for Strategic and International Studies, Jakarta: Accessed August 13, 2023. https://www.csis.or.id/publications/perceptions-and-readiness-of-indonesia-towards-the-belt-and-road-initiative.

Das, S. B. 2017. OBOR's digital connectivity offers both benefits and risks (Perspective No. 60). Singapore: ISEAS - Yusof Ishak Institute. Accessed August 13, 2023. https://www.iseas.edu.sg/images/pdf/ISEAS_Perspective_2017_60.pdf.

De Graaff, N. 2020. China Inc. goes global: Transnational and national networks of China's globalizing business elite. *Review of International Political Economy* 27 (2):208–33. doi:10.1080/09692290.2019.1675741.

Diao, W., and A. Park. 2021. Which countries have benefited most from China's Belt and Road Initiative? (HKUST IEMS Working Paper No. 2021-79). Hong Kong: Institute for Emerging Market Studies, Hong Kong University of Science and Technology. Accessed August 16, 2023. https://iems.ust.hk/publications/iems-working-papers/wentian-dao-albert-park-which-countries-benefited-belt-and-road-wp79.

Diela, T. 2019. Indonesia relaxes data storage rules to allow placement abroad. *Reuters,* October 24. Accessed August 16, 2023. https://www.reuters.com/article/us-indonesia-tech-data/indonesia-relaxes-data-storage-rules-to-allow-placement-abroad-idUSKBN1X31P5

Drahokoupil, J., A. McCaleb, P. Pawlicki, and Á. Szunomár. 2017. Huawei in Europe: Strategic integration of local capabilities in a global production network. In *Chinese investment in Europe: Corporate strategies and labour relations*, ed. J. Drahokoupil, 211–29. Brussels: European Trade Union Institute.

Du, X. 2017. Alibaba's Jack Ma: "Belt and Road" a more inclusive globalization. *People's Daily*, May 15. Accessed August 20, 2023. http://en.people.cn/n3/2017/0515/c90000-9215677.html.

Erie, M. S., and T. Streinz. 2021. The Beijing effect: China's Digital Silk Road's transnational data governance. *New York University Journal of International Law and Politics* 54 (1):1–91.

EY. 2021. Overview of China's outbound investment of 2020. EY Greater China, Hong Kong. Accessed August 13, 2023. https://www.ey.com/en_cn/china-overseas-investment-network/overview-of-china-outbound-investment-of-2020.

Fossati, D. 2019. Embedded diasporas: Ethnic prejudice, transnational networks and foreign investment. *Review of International Political Economy* 26 (1):134–57. doi:10.1080/09692290.2018.1543721.

Foster, C., and S. Azmeh. 2020. Latecomer economies and national digital policy: An industrial policy perspective. *The Journal of Development Studies* 56 (7):1247–62. doi:10.1080/00220388.2019.1677886.

Freedman, A. 2003. Political institutions and ethnic Chinese identity in Indonesia. *Asian Ethnicity* 4 (3):439–52. doi:10.1080/1343900032000117259.

Freischlad, N. 2018. Indonesian automotive group Astra boosts Fintech plan with help from China. Accessed August 20, 2023. https://kr-asia.com/indonesian-automotive-group-astra-boosts-fintech-plan-with-help-from-china.

Gagliardone, I. 2019. *China, Africa, and the future of the Internet.* London: Bloomsbury Publishing.

Google, Temasek, and Bain & Company. 2021. e-Conomy SEA 2021. Mountain view, CA: Google. Accessed August 27, 2023. https://economysea.withgoogle.com/.

Gray, J. E. 2021. The geopolitics of "platforms": The TikTok challenge. *Internet Policy Review* 10 (2):1–26. doi:10.14763/2021.2.1557.

Greene, R., and P. Triolo. 2020. Will China control the global Internet via its Digital Silk Road? Accessed August 19, 2023. https://carnegieendowment.org/2020/05/08/will-china-control-global-internet-via-its-digital-silk-road-pub-81857.

Gu, J. 2009. China's private enterprises in Africa and the implications for African development. *The European Journal of Development Research* 21 (4):570–87. doi:10.1057/ejdr.2009.21.

Harwit, E. 2013. Chinese and Japanese investment in Southeast and South Asia: Case studies of the electronics and automobile industries. *The Pacific Review* 26 (4):361–83. doi:10.1080/09512748.2013.788068.

Hawes, C. 2021. Why is Huawei's ownership so strange? A case study of the Chinese corporate and socio-political ecosystem. *Journal of Corporate Law Studies* 21 (1):1–38. doi:10.1080/14735970.2020.1809161.

He, L. 2021. China's big tech companies are now fighting with each other. *CNN.com,* February 3. Accessed August 20, 2023. https://www.cnn.com/2021/02/03/tech/bytedance-tencent-lawsuit-intl-hnk/index.html.

He, Y. 2019. Connecting the emerging markets: China's growing role in global digital infrastructure (HKUST IEMS Thought Leadership Brief No. 26). Hong Kong: Institute for Emerging Market Studies, Hong Kong University of Science and Technology. Accessed August 13, 2023. https://hdl.handle.net/1783.1/107796.

He, Y., and A. Tritto. 2022. Urban utopia or pipe dreams? Examining Chinese-invested smart city development in Southeast Asia. *Third World Quarterly* 43 (9):2244–68. doi:10.1080/01436597.2022.2089648.

Hernandez, K. 2019. Achieving complex development goals along China's Digital Silk Road (K4D Emerging Issues Report). Brighton, UK: Institute of Development Studies. Accessed August 20, 2023. https://opendocs.ids.ac.uk/opendocs/handle/20.500.12413/14396.

Hong, Y. 2017. Networking China: The digital transformation of the Chinese economy. Champaign: University of Illinois Press.

Horwitz, J. 2023. 2023. China's Alibaba to break up empire into six units as Jack Ma returns home. *Reuters,* March 29. Accessed August 20 https://www.reuters.com/markets/deals/alibaba-splits-into-six-units-that-may-pursue-individual-ipos-bloomberg-news-2023-03-28/

HSF (Herbert Smith Freehills). 2021. Foreign investment in technology, media and telecommunications liberalised in Indonesia. Accessed August 20, 2023. https://hsfnotes.com/indonesia/2021/03/05/foreign-investment-in-technology-media-and-telecommunications-liberalised-in-indonesia/

Hsueh, R. 2011. *China's regulatory state: A new strategy for globalization.* Oxford, UK: Oxford University Press.

Huang, C., and N. Sharif. 2015. Global technology leadership: The case of China. *Science and Public Policy* 43 (1):62–73. doi:10.1093/scipol/scv019.

Huang, X., and R. Chi. 2014. Chinese private firms' outward foreign direct investment: Does firm ownership and size matter? *Thunderbird International Business Review* 56 (5):393–406. doi:10.1002/tie.21629.

IISS (International Institute for Strategic Studies). 2021. China's Digital Silk Road: Integration into national IT infrastructure and wider implications for Western defence industries. London: International Institute for Strategic Studies. Accessed August 20, 2023. https://www.iiss.org/research-paper//2021/02/china-digital-silk-road-implications-for-defence-industry.

Indian Ministry of External Affairs. 2017. Official spokesperson's response to a query on participation of India in OBOR/BRI Forum. Accessed August 20, 2023. https://mea.gov.in/media-briefings.htm?dtl/28463/Official_Spokespersons_response_to_a_query_on_participation_of_India_in_OBORBRI_Forum.

Indonesia Investment Coordinating Board. 2021. Indonesia investment handbook. Jakarta: Indonesia Investment Coordinating Board. Accessed August 20, 2023. https://www.bkpm.go.id/images/uploads/printing/Indonesia_Investment_Guidebook.pdf.

iPriceInsights. 2021. The map of e-commerce in Indonesia. Kuala Lumpur, Malaysia: iPriceInsights. Accessed August 13, 2023. https://iprice.co.id/insights/mapofecommerce/en/.

Jakarta Post. 2019. Jokowi issues rule on tax deductions of up to 300% of R&D cost. *Jakarta Post*, July 9. Accessed August 20, 2023. https://www.thejakartapost.com/news/2019/07/09/jokowi-issues-regulation-on-tax-deductions-up-to-300-percent.html.

Jakarta Post. 2020. Alibaba teams up with Indonesian universities, tech providers, incubator to offer cloud tech training. *Jakarta Post*, January 20. Accessed August 30, 2023. https://www.thejakartapost.com/news/2020/01/20/alibaba-teams-up-with-universities-tech-providers-incubator-to-offer-cloud-tech-training.html

Jenkins, R. 2022. China's Belt and Road Initiative in Latin America: What has changed? *Journal of Current Chinese Affairs* 51 (1):13–39. doi:10.1177/18681026211047871.

Jia, K., M. Kenney, and J. Zysman. 2018. Global competitors? Mapping the internationalization strategies of Chinese digital platform firms. In *International business in the information and digital age*, ed. R. Tulder, A. Verbeke, and L. Piscitello, 187–215. Bingley, UK: Emerald. doi:10.1108/S1745-886220180000013009.

Jia, L., and D. Winseck. 2018. The political economy of Chinese Internet companies: Financialization, concentration, and capitalization. *International Communication Gazette* 80 (1):30–59. doi:10.1177/1748048517742783.

Jia, L., and F. Liang. 2021. The globalization of TikTok: Strategies, governance and geopolitics. *Journal of Digital Media & Policy* 12 (2):273–92. doi:10.1386/jdmp_00062_1.

Jones, L., and J. Zeng. 2019. Understanding China's "Belt and Road Initiative": Beyond "grand strategy" to a state transformation analysis. In *Rising powers and state transformation*, ed. S. Hameiri, L. Jones, and J. Heathershaw, 19–43. London: Routledge.

Kawakami, T. 2019. Wave of layoffs washes over China's tech giants. Accessed August 20, 2023. https://asia.nikkei.com/Business/China-tech/Wave-of-layoffs-washes-over-China-s-tech-giants.

Keane, M., and H. Wu. 2018. Lofty ambitions, new territories and turf battles: China's platforms "go out". *Media Industries* 5 (1):51–68.

Keane, M., and H. Yu. 2019. A digital empire in the making: China's outbound digital platforms. *International Journal of Communication* 13:4624–41.

Kharpal, A. 2020. "Chinese firms are learning a painful lesson": India's app crackdown opens doors for U.S. *CNBC.com*, September 4. Accessed August 13, 2023. https://www.cnbc.com/2020/09/04/india-crackdown-on-chinese-tech-opens-doors-for-us-giants.html.

Kirkegaard, J. F. 2019. Chinese investments in the US and EU are declining – for similar reasons (Policy brief). Washington, DC: Peterson Institute for International Economics. Accessed August 21, 2023. https://www.piie.com/sites/default/files/documents/pb19-12.pdf.

Kohpaiboon, A. 2020. Industry 4.0 policies in Thailand (ISEAS Economics Working Paper No. 2020-02). Singapore: ISEAS - Yusof Ishak Institute. Accessed August 21, 2023. https://www.iseas.edu.sg/images/pdf/ISEAS_EWP_2020-2_Archanun.pdf.

Kumar, K. 1989. Conducting key informant interviews in developing countries (A.I.D. Program Design and Evaluation Methodology Report No. 13). Washington, DC: USAID. Accessed August 25, 2023. https://pdf.usaid.gov/pdf_docs/PNAAX226.PDF.

Lai, K. P., S. Lin, and J. D. Sidaway. 2020. Financing the Belt and Road Initiative (BRI): Research agendas beyond the "debt-trap" discourse. *Eurasian Geography and Economics* 61 (2):109–24. doi:10.1080/15387216.2020.1726787.

Lee, S. 2016. International reactions to U.S. cybersecurity policy: The BRICS undersea cable. Accessed August 21, 2023. https://jsis.washington.edu/news/reactions-u-s-cybersecurity-policy-bric-undersea-cable/.

Li, X., and K. Zeng. 2019. To join or not to join? State ownership, commercial interests, and China's belt and road initiative. *Pacific Affairs* 92 (1):5–26. doi:10.5509/20199215.

Liu, H., and G. Lim. 2019. The political economy of a rising China in Southeast Asia: Malaysia's response to the Belt and Road Initiative. *Journal of Contemporary China* 28 (116):216–31. doi:10.1080/10670564.2018.1511393.

Liu, H., and Y. Zhou. 2019. New Chinese capitalism and the ASEAN Economic Community. In *The sociology of Chinese capitalism in Southeast Asia: Challenges and prospects*, ed. Y. Santasombat, 55–73. Singapore: Palgrave Macmillan. doi:10.1007/978-981-13-0065-3_3.

Logan, S. 2015. The geopolitics of tech: Baidu's Vietnam. Philadelphia: Center Global Communication Studies, University of Pennsylvania. Accessed August 21, 2023. https://repository.upenn.edu/entities/publication/dbb0b0ea-5f59-4a97-bd33-25eb505d0cac

Logan, S., B. Molloy, and G. Smith. 2018. Chinese tech abroad: Baidu in Thailand. Accessed August 21, 2023. doi:10.2139/ssrn.3810369.

Loughlin, N., and M. Grimsditch. 2021. How local political economy dynamics are shaping the Belt and Road Initiative. *Third World Quarterly* 42 (10):2334–52. doi:10.1080/01436597.2021.1950528.

Martinus, M. 2020a. ASEAN Smart Cities Network: A catalyst for partnerships (ISEAS Perspective Issue 2020 No. 32). Singapore: ISEAS - Yusof Ishak Institute. Accessed August 21, 2023. https://www.iseas.edu.sg/wp-content/uploads/2020/02/ISEAS_Perspective_2020_32.pdf.

Martinus, M. 2020b. China can boost ASEAN's smart-city dreams but, first, it needs to earn some trust in Southeast Asia. *South China Morning Post*, January 12. Accessed August 21, 2023. https://www.scmp.com/comment/opinion/article/3045414/china-can-boost-aseans-smart-city-dreams-first-it-needs-earn-some.

Martinus, M. 2020c. The intricacies of 5G development in Southeast Asia (ISEAS Perspective Issue 2020 No. 130). Singapore: ISEAS - Yusof Ishak Institute. Accessed August 21, 2023. https://www.iseas.edu.sg/wp-content/uploads/2020/11/ISEAS_Perspective_2020_130.pdf.

McMorrow, R., and S. Findlay. 2020. Chinese tech companies write off India. *Financial Times*, November 20. Accessed August 21, 2023. https://www.ft.com/content/eccb0eab-c99a-471a-b49b-dd380a1f6244.

McMorrow, R., N. Liu, H. Lockett, and Q. Liu. 2023b. Chinese tech groups suffer as foreign investors take flight. *Financial Times,* June 12. Accessed August 21, 2023. https://www.ft.com/content/7d6c3c8a-97dc-4b98-8421-f881f185661e

McMorrow, R., Q. Liu, and C. Leng. 2023a. China moves to take "golden shares" in Alibaba and Tencent units. *Financial Times,* January 13. Accessed August 21, 2023. https://www.ft.com/content/65e60815-c5a0-4c4a-bcec-4af0f76462de

Mochinaga, D. 2020. The expansion of China's Digital Silk Road and Japan's response. *Asia Policy* 15 (1):41–60. doi:10.1353/asp.2020.0005.

Monk's Hill Ventures & Glints. 2021. The Southeast Asia tech talent compensation report. Accessed August 25, 2023. https://ebook.glints.com/techtalentreport2021/

Namingit, S., and S. Al Haddad. 2020. Huawei's carrier business in Southeast Asia. In *Huawei goes global*, ed. W. Zhang, I. Alon, and C. Lattemann, 207–30. Cham, Switzerland: Palgrave Macmillan.

Naughton, B. 2020. Chinese industrial policy and the Digital Silk Road: The case of Alibaba in Malaysia. *Asia Policy* 15 (1):23–39. doi:10.1353/asp.2020.0006.

Nicholson, B., P. Nielsen, and J. Saebo. 2021. Editorial: "Special issue: Digital platforms for development. *Information Systems Journal* 31 (6):863–8. doi:10.1111/isj.12364.

Oh, Y. A., and S. No. 2020. The patterns of state-firm coordination in China's private sector internationalization: China's mergers and acquisitions in Southeast Asia. *The Pacific Review* 33 (6):873–99. doi:10.1080/09512748.2019.1599410.

Olcott, E., and Q. Liu. 2023. Tencent accelerates investment in overseas gaming studios. *Financial Times,* April 26. Accessed August 25, 2023. https://www.ft.com/content/6921a1cc-9874-4258-8fe8-3d01f5648a1e

Oliveira, G. d L. T., G. Murton, A. Rippa, T. Harlan, and Y. Yang. 2020. China's Belt and Road Initiative: Views from the ground (Guest editorial). *Political Geography* 82:102225. doi:10.1016/j.polgeo.2020.102225.

Oreglia, E., H. Ren, and C.-C. Liao. 2021. The puzzle of the Digital Silk Road. In *Digital Silk Road in Central Asia: Present and future (report)*, ed. N. Kassenova and B. Duprey, 1–8. Cambridge, MA: Davis Center for Russian and Eurasian Studies, Harvard University. Accessed August 25, 2023. https://daviscenter.fas.harvard.edu/digital-silk-road.

Paulo, M. 2018. China-Europe investment cooperation: A Digital Silk Road. In *The Belt and Road Initiative in the global arena: Chinese and European perspectives*, ed. Y.

Cheng, L. Song, and L. Huang, 177–204. Singapore: Palgrave Macmillan.

Pranata, N. 2019. The role of digital payments fintech in accelerating the development of MSMEs in Indonesia. In *Fintech for Asian SMEs*, ed. N. Nemoto and N. Yoshino, 145–66. Tokyo, Japan: Asian Development Bank Institute. Accessed August 25, 2023. https://www.adb.org/sites/default/files/publication/502781/adbi-fintech-smes.pdf.

PRC Ministry of Foreign Affairs. 2020. Opening speech by State Councilor Wang Yi at the meeting of the Advisory Council of The Belt and Road Forum for International Cooperation. Accessed August 13, 2023. http://en.cidca.gov.cn/2020-12/21/c_576318.htm

PRC Ministry of Science and Technology (MOST). 2016. Plan on cooperation in science, technology and innovation under the Belt and Road Initiative (in Chinese). Accessed August 13, 2023. https://www.most.gov.cn/tztg/201609/W020160914524313282596.doc

PRC MOST (Ministry of Science and Technology). 2017. China Science & Technology Newsletter No. 10. Accessed August 13, 2023. http://www.china-un.org/eng/chinaandun/P020170617169003317276.pdf.

PRC NDRC (National Development and Reform Commission). 2015. Vision and actions on jointly building Silk Road Economic Belt and 21st-century maritime Silk Road (news release). Accessed August 13, 2023. https://eng.yidaiyilu.gov.cn/p/1084.html

Priyandita, G. 2018. Belt and Road investment under fire in Indonesia's presidential elections. August 23, 2023. https://www.eastasiaforum.org/2018/11/20/belt-and-road-investment-under-fire-in-indonesias-presidential-elections/.

Reuhl, M., and L. Lewis. 2022. Chinese companies set up in Singapore to hedge against geopolitical risk. *Financial Times*, November 30. Accessed August 25, 2023. https://www.ft.com/content/a0c11e3e-ab72-4b4b-a55c-557191e53938

Reuters. 2018. Indonesia's Lippo Group says invests $44 million in China's Tencent. https://www.reuters.com/article/us-lippo-group-tencent-holdings-idUKKBN1JM08Z.

Reuters. 2019. Jokowi proposes moving Indonesia's capital from Jakarta to Borneo Island. *South China Morning Post*, August 16. Accessed August 25, 2023.https://www.scmp.com/news/asia/southeast-asia/article/3023058/indonesias-president-formally-proposes-relocating-capital.

Reuters. 2021. Indonesia sets new rules on payments systems. Accessed August 25, 2023. https://www.reuters.com/article/indonesia-economy-payments/indonesia-sets-new-rules-on-payments-systems-idUSL4N2JJ1HN.

Rolland, N. 2017. China's Eurasian century? Political and strategic implications of the Belt and Road initiative. Seattle, WA: National Bureau of Asian Research.

Roumeliotis, G. 2018. U.S. blocks MoneyGram sale to China's Ant Financial on national security concerns. Accessed August 25, 2023. https://www.reuters.com/article/usmoneygram-intl-m-a-ant-financial-idUSKBN1ER1R7.

Shen, H. 2017. Across the Great (fire) Wall: China and the global Internet. Doctoral dissertation, University of Illinois Urbana-Champaign.

Shen, H. 2018. Building a Digital Silk Road? Situating the Internet in China's Belt and Road Initiative. *International Journal of Communication* 12:2683–701.

Shen, H. 2021. *Alibaba: Infrastructuring global China*. New York: Routledge.

Shen, H., and Y. He. 2022. The geopolitics of infrastructuralized platforms: The case of Alibaba. *Information, Communication & Society* 25 (16):2363–80. doi:10.1080/1369118X.2022.2128599.

Su, C., and T. Flew. 2021. The rise of Baidu, Alibaba and Tencent (BAT) and their role in China's Belt and Road Initiative (BRI). *Global Media and Communication* 17 (1):67–86. doi:10.1177/1742766520982324.

Sutherland, D., and L. Ning. 2011. Exploring "onward-journey" ODI strategies in China's private sector businesses. *Journal of Chinese Economic and Business Studies* 9 (1):43–65. doi:10.1080/14765284.2011.542885.

Tani, S. 2019. Jokowi vows to invest in tech skills for an Indonesian "golden age". Accessed August 25, 2023. https://asia.nikkei.com/Spotlight/The-Big-Story/Jokowi-vows-to-invest-in-tech-skills-for-an-Indonesian-Golden-Age

Tapsell, R. 2017. The political economy of digital media. In *Digital Indonesia: Connectivity and divergence*, ed. E. Jurriens, 56–72. Singapore: ISEAS Publishing.

Thomas-Noone, B. 2018. ASEAN and China's Digital Silk Road. Accessed August 16, 2023. https://www.iiss.org/blogs/analysis/2018/07/asean-and-china-digital-silk-road.

Timmerman, A. 2022. As GoTo slashes 12% of workforce, massive tech layoffs hit Southeast Asia. Accessed August 25, 2023. https://restofworld.org/2022/goto-layoffs-indonesia/

Tritto, A. 2019. The Belt and Road Initiative as a catalyst for institutional development (HKUST IEMS Thought Leadership Briefs No. 30). Hong Kong: Institute for Emerging Market Studies, Hong Kong University of Science and Technology. Accessed August 25, 2023. https://iems.ust.hk/publications/thought-leadership-briefs/tritto-belt-and-road-initiative-institutional-development-tlb30.

Tritto, A., Y. He, and V. A. Junaedi. 2020. Governing the gold rush into emerging markets: Indonesia's regulatory responses to the expansion of Chinese-backed online P2P lending. *Financial Innovation* 6 (1):1–24. doi:10.1186/s40854-020-00202-4.

U.S. Department of Justice. 2020. Attorney General William P. Barr delivers remarks on China policy at the Gerald R. Ford Presidential Museum. July 16. https://www.justice.gov/opa/speech/attorney-general-william-p-barr-delivers-remarks-china-policy-gerald-r-ford-presidential.

UNESCAP (United Nations Economic and Social Commission for Asia and the Pacific). 2017. A study of ICT connectivity for the Belt and Road Initiative (BRI): Enhancing the collaboration in China-Central Asia corridor (Working paper of the Information and Communications Technology and Disaster Risk Reduction Division). Bangkok, Thailand: UNESCAP. Accessed August 25, 2023. https://www.unescap.org/sites/default/files/BRI.pdf.

van der Lugt, S. 2021. Exploring the political, economic, and social implications of the Digital Silk Road into East Africa. In *Global perspectives on China's Belt and Road Initiative: Asserting agency through regional connectivity*, ed. F. Schneider, 315–46. Amsterdam: Amsterdam University Press.

Vila Seoane, M. F. 2020. Alibaba's discourse for the Digital Silk Road: The electronic world trade platform and "inclusive globalization". *Chinese Journal of Communication* 13 (1):68–83. doi:10.1080/17544750.2019.1606838.

Wen, Y. 2020. *The Huawei model: The rise of China's technology giant*. Champaign: University of Illinois Press.

Woon, C. Y. 2021. "Provincialising" the Belt and Road Initiative: Theorising with Chinese narratives of the

"Digital Silk Road"(数字丝绸之路). *Asia Pacific Viewpoint* 62 (3):286–90. doi:10.1111/apv.12320.

World Bank. 2020. Digital development: Overview. Accessed August 25, 2023 https://www.worldbank.org/en/topic/digitaldevelopment/overview#1.

World Bank. 2021. World development report 2021: Data for better lives (World development report). Washington, DC: World Bank. Accessed August 25, 2023. https://openknowledge.worldbank.org/bitstream/handle/10986/35218/9781464816000.pdf.

Xinhua. 2017a. Full text: Joint communique of leaders roundtable of Belt and Road forum. Accessed August 25, 2023. http://www.xinhuanet.com//english/2017-05/15/c_136286378.htm.

Xinhua. 2017b. China, ASEAN to advance trade, investment with upgraded. August 25, 2023. http://www.chinadaily.com.cn/business/2017-09/14/content_31978084.htm.

Xinhua. 2017c. Full text of President Xi's speech at opening of Belt and Road Forum. August 25, 2023. http://www.xinhuanet.com/english/2017-05/14/c_136282982.htm.

Xinhua. 2018. China to set up new comprehensive cross-border e-commerce pilot zones for greater opening-up. August 25, 2023. http://www.xinhuanet.com/english/2018-07/14/c_137322643.htm.

Xinhua. 2019. China, ASEAN vow to strengthen cooperation in smart city policy making, Lanning. August 25, 2023. http://www.xinhuanet.com/english/2019-11/03/c_138525333.htm.

Xinhua. 2020. JD.com Indonesia: Promoting Chinese brands "going global" with infrastructure advantages. August 25, 2023. http://digital.china.com.cn/2020-03/31/content_41108101.htm

Yean, T. S. 2018. The Digital Free Trade Zone (DFTZ): Putting Malaysia's SMEs onto the Digital Silk Road (ISEAS Perspective Issue 2018 No. 17). Singapore: ISEAS - Yusof Ishak Institute. Accessed August 25, 2023. https://www.iseas.edu.sg/images/pdf/ISEAS_Perspective_2018_17@50.pdf.

Yean, T. S. 2020. Alibaba's expansion into Malaysia: A double-edged sword? (ISEAS Commentary - 2020/205). Singapore: ISEAS - Yusof Ishak Institute. https://www.iseas.edu.sg/media/commentaries/alibabas-expansion-into-malaysia-a-double-edged-sword/.

Yin, R. K. 2003. *Case study research: Design and methods*. Thousand Oaks, CA: SAGE.

Zeng, J. 2019. Narrating China's Belt and Road Initiative. *Global Policy* 10 (2):207–16. doi:10.1111/1758-5899.12662.

Zhao, E. J. 2018. Negotiating state and copyright territorialities in overseas expansion: The case of China's online video streaming platforms. *Media Industries Journal* 5 (1):106–21. doi:10.3998/mij.15031809.0005.107.

Zhu, J., W. Lan, and X. Zhang. 2021. Geographic proximity, supply chain and organizational glocalized survival: China's e-commerce investments in Indonesia. *PloS One* 16 (9):e0256837. doi:10.1371/journal.pone.0256837.

Zinser, S. 2021. The global reach of China's venture capital. *The Diplomat*, January 21. Accessed August 27, 2023. https://thediplomat.com/2021/01/the-global-reach-of-chinas-venture-capital/.

Alibaba in Mexico: adapting the digital villages model to Latin America

Guillermo J. Larios-Hernandez

ABSTRACT

Based on experiences in China where rural development has reputedly been accelerated through use of its e-commerce platforms to create Taobao Villages, Chinese digital conglomerate Alibaba has sought to export its vision of "inclusive globalisation" to other economies in the Global South. Its initiatives intended to reduce inequality by specifically supporting small enterprises. Some research has already charted its multi-dimensional Electronic World Trade Platform approach. However, its more narrowly-focused Digital Villages approach, currently being implemented in Latin America, has still not been analyzed. Drawing on data from interviews and documentary sources, this article analyses the activities of Atomic88, an Alibaba subsidiary in Mexico, which (initially) focused on digitally-enabled development of small enterprise. It finds that Alibaba's nascent position in an e-commerce market dominated by US and Latin American platforms led it to follow a quite different path from the Chinese Taobao Village Model. It sought out the action areas – training and consultancy – that would not directly compete with incumbents, and worked as an indirect facilitator of local actors, rather than directly intervening. While short-term inequality-reduction impact of Alibaba's approach could be called into question, what it has done is build relationships with key digital economy stakeholders in Mexico. These show signs of providing valuable stepping stones toward a larger and more direct presence of Alibaba in the Mexican market.

Introduction

Many have hoped that digital technologies can reduce the serious economic inequalities that face all countries of the Global South, among other things, by providing internal efficiencies and offering access to wider markets for enterprises of all sizes (e.g., Tapscott and Williams 2010). In practice, though, this has typically not been the case, with larger companies appearing to be the winners from adoption of digital technologies, in comparison with smaller enterprises (OECD 2021a). This disparity is representative of the digital divide – the gaps between individuals, households, businesses, and territories of different socio-economic levels with respect to the opportunities that digital technologies can offer (OECD 2001). It is understood to arise not just from differentials in access to the technology but also in relation to other factors such as the knowledge necessary to make effective use of digital technologies, and the resources necessary to turn digitally-enabled decisions into actions (Pisanty Baruch 2005).

China is often held up as an exception, given the enormous progress it has made in application of digital technology not just in its metropolitan centers but right across the country (Wang and Liu 2021). Best known of its digitally-enabled rural development initiatives is the development of Taobao Villages, where e-commerce on Taobao has reached a critical mass, as per the parameters determined by AliResearch (e.g. number of online businesses, aggregate e-commerce revenue), a branch of Alibaba, Chinese technology conglomerate. By 2022, there were more than 7,000 such villages in China, and studies reported that they gained significant economic benefits *via* small and micro-enterprise development (Boufflet 2022; Fan 2019; Leong et al. 2016).

Because of its perceived success in China, the Taobao Village Model has been promoted in other developing countries as a model for inclusive digital development. This promotion has particularly been by Alibaba itself, especially through its CEO, Jack Ma, who has incorporated experiences in China into the concept of "inclusive globalisation" (Vila Seoane 2020). Adopted more widely as a slogan for China's digital outreach to developing countries, this is claimed to be a counter-hegemonic approach which seeks to use digital technologies to empower those who have been left behind by Western globalization; notably small enterprises, women, and young people. The highest-profile encapsulation of inclusive globalization is the Electronic World Trade Platform (eWTP), which aims to deliver an entire e-commerce ecosystem – physical infrastructure, financial and logistical services, training, new institutional arrangements, etc. – with Alibaba's own e-commerce platform at its heart (Hernandez 2019).

eWTP has been implemented in a number of developing countries, which researchers have examined in a few general analyses (Johnston 2021; Lefevre and Wiart 2020; Vila Seoane 2020) and specific studies relating to individual countries such as Malaysia (Naughton 2020) and Rwanda (Hamersma 2021). Much less attention has been given to alternative approaches that Alibaba has used in countries less immediately amenable to its eWTP approach. In Latin America, for example, Alibaba has been using a more incremental Digital Villages strategy that seeks to support local small enterprises using digital technology.

Given the lack of existing research, this article addresses three quite broad-ranging research questions (RQs), using the example of Alibaba's inclusive digital development strategy in Mexico, implemented through its local subsidiary, Atomic88:

RQ1 - Strategy description: What is Alibaba's strategy in seeking to achieve the objective of more inclusive digital markets in Mexico?
RQ2 - Comparative analysis: How and why is Alibaba's inclusive digital markets strategy in Mexico similar to and different from its Taobao Village initiative in China?
RQ3 - Outcome: What has so far been achieved by Alibaba's initiative in Mexico?

To address these questions, the article first reviews existing literature about small enterprise digitalization initiatives in Mexico, in China, and exported from China to other developing countries. Following an explanation of research methods, it analyses Alibaba's Digital Villages project in Mexico and ends with discussion and conclusions.

Literature review

Globalization has been one of the most powerful developmental forces of the past decades. However, the current dominant form of globalization has left segments of society behind, including the majority of small enterprises (Gamage et al. 2020; Hilbert 2001). Given the association of digital technologies with efficiency, growth, and globalization, digitalization of small enterprises has been expected to help close inequalities, shaping strategies that governments, development agencies, and others in the Global South have pursued for many years (Al Busaidi, Bhuiyan, and Zulkifli 2019; Southwood 2004).

However, such initiatives have often run into difficulties, with a range of factors constraining the potential of digitalization to foster small enterprise growth and globalization. Some problems can be seen as content-related; that is, concerned with what initiatives have sought to do. Small enterprise digitalization has often been techno-centric, focusing solely (or largely) on providing Internet connectivity, and less often also on providing software applications for the enterprises (Samara and Terzian 2021). Yet, studies have consistently shown that small enterprises require a set of complementary inputs if they are to make effective use of digital technologies (Schia 2018; World Bank 2016). These inputs particularly include human capabilities: not just use-skills for digital systems but also knowledge of schemes and technologies, and abilities to contextualize generic understandings to the specifics of a particular enterprise (Akpan, Udoh, and Adebisi 2022). They can include physical and logistics infrastructure too: for example, the roads and delivery systems to take goods ordered online from an enterprise to the customer (Chege and Wang 2020). They also include institutional support services such as finance and legal infrastructure for online contracts (Meltzer 2014).

Other problems can be seen as process-related; that is, concerned with how initiatives are implemented albeit with a knock-on impact on inputs. Three will be identified here: motivation, leadership, and value network. All in some ways arise from the fact that initiatives tended to be top-down and supply- rather than demand-driven; that is designed from the perspective of the implementing government or other development agency, rather than from the perspective of entrepreneurs (Cave and Flores-Roux 2017; Curtis 2016; Heeks and Duncombe 2001; Samara and Terzian 2021; World Bank 2016). There has been insufficient attention to mechanisms to motivate those involved to take new actions or to see them through sustainability; especially a lack of incentives for entrepreneurs to give their time and energy. Leadership of initiatives has been remote and needed to do more to involve entrepreneurs. Also, formation of new stakeholder relations has been lacking; particularly the kind of new commercial relationships (e.g. with new suppliers or traders or customers) that could form a new value network for the small enterprises involved (Christensen, Ojomo, and Dillon 2019).

Alibaba and inclusive globalization

Into this domain, with its own logic for small enterprise globalization and digitalization, has stepped the Chinese model, promoting what it claims to be a new approach: that of "inclusive globalisation" (Hernandez 2019; Neilson 2022; Shen 2018).[1] Of all China's tech firms operating in the Global South, it is Alibaba which has been most-associated with inclusive globalization for small enterprise (Hong and Harwit 2020; Vila Seoane 2020).

Alibaba's approach to digitalization of small enterprise began with, and is epitomized by, its Taobao Villages in China. With this approach, it claims to have significantly addressed many of the shortcomings of prior interventions that sought to drive forward small enterprise digitalization. Analysis of Taobao Villages, for example, shows a strong commitment, not just to the provision of applications in the form of Alibaba's e-commerce platform Taobao and supporting systems (e-payments, e-shop, etc.), but also to a slew of complementary inputs. Alibaba itself provides direct training for local entrepreneurs, site visits to successful role models, free wireless Internet connectivity, and support services such as finance and logistics (Leong et al. 2016; Neilson 2022; Wei, Lin, and Zhang 2020). It has stimulated local governments in rural China to deliver physical infrastructure (telecommunications and transport links), and to develop favorable tax and other policies to help incentivise not just local entrepreneurship but also inflow of related finance providers, suppliers, traders, and auxiliary services (Boufflet 2022; He 2019; Wei, Lin, and Zhang 2020). Site visits, alongside financial incentives, motivate entrepreneurs to participate, which, in turn, give them experiential learning about best practices for production, online marketing, and sales of local goods (Li et al. 2018).

The successful role models do not enforce particular commercial relations to aspiring Taobao entrepreneurs. They instead arise from local service providers (e.g. packaging, marketing, logistics) and from local e-commerce intermediaries (He 2019; Leong et al. 2016). While many entrepreneurs set up their own individual e-shop on Alibaba's platforms – about three million on Taobao (AliResearch 2021) – many others sell *via* an e-shop shared by the local community and run by an intermediary who acts as a local facilitator, offering advice on everything from quality control of production to how best to market and sell products *via* the Taobao platform (He 2019). Lack of knowledge of such broader issues is a greater barrier to e-commerce than understanding the technical functionalities of the platform, and incorporation of a basis for learning such knowledge is a key benefit of the Taobao Village Model (Li et al. 2018).

Another key feature is the profile of entrepreneurs: young people have been the specific focus of the initiative with three quarters of Chinese rural e-entrepreneurs being in their twenties; something that likely correlates more positively with a higher level of motivation and of self-learning capabilities than might be the case with an older cohort (Boufflet 2022; World Bank and Alibaba Group 2019). Although Alibaba is obviously a key facilitator, entrepreneurs drive the process along (often part of a network of family businesses), alongside the local e-shop intermediaries, and other grassroots leaders and local government officials, with all being aligned to achieve a common goal of growing the local economy (He 2019; Leong et al. 2016). Notwithstanding the image of China as a model of top-down policy decision-making, the freedom allowed for local economic initiatives such as these is key to its recent economic success (Ding, McQuoid, and Karayalcin 2019; Li 2017). In this and other ways, then, the Taobao Villages approach to small enterprise digitalization differs from that typically and historically seen in other developing countries; as summarized in Table 1.

On the other hand, Taobao Villages are not without their downsides. Growth in local production and incomes has been linked to: inequalities between the younger villagers who participate and the older ones who do not, disruptive in-migration, and higher levels of pollution (Leong et al. 2016; Tang and Zhu 2020; Wang et al. 2021). They have also been criticized for relentless positive publicity from stakeholders with vested interests that has exaggerated and almost mythologized Taobao Villages (Couture et al. 2021). Nonetheless, they have undoubtedly had a transformative economic impact on locations in China that were previously marginalized: Taobao more generally has enabled millions of small entrepreneurs in China to be inducted into e-commerce, with their annual gross sales volume exceeding US$700 billion by 2022 (AliResearch 2021; Risley 2023; Zhou, Yu, and Choguill 2021).

The scale of this growth has been sufficient to convince Alibaba and, in particular, its CEO, Jack Ma, that experiences in China could form the basis

Table 1. Comparing the Taobao Village Model with traditional approaches to small enterprise digitalization.

Category	Dimension		Description	Chinese Taobao Villages Model	Traditional Approaches to Small Enterprise Digitalization
Content	Digital systems		Systems that facilitate value creation for small enterprises	Constellation of integrated systems focused around Alibaba e-commerce platform: e-payments, e-shop development tools, etc.	Techno-centric focus, particularly on Internet connectivity
	Complementary inputs	Human capabilities	Knowledge and skills for effective use of digital systems by entrepreneurs	Development of entrepreneurs' e-commerce capabilities *via* direct training and indirect exposure, e.g. intermediary support and site visits	Training and learning not particularly considered
		Infrastructural enablers	Factors required to enable effective use of digital systems by small enterprises	Physical infrastructure (Internet connectivity, roads); support services (finance, logistics, intermediation, and e-commerce facilitation); institutions (local government tax, regulation)	Not considered other than Internet connectivity
Process	Motivation		Incentives for participation and action of stakeholders	Financial and experiential incentives bringing gains for core and support-service entrepreneurs; market pull as core driver	No additional incentives beyond assumption that benefits of digitalization were convincing enough
	Leadership		Nature of core direction and drive for initiative	Market-led, demand-pull model that is government-enabled, with local stakeholder engagement	Government-led; top-down initiatives with little or no participation from local stakeholders
	Value network		Formation of new commercial relationships	Creates new digital ecosystem and economic value network for small enterprises centered on e-shop intermediaries	Focuses on existing value network and relationships

for a new model of digital development. It has therefore aligned itself with the wider rhetoric that arises from the Chinese model of inclusive globalization (Vila Seoane 2020). It aims to use the power of e-commerce, specifically Electronic World Trade Platform (eWTP), to close inequalities by accelerating integration of those relatively-excluded by extant globalization: small enterprise, youth, women, and others. While eWTP recognizes that the context in China is different from that in other developing countries (World Bank and Alibaba Group 2019), it has essentially sought to replicate the Chinese Taobao experience in other countries, bringing together as many of the features mentioned in Table 1 as possible to create an entire digital trade ecosystem for facilitating the growth of local small enterprises (Johnston 2021). Setting aside questions of whether eWTP will actually deliver inequality-reducing development of local small enterprises (Hernandez 2019), tailored versions of this full-ecosystem approach have been limited so far to just a few developing countries – namely, Malaysia, Rwanda, and Ethiopia. Factors that were conducive in these economies include strong central government support and an existing presence of Alibaba in the e-commerce market or the existence of local commodities demanded by China, which could be commercialized *via* Alibaba's platform (Lefevre and Wiart 2020; Naughton 2020; Yean 2018).

But such conditions do not exist in many developing countries; for example, in much of Latin America, where e-commerce markets have been relatively well-developed for some years, Alibaba has historically had a very limited presence, and political pressures (e.g., from the US) may not always be conducive to high-profile central government collaborations with Chinese entities (Geldman 2021; Malena 2021). In these circumstances, Alibaba has taken an alternative approach that, while informed by the eWTP vision, is much less ambitious in its initial scope. Mexico is one such example, where Alibaba is working through its local subsidiary, Atomic88, and other local institutions to support digital inclusion, involving particularly a Digital Villages project.

While, as reviewed above, there is some literature discussing and assessing China's role vis-à-vis inclusive globalization in a general sense, there has been little research specifically on Alibaba's actualization of the concept through its eWTP programme – despite it involving thousands of small enterprises, and hundreds of millions of dollars-worth of investments around the world (Alizila 2018; Chin, Foo, and Falahat 2023; Fortune 2022). As for Alibaba's activities in Latin America, there has been no academic analysis to date. This knowledge gap provides the impetus for the current research described next, which focuses on the Mexico Digital Villages project.

Methods

The research strategy adopted here was that of a single exploratory case study; with the case in question being the activities of Atomic88 in Mexico. Consistent with the tenets of case study research, a multi-method, qualitative methodology was adopted that sought triangulation of methods and data sources (Rashid et al. 2019; Yin 2013, 2018).

The first method adopted was semi-structured interviews. Following the rationale of Brunetti et al. (2020), this study adopted a multi-stakeholder approach, gathering responses from at least one representative of each key stakeholder group that could be identified; thus triangulating between different sources. In effect, it was a purposive sampling approach that covered the following stakeholders: Atomic88, small enterprise owners, mentors, government officials, and educators (see below for further explanation of roles). In addition, a structured questionnaire was administered to three trainee consultants, products of the core training initiative of Atomic88. Table 2 provides a summary overview and the codes for respondents, which are used in the findings section. All respondent contacts were undertaken in the first half of 2022. The final method and data source were gathering of primary documentation: webpages, newsletters, reports, etc., of specific relevance to Alibaba's objectives and actions in Mexico, and in accordance with principles of documentary research (Bowen 2009).

Design of the interview and questionnaire content and analytical frame for these and the primary documentation data was centered on the three research questions. This entailed use of both inductive and deductive logics. Given the lack of existing insights into Alibaba's strategy in Latin America, and the implications of that strategy, RQ1 and RQ3 were approached inductively. By contrast, given the analytical frame for Taobao Villages derived above, it was used as a deductive starting point for RQ2. Data from the multiple methods and sources were incorporated into a single corpus that was analyzed using *in vivo* coding; either matching or deriving concepts and patterns depending on use of deductive or inductive logic for the different research questions (Auerbach and Silverstein 2003; Gioia, Corley, and Hamilton 2013).

Findings

The Digital Villages initiative in Mexico

In 2019, Mexico's e-commerce market with potential for local small enterprise involvement was dominated by Argentina-based Mercado Libre and US-based Amazon, alongside the websites of major retailers – Mexican subsidiaries of major chains like Walmart and Sears, and local firms like Coppel and Liverpool (George 2019). Alibaba itself had no real profile or presence *via* a subsidiary, nor had it built up any strong relationships with local actors, particularly at federal level. As a result, although guided by the logics and a narrative of inclusive globalization and seeking to digitalize local small enterprises, it could not adopt the type of maximalist approach inherent to Taobao Villages or their global variant, eWTP.

Instead, Alibaba focused at state level, signing memorandums of understanding (MOUs) with a number of state governments, which sought to impact small enterprises mainly through the agency of state-level higher education institutions (HEIs). This was a Digital Villages model that originated from use of Taobao in rural China but was then modified through experiences in Africa and other Global South locations during the late 2010s. The model provided e-commerce training for local entrepreneurs who were then to act as catalysts for further small enterprise digitalization in their home countries (Vanek 2018). Alibaba had itself directly funded and delivered this training but had learned this approach did not generate local ownership and collaboration (*A8*). The strategy adopted in Mexico was therefore one that relied much more on the actions of, and funding from, local stakeholders.

Table 2. Interview/questionnaire stakeholders.

Institution	Role description	Code
Atomic88	Manager in Alibaba Group subsidiary in Mexico	A8
ITESM Puebla	Alibaba Global Digital Talent (GDT)-certified educator in Puebla	CI
Tecnológico de Teziutlán	GDT-certified educator in Puebla	CT
Universidad Tecnológica de Querétaro	GDT-certified educator in Queretaro	CU
"Herbea"	Small enterprise owner in Mexico City producing beauty and personal health products	EH
"Viva Bacanora"	Small enterprise owner in the State of Sonora producing *bacanora* alcoholic beverages	EV
State Government of Guanajuato	Government official in Office for Coordination of Foreign Trade Promotion of the State of Guanajuato	GG
State Government of Puebla	Government official in General Office for Entrepreneurship, Competitiveness and Business Development of the State of Puebla	GP
"Poderosa"	GDT-certified mentor	MP
Tecnológico de Teziutlán	Trainee consultant	TC1
Tecnológico de Teziutlán	Trainee consultant	TC2
Tecnológico de Teziutlán	Trainee consultant	TC3

Notes. Names of enterprises have been pseudonymised; small enterprises are taken to be those employing fewer than 50 employees (OECD 2021b).

The Digital Villages model within the MOU incorporated a staged process starting with identification, in collaboration with local stakeholders (e.g., government agencies or business associations), of small enterprises deemed to have marketable products but lacking digital systems and capabilities (Atomic88 n.d.). This was then followed by identification of a nearby HEI where staff would be trained to obtain certification in Alibaba's Global Digital Talent (GDT) programme (formerly known as Global eCommerce Talent). That training would usually be paid for by the state government. The HEI educators would then cascade this training to their students who would become "trainee consultants" sent out to support the implementation of new digital systems in the identified small enterprises. Based on their training and consulting interventions, the students would receive academic credits for their particular degree course.

State governments are well aware of the contextual differences between China and Mexico (*GP*), yet they are attracted to Taobao Villages' aforementioned success, given the relative failure of previous attempts to support small enterprise in Mexico. The first MOU was signed in August 2019 with the Guanajuato state government, which was motivated by the potential for local small enterprises to export goods including shoes, handicrafts, and agri-food to China. The local HEIs included Instituto Tecnológico de León and Universidad de Celaya (*GG*). In 2020, a similar MOU was signed with Sonora state with local HEIs training nearly 1,000 students working in teams of four to support digitalization of more than 200 local small enterprises (though a planned second phase was canceled in 2021 following a change of government).

The GDT training curriculum implemented in Mexico was a generic one developed by the Hangzhou-based Alibaba Business School on the basis of experiences with Taobao Villages. This curriculum has been delivered worldwide through the Alibaba Global Initiative, which is the main vehicle for promotion *via* education and training programmes of the Alibaba inclusive globalization model (eWTP 2021). In August 2020, Alibaba determined that delivery of this certificated trainer training and the other support outlined within its MOUs would best be undertaken through the creation of a local subsidiary that would bundle it as part of a Digital Villages project as well as work to advance Alibaba's position in Mexico in other ways. That subsidiary was called Atomic88, which was also intended to provide a locally-associated "neutral space" through which local partners could potentially work more comfortably rather than directly interact with Alibaba (*A8*). Alongside the Digital Villages project, Atomic88 also provides more general GDT training and e-commerce consulting services.

Following the formation of Atomic88, two other MOUs were signed in 2021. The Queretaro state government engaged just one HEI: Universidad Tecnológica de Querétaro from which 50 staff were trained by Atomic88 and then cascaded this to 1,000 students as trainee consultants to work with 50 small enterprises. In 2022, this was expanded to include five other universities, with their students reaching out to 200 enterprises. The government of Puebla state involved 15 different HEIs from which 37 staff members were trained by Atomic88, and in turn trained more than 800 students to work as consultants, supporting 180 small enterprises (*GP*). In addition, and without any direct state government involvement, one of Mexico's largest universities, Instituto Tecnológico y de Estudios Superiores de Monterrey (ITESM), which has campuses across the country, signed a direct agreement by which it would pay Atomic88 to train its staff, and knowledge so acquired would then be cascaded into small enterprises *via* the student trainee-consultant model (Tec Review 2021). In terms of overall metrics, as of May 2022, Atomic88 states that the Digital Villages initiative in Mexico had thus far trained around 400 HEI educators, who had in turn trained 8,000 students as trainee-consultants, who had in turn supported 1,500 small enterprises (Atomic88 2022). It further cites a claim from the Guanajuato state government that participating handicraft small enterprises had seen their income increase between 200–300%, though that outcome can also be attributable to the actions of the state's export agency (*GG*).

Though each state decided to implement Digital Villages variously, this, then, represents the dominant model being used by Alibaba in Mexico to support small enterprise; a key feature of which has been the lack of direct promotion of Alibaba's own e-commerce platforms. The local version of GDT training provided to the higher education staff – and thence to their students and through them as solutions offered to local small enterprise – does use Alibaba digital content for discussing some of the more theoretical topics (*GP*). But it has otherwise been customized by Atomic88 to the Mexican context with incorporation of the locally-available applications, e.g., e-commerce platforms (e.g. Mercado Libre), e-commerce shop/marketing development applications (e.g. Shopify), logistics applications (e.g. 99minutos), and financial services (e.g. Dapp) (*A8*). Another key feature is Alibaba's relatively arms'-length role. Although the key inspiration for the initiative may be the company's development of the Taobao Villages in China, it acts only indirectly in Mexico in two senses. One, it acts *via* a local subsidiary run by Mexican staff, and it provides only the first top-level training. Two, the other steps – from funding and small enterprise identification through to the cascade of knowledge *via* HEIs into the small enterprises – come entirely from Mexican organizations and individuals: small business associations, state governments, higher education institutions, local digital solution providers, students, and entrepreneurs.

Since 2022, Alibaba has been able to expand to a broader strategy in Mexico, with initiatives aimed at larger and/or more export- or growth-focused enterprises (*GG*). Using the eWTP label, Alibaba has signed an agreement with CONAGO, the Mexican Confederation of State Governors, to roll out e-commerce to a greater number of Mexican enterprises. It has also signed MOUs with individual state governments aiming to connect Mexican enterprises – especially larger, urban-based, export-ready firms – to exporters *via* the alibaba.com platform. Atomic88 set a goal of 300 exporters participating in a Mexican "pavilion" on the platform by the end of 2022 (Campus 2021). New training programmes for business owners were launched such as the Alibaba Netpreneur Masterclass for Latin America, and the e-Founders Fellowship that provides e-commerce training. It has also opened its first import logistics distribution center, to service Mexican consumers purchasing Chinese products through its AliExpress platform (Juarez 2022).

Having outlined the Digital Villages strategy used by Alibaba in Mexico, we move next to analyze what is being done in more detail; particularly in comparison to the original Taobao Villages Model. In accordance with Table 1, we begin with content elements before then moving on to discuss process elements.

Content features

Alibaba's Digital Villages initiative in Mexico is guided by the same logic as that of the Taobao Villages in recognizing the value of, and need for, small enterprise digitalization in order to increase market access and growth, and to reduce socio-economic inequalities. Atomic88 thus echoes the sentiments of Taobao Villages, seeing the Mexican project as an exercise in inclusive digital transformation focused on bottom-of-the-pyramid empowerment (*A8*), and providing more than digital technologies. In other ways, though, Alibaba's strategy in Mexico is different from that in China.

Digital systems. As described above, Alibaba's platform is the centerpiece of Taobao Villages: not just the core focus for e-commerce activities but also the site for digital intermediaries running e-shops, and the basis for other services such as payment and logistics. By contrast, Alibaba seems to have no direct interest in promoting use of its platforms such as Alibaba.com or AliExpress to Mexican small enterprises, and does not seek to impose a standardized, one-size-fits-all model. What is offered instead within the GDT training is much more of a patchwork of stand-alone services based on different applications already widely-used in Mexico, such as Mercado Libre, Spotify, and other solutions (*A8*).

Hence, the link from Alibaba to the small enterprises is even more indirect: the educators and student trainee-consultants adapt the GDT training to the context of the small enterprises they seek to assist. As noted, the training focuses on e-commerce particularly but also on other relatively sophisticated applications of digital technology: e-payments, network risk management, development of IT services, ensuring systems compatibility, etc. (*MP*). The staff and students of HEIs are not often that familiar with the circumstances of small enterprises, but they rapidly become aware that much of this content has limited relevance to the much more basic digitalization level and infrastructure of Mexican small enterprise (*CI*). To fully apply the digital systems covered by GDT training would require understanding, sometimes paying for, and integrating a series of different applications. This would create complexity and increase the capability requirements for those involved. Given the limited digital capabilities and financial resources of the Mexican entrepreneurs (*CI*), this is then more likely to exceed what the entrepreneurs themselves might be capable.

As a result, the consulting inputs to small enterprise typically focus on much simpler levels of digitalization and look for applications that cost little or nothing: "good-enough" application solutions, rather than intending to be world-class or cutting-edge (*A8, MP*). For example, they might help the small enterprise to set up a Facebook page or use a trial version of a web development tool to build a web page in order to create a first Internet presence. In contrast to the situation with Taobao Villages, this has been rather a patchwork of stand-alone services and one does not therefore find development of e-shop intermediaries, e-payment systems, business networking, etc. (*GP*).

Complementary inputs. As discussed above, the Taobao Villages initiative was particularly strong at delivering a series of complementary inputs beyond just software applications, which were necessary to ensure the development of e-commerce in communities. Such inputs are much needed in parts of Mexico where there is a lack of human, financial, physical (e.g., roads, logistics), and digital infrastructure (Aguerrebere and Bustos 2021; IFAD 2017; Martínez-Domínguez and Mora-Rivera 2020).

Alibaba has focused on the development of the one input that it can fairly readily influence given its role in Mexico: human capabilities. Even then, the Digital Villages initiative is not providing direct training to entrepreneurs as was the case in China, in part, perhaps, because all training materials are currently in English (*A8, CT*). Instead, the project is seeking to indirectly insert additional knowledge and skills *via* the student trainee-consultants. This itself has been somewhat hampered because many interactions between students and entrepreneurs had been taking place by phone or online due to Covid-19, which is seen to have affected the engagement of the entrepreneurs (*CT, GP*). This sets it further from the Taobao Village approach where site visits and other direct interactions enabled an experiential learning approach.

Development of other inputs such as physical and institutional infrastructure were not part of the programme, which has therefore not adapted itself to the full range of local requirements, representing much more of a challenge (*GP*). This has led to difficulties because a minimum requirement for participation was that small enterprises would have Internet connectivity (*A8, GP*), and yet several segments in Mexico do not. As a result, some state governments such as Puebla and Querétaro had to reorient their programmes (*CU, GP*). Their original intention had been to prioritize particularly marginalized small enterprises or those making traditional products. But many of these were in rural areas without Internet access, alongside lacking other elements necessary for effective growth in commerce. Hence the programmes had to refocus on enterprises in urban and sub-urban locations that were somewhat larger, more-formalised, and digitally-connected.

Urban locations and formal enterprises are already better provided with physical and institutional infrastructure and support services. For the initiatives that stayed focused on rural areas, the government of Guanajuato decided to supplement the Digital Villages project with additional inputs including facilitation of logistics and financial services, provision of physical spaces for enterprises, and arranging direct, customized training of entrepreneurs (*GG*). Although these were not part of what Alibaba provided *via* Atomic88, they did come a bit closer to the provisions of the original Taobao Villages Model.

Process features

Alongside provision of digital applications and complementary inputs, the Taobao Villages projects involved presence of strategic processes to develop rural e-commerce. The presence or absence of these in Mexico's Digital Villages project is analyzed next.

Motivational incentives to participate. In conjunction with the framework and inputs provided within the Taobao Villages initiative, its design motivated those involved to participate. The case in Mexico was different: some entrepreneurs had low expectations about the programme, which therefore did not particularly affect their initial motivation. Some others came to the programme with a preexisting motivation for higher sales and income through digitalization; something to which Covid-19 had added a sense of urgency and opportunity (*A8, CI*, Chiatchoua and Lozano Arizmendi 2021). Other entrepreneurs would potentially have digitalized their small enterprises without Digital Villages, but the programme may have been attractive to them because they expected exports. Viva Bacanora, for example, a *bacanora* alcoholic beverage producer based in Sonora joined the initiative seeking better export opportunities (*EV*). With cancelation of the Digital Villages programme in 2021, after the change in government in Sonora, Viva Bacanora kept engaged with state officials in seeking help with exports because its owner was internally motivated. For many other entrepreneurs, though, that preexisting internal motivation was not there: they had little appreciation of the role of digital technologies, they were very busy with the day-to-day activities of their enterprise, and they were reluctant to get involved (*A8, CI, CT, CU*). But in some other cases they did, for example, with the persuasion of the local HEI or government, though it is not clear that the internalization of motivation is strong enough to enable the consulting interventions to be sustained into longer-term digitalization – especially for older entrepreneurs – (*CT, CU, GG, GP*).

As noted above, the Digital Villages project adopted a trickle-down model of capability-building with existing small enterprises *via* the HEIs, rather than seeking either to directly train entrepreneurs or to stimulate the formation of new enterprises, both of which were features of Taobao Villages. Within the trickle-down model, the trainee-consultants were the main carrier of capabilities into the enterprises. There was no financial motivation for them and the only direct incentive was to receive GDT certification and grades for their courses. As a result, their focus was on course requirements more than delivering particular improvements for the small enterprises (*CT, EB, EV*). While some were keen to support the small enterprises, they have little or no experience with business, and this was at best a temporary activity with no clear path to sustainable intervention (*TC1, TC2, TC3*). The presumption was that any support was transitory: it would not sustain once the students had completed the particular degree course unit, and succeeding cohorts of students would engage with new enterprises rather than continue to work with enterprises already supported by earlier students (*CT*). One could thus contrast this with the long-term presence, and hence potential support for local enterprise, provided by e-shop and other intermediaries in Taobao Villages.

As with the absence of complementary inputs, these issues had led the Guanajuato government to adopt a somewhat different approach. In seeking greater sustainability for their Digital Villages intervention, this government used HEI educators as the consultants working directly with small enterprises (*GG*). Students were used only in support roles and responsibility for digitalization was, where feasible, given to young family members within the target small enterprises. For educators, the programme could help build new capabilities especially if, as in Guanajuato, these can be built by direct interaction with the enterprises and hence offer experiential learning (*CI, MP*). For their institutions, there was potential for attainment of institutional goals such as building university-industry links or delivering social impact or employability indicators (*CT, CU*). But this highlights that the Digital Villages project is dependent on motivations of higher education institutions, their staff and students who are all at least one step removed from the small enterprises, whereas the Taobao Villages project is more directly centered on entrepreneur motivations.

Leadership. In China, the Taobao Villages develop through a demand-pull model in which local government and other local actors remove barriers and provide the necessary complementary inputs to small enterprises being guided by market signals. By contrast, in Mexico, and following a historical pattern of digital and small enterprise interventions in the country, the model is more supply-push, with operational leadership coming from a combination of the state governments and higher education institutions.

Alibaba itself, *via* local subsidiary Atomic88, is the initial orchestrator that then takes a relative back seat. It had originally considered funding the Digital Villages initiative but, as noted above, had not done this following earlier negative experiences in Africa, where Alibaba funding failed to secure effective local ownership of and collaboration in the initiative (*A8*). Instead, and more akin to the original Taobao Villages approach, the local state governments – or the education institution in the case of ITESM – have come up with the funding for the project; something which ensures their engagement. As evidenced above, supply-push projects can suffer from not creating sufficient market incentives to induce entrepreneurial action. However, government leadership has a number of advantages since it allows for the programme to be delivered at scale and reaching out to locations in ways not possible if the project had been led by a commercial partner (*CI, CT*). Government leadership and funding has also ensured that other actors – the higher education institutions, business associations, even some of the individual small enterprises – have been readier to involve themselves than they otherwise might (*A8, GG, GP*).

Value network. In China's Taobao Villages, a new digital ecosystem has been created, centering around the small enterprises. Not just an ecosystem but, within that, a new value network of suppliers, buyers and supporting services that is essential for any enterprise to create significant new value and, hence, greater income and growth (Christensen, Ojomo, and Dillon 2019). In Mexico, the Digital Villages project has brought new connections for the small enterprises. However, these connections are with student or educator consultants, not with new value chain stakeholders. Such consultants bring technical skills rather than a profound understanding of business, and, as seen, they come with uneven motivations for involvement (*GP, TC1, TC2*). Given the relative absence of links to new suppliers and buyers or to local digital intermediaries like those in China who run platform e-shops, the project in Mexico can be seen more as an impetus for internal digitalization of enterprises rather than to the insertion of enterprises into new e-commerce, let alone export networks.

Guanajuato state again presents a somewhat different picture in that – moving beyond the initial remit of Atomic88's project – it has given its export promotion agency an ensuing orchestrating role (*GG*). The aim has been to facilitate the supply chain linkages and logistics for small enterprises *via* e-commerce, and to boost the ability of local enterprises to export their goods. Universidad Tecnológica de Querétaro had similarly recognized some limitations of the current approach and was exploring how to put small enterprises together on a sectoral basis, and then create an e-shop through which their goods could be sold (*CU*).

This is not to say that the Digital Villages project failed to create a new value network. The initiative brought together Alibaba (in the form of Atomic88), local governments, local business associations, and local HEIs; creating a collaborative network both at an institutional level as well as at the level of personal relationships. While the prime mover in implementation may be the educational establishments – this is, in essence, an educational ecosystem – and while there was evidence of some new relationships being formed for the state governments (*A8, GG, GP*), it is Alibaba that has benefited too. Atomic88 has built both social and political capital from this; developing knowledge, trust, and relationships. Where Taobao Villages create an economic value network at the level of small enterprise, the Digital Villages project has been more notable for creating a socio-political value network at a higher, institutional level.

Discussion

China is seen as an exemplar of how a developing country may overcome the capital and institutional deficits that have perpetuated poverty across the Global South (Chow 2015; Santos-Paulino 2013). Significant use of digital technologies within its rapid economic growth has led China to be a digital role model and, within this, the Alibaba Taobao Villages have been of particular interest in developing countries (Kshetri 2018). Alibaba has built its experiences in China into what it claims to be an alternative development model of inclusive globalization; one that particularly pays attention to groups relatively excluded from the benefits of development to date, including small enterprises.

Given limited analysis to date of Alibaba's attempts to roll out this model across the Global South, this article focuses on analysis of its Digital Villages initiative in Mexico. In addressing the first research question posed above, we find that Alibaba has adopted a localized and tightly-focused strategy that can be contrasted with the approach used with its eWTP initiatives in Malaysia and elsewhere (Johnston 2021; Lefevre and Wiart 2020). Rather than seeking an immediate, high-profile presence for the Alibaba brand, it has worked through local subsidiary, Atomic88. Rather than operating at national level, it has worked with state governments. Rather than acting directly, it has adopted an indirect, trickle-down model. Rather than funding the initiative, it has persuaded local actors to spend their funds. And rather than undertaking a multi-dimensional intervention that would build a new digital ecosystem, it has concentrated only on training and consultancy.

We can expand these latter points by addressing the second research question, that compares the Digital Villages project in Mexico with the original Taobao Villages template from China; a comparison summarized in Table 3. As shown, the Mexican Villages project is significantly different, with a number of elements found in Taobao Villages either absent or more limited in Mexico: many complementary inputs, site visits, local intermediary facilitators, entrepreneurship incentives and facilitation, nature of leadership, etc. Where Taobao Villages create a new digital ecosystem and concentrate on use of e-commerce to insert enterprises into new economic value networks, Digital Villages creates a new educational ecosystem that inserts higher education institutions, their staff and students into new learning opportunities. The Mexican projects have also been much more incremental and diverse in their digital interventions; helping enterprises with individual priorities rather than following a template.

This explains why some actors – the Guanajuato state government most notably but also in the plans of Universidad Tecnológica de Querétaro – have supplemented the Digital Villages model. They have provided some absent elements or strengthened some more limited elements and thus brought their interventions closer to the original Chinese model. Other states have reoriented from rural areas to locations which already have a greater presence of complementary inputs. Alibaba's own role is also quite different. In China, Alibaba stands at the heart of the digital ecosystem and the new value networks through its e-commerce platform and it is an institutional and educational prime mover. In Mexico, by contrast, Alibaba plays no role as digital platform provider, and stands almost off-stage as a facilitator of knowledge spillovers that are primarily driven by local actors, especially universities.

This explains how Digital Villages differs from Taobao Villages, but the second part of the research question seeks to understand *why* this should be the case. In a general sense, it is understood that all countries are different and that China's particular characteristics make it more different than most. Hence, any Chinese initiative would need to be customized in

Table 3. Comparing the Taobao Village Model with the Mexican Digital Villages project.

Category	Dimension		Description	Chinese Taobao Villages Model	Mexican Digital Villages Model
Content	Digital systems		Systems that facilitates value creation for small enterprises	Constellation of integrated systems focused around Alibaba e-commerce platform: e-payments, e-shop development tools, etc.	Focus on stand-alone, locally-available digital systems with Alibaba only as a theoretical example. Consulting focus on basic digitalization of small enterprises using individual, simple, often cost-free systems
	Complementary inputs	Human capabilities	Knowledge and skills for effective use of digital systems by entrepreneurs	Development of entrepreneur e-commerce capabilities *via* direct training and indirect exposure, e.g. intermediary support and site visits	Development of HEI staff digitalization knowledge *via* direct training, with subsequent trickle-down (Covid-impacted) into small enterprises *via* student consulting
		Infrastructural enablers	Factors required to enable effective use of digital systems by small enterprises	Physical infrastructure (Internet connectivity, roads); support services (finance, logistics, intermediation, and e-commerce facilitation); institutions (local government tax, regulation)	Not considered in the standard model, so dependent on existing presence. Some exceptions to standard model
Process	Motivation		Incentives for participation and action of stakeholders	Financial and experiential incentives bringing gains for core and support-service entrepreneurs; market pull as core driver	Covid crisis and export expectations, reliant on temporary education-related incentives of HEIs, staff and students
	Leadership		Nature of core direction and drive for initiative	Market-led, demand-pull model that is government-enabled, with local stakeholder engagement	Supply-push model that is local government-/HEI-led
	Value network		Formation of new commercial relationships	Creates new digital ecosystem and economic value network for small enterprises centered on e-shop intermediaries	Creates new institutional ecosystem and educational value network centered on HEIs

some ways to the local context of another country and this becomes more likely when the interests and objectives of local stakeholders – here the state governments – are taken into account. Some of the customizations can therefore be seen as planned: for instance, the interest of state governments to use public sector bodies as the implementing agencies for the project. Other customizations have been more emergent; for instance, the consultants' translation of GDT content to the conditions and priorities they met when interacting with the small enterprises; a translation that meant they might well diverge from the solutions covered within their training in order to fit the situation and priorities of the enterprises.

On the other hand, Digital Villages reflect a path-dependency from earlier digital initiatives in Mexico, which differ from the original Taobao Villages Model; particularly because of the top-down involvement of government. There are certainly many similarities between the Digital Villages project and earlier initiatives (summarized in a comparison of the right-hand columns of Tables 1 and 3): the supply-push, top-down design; the lack of action on other complementary inputs; the lack of attention to entrepreneurship incentives and facilitation or to creation of new enterprise value networks; etc.

Of course, one key difference from earlier initiatives is the core of Digital Villages – training, consulting, and capability development. Given Alibaba's position as a relatively new entrant in a market already dominated by Latin American or US digital firms, rather than seeking to immediately compete with them head-to-head, Alibaba developed a strategy at the intersection of two niches largely ignored by existing players: small enterprise and digital capabilities development. This follows a more general pattern of Chinese digital firms targeting market segments in developing countries that existing (typically Western) incumbents were neglecting (Djan and Owusu-Ansah 2020). Looking across the various elements of Taobao Villages – centrality of Alibaba's own platforms, induced investment in physical infrastructure, development of rural digital support services – most would have been well beyond its capacities to deliver in Mexico. It instead chose an intervention within its zone of feasibility that was well-bounded, sensibly leaving the "last-mile" direct engagement with small enterprises to local actors, given its own limited knowledge of the particular circumstances of small enterprises. In effect, Alibaba choose what it is able to do given the local context rather than what it might ideally wish to do.

What of the outcome of Digital Villages; the third research question? One thing is clear: significantly greater levels of exports could not be expected of small enterprises involved, unless and until the content and process features presented in this article are addressed. Of those small enterprises contacted by state governments and HEIs within Digital Villages, many have been reluctant to, or unable to, engage in the initiative. Some of the remainder have been assisted to enhance their level of digitalization, at least temporarily during the interaction with the students, albeit with a lack of clarity as yet about its sustainability. But there still remains a shortfall in transforming even these enterprises into digitally-enabled exporters. Digital Villages project's impact has been more in educational and institutional than enterprise terms. Alibaba has certainly succeeded in building digital capabilities in the HEI educators it has trained and, through them, their students. Whether or not the current initiative sustains over the long-term, these educators will train many more student cohorts.

Institutionally, the Digital Villages project helped Alibaba "find its feet" in the Mexican market: building knowledge, trust and relationships, all of which build a valuable foundation for future expansion. All this would have been at risk if the Digital Villages project were to fail, but the outsourcing of implementation to local actors in some sense outsourced this risk. In any case, risks of overt failure are small. The digitalization of small enterprise occurs largely behind closed doors of the enterprise, and the worst thing likely to happen from the consulting is a lack of progress with digitalization rather than any actual damage to the enterprise. Far from any risk of reputational damage, the Alibaba brand seems to have benefited from the project. Alongside the building of social and political capital, this can be seen as partly explaining the company's ability to expand to a broader strategy from 2022 onwards. As outlined previously, this moves closer to the kind of eWTP approach seen in Asia and Africa, and closer to the Taobao Villages Model with a greater focus on the Alibaba platform, on e-commerce, on more export- and growth-oriented local enterprises, and on direct training from Alibaba. All of this involves Alibaba and its platforms more centrally than the Digital Villages project. From this perspective, the Digital Villages project can be understood as an initial market entry strategy and stepping stone toward the kind of Alibaba presence seen in other markets. That presence has included sales to Mexican consumers *via* AliExpress, which had grown to become one of the top 10 Mexican e-commerce sites by 2021 (Statista 2021).

Conclusions

Many aspects of Chinese digital engagement in the Global South have been loosely associated with a strategy of inclusive globalization, but there has been little analysis to date of what that means in practice. The main contribution of this article is to provide that analysis; exposing the details of activities most-closely associated with inclusive globalization: Alibaba's actions to develop digitalization for small enterprise and other marginalized groups in the Global South. While there have been a handful of papers discussing Alibaba's eWTP initiative in Asia and Africa, the research reported here analyses the knowledge gap around Alibaba's activities in Latin America – specifically, its Digital Villages project in Mexico.

Three research questions were addressed: on strategy; differences from the Chinese Taobao Villages Model; and impact. Regarding strategy, one view of Chinese multinationals in the Global South is that they adopt a Sino-centric strategy; using Chinese funding to buy Chinese goods that are installed and run by Chinese labor (Tugendhat and Voo 2021). There has been evidence of this in some projects of digital companies such as Huawei and ZTE (Erie and Streinz 2021; Makundi, Huyse, and Develtere 2016). Alibaba, though, has taken a rather different approach. Consistent with findings about its eWTP initiatives (Neilson 2022; Yean 2018), analysis of the Digital Villages projects in Mexico shows its use of a local subsidiary to collaborate with local stakeholders who fund the activity and implement key parts of it. Beyond that, though, the Mexican Digital Villages experience differs from that seen under eWTP. The platforms and systems of local and US competitors substitute for Alibaba's platforms as the advocated and implemented solutions; there is a singular orientation toward human capabilities; and Alibaba has taken a much smaller and more indirect role.

These and other elements add together to an approach quite different from the original Taobao Villages blueprint that has guided Alibaba's engagement with the Global South. Whereas elsewhere Alibaba has created a whole new digital ecosystem, in Mexico, its main aim was contributing to the educational ecosystem. This difference arose because of context sensitivity, including the specific nature of small enterprise in Mexico; the past history of digital interventions to support small enterprise; the priorities of local stakeholders, most especially state governments; and Alibaba's position as a relatively new entrant to a relatively mature e-commerce market. From that latter dimension, the rather uncertain impact of Digital Villages on Mexican small enterprise likely is of less concern to Alibaba than the success of the programme in relationship- and reputation-building, and in helping it move on to later-stage market strategies.

More broadly, this article's contribution to scholarship on China's digital expansion in the Global South is two-fold. First, it offers a detailed analysis of the realities of China's inclusive globalization efforts in practice; an inclusivity that materializes in involvement of key local stakeholders if not yet major enhancement of small enterprises into exports ventures. Second, it provides a contrary case to the widespread notion that China's digital expansion is a top-down, state-directed, one-size-fits-all activity (Hernandez 2019; Luo 2019). In this case, the Chinese state played little role and Alibaba diverged strongly from the eWTP-type approach it had used elsewhere in the Global South. Its approach was heavily shaped by local context and heavily involved local actors and their priorities and other characteristics.

One can look at the gaps between Digital Villages and Taobao Villages and use them to make a series of recommendations: development of local intermediaries; use of site visits to motivate and educate entrepreneurs; direct training for entrepreneurs; provision of training materials in the local language; greater investment in complementary inputs; greater integration of enterprises into new value networks that provide access to new markets; and so forth. From Mexico's perspective, these will be developmentally valuable and this explains why some local stakeholders are trying to provide some of these gap-filling interventions. Their iterative approach – learning from the initial formulation of the Digital Villages programme and then revising that formulation on the basis of its impact – is also something that could be copied more broadly. It would enable a better match to the heterogeneity of context and experiences within each of Mexico's states; though it is an approach that can be challenged by the changes in state government and which can disrupt continuity of long-term initiatives, as seen by the experiences of Sonora state. From Alibaba's perspective, however, the necessity for change to Digital Villages may be more questionable given that the programme in its current form appears to be delivering strategic benefits for the company.

Looking beyond Mexico, the analysis provided here can be of value in other developing countries. This may be especially so in Latin America given expectations that the Digital Villages/Atomic88 approach can be replicated in other countries such as Chile and Bolivia. Given the crucial importance of local context that has emerged from this study, application in other countries needs to factor in the elements just listed: the status of small enterprise, the priorities of local stakeholders, and Alibaba's market position and strategy. Future research can track the progress of Digital Villages initiatives in other countries and, more generally, undertake further investigation of the nature, causes, and outcomes of digital inclusion strategies adopted by Alibaba and other Chinese tech firms in other developing countries.

Notes

1. Inclusive globalisation has at times been more broadly associated with the entirety of China's Belt and Road Initiative (Liu, Dunford, and Gao 2018; Weidong 2017).

Acknowledgements

This research was developed as part of the project, "China's Digital Expansion in the Global South", funded by the Faculty of Humanities, University of Manchester, UK. Richard Heeks and Chris Foster of the Centre for Digital Development, University of Manchester, were the facilitating editors.

Disclosure statement

No potential conflict of interest was reported by the author(s)

ORCID

Guillermo J. Larios-Hernandez http://orcid.org/0000-0002-8288-7981

References

Aguerrebere, R., and A. Bustos. 2021. The challenges of rural transportation in Mexico. *ReVista (Cambridge)* 21 (1):1–23.

Akpan, I. J., E. A. P. Udoh, and B. Adebisi. 2022. Small business awareness and adoption of state-of-the-art technologies in emerging and developing markets, and lessons from the COVID-19 pandemic. *Journal of Small Business & Entrepreneurship* 34 (2):123–40. doi:10.1080/08276331.2020.1820185.

Al Busaidi, N. S., A. B. Bhuiyan, and N. Zulkifli. 2019. The critical review on the adoption of ICTs in the small and medium enterprises (SMEs) in the developing countries. *International Journal of Small and Medium Enterprises* 2 (2):33–40. doi:10.46281/ijsmes.v2i2.437.

AliResearch. 2021. China Taobao Village report 2020. Accessed April 30, 2022. http://www.aliresearch.com/en/Reports/Reportsdetails?articleCode=167153834769125376

Alizila. 2018. Rwanda first in Africa to join Alibaba-led eWTP. Accessed June 26, 2023. https://www.alizila.com/rwanda-first-in-africa-to-join-alibaba-led-ewtp/

Atomic88. 2022. Foro de Inclusión Digital 2022 (Digital Inclusion Forum 2022). LinkedIn video post, May 9. Accessed June 26, 2023. https://www.linkedin.com/video/event/urn:li:ugcPost:6926991587633754112/

Atomic88. n.d. Aldeas Digitales (Digital Villages). Accessed April 30, 2022. https://atomic88.com/a88/aldeas-digitales/

Auerbach, C., and L. B. Silverstein. 2003. *Qualitative data: An introduction to coding and analysis*. New York: NYU Press.

Boufflet, S. 2022. Chinese rurality 2.0. Taobao Village 2.0. The unicorn as a model! Accessed September 10, 2022. https://hal.science/hal-03617811/document

Bowen, G. A. 2009. Document analysis as a qualitative research method. *Qualitative Research Journal* 9 (2):27–40. doi:10.3316/QRJ0902027.

Brunetti, F., D. T. Matt, A. Bonfanti, A. De Longhi, G. Pedrini, and G. Orzes. 2020. Digital transformation challenges: Strategies emerging from a multi-stakeholder approach. *The TQM Journal* 32 (4):697–724. doi:10.1108/TQM-12-2019-0309.

Campus. 2021. Atomic88 detonará exportaciones mexicanas ante 26 millones de empresas compradoras del mundo (Atomic88 will detonate Mexican exports before 26 million buying companies in the world). Accessed March 28, 2022. https://suplementocampus.com/atomic88-detonara-exportaciones-mexicanas-ante-26-millones-de-empresas-compradoras-del-mundo/

Cave, M., and E. Flores-Roux. 2017. How Mexico can Benefit from the Digital Economy. Accessed April 29, 2022. https://ceeg.mx/publicaciones/CEEG-Final-Version-25-jan-2017.pdf

Chege, S. M., and D. Wang. 2020. Information technology innovation and its impact on job creation by SMEs in developing countries: An analysis of the literature review. *Technology Analysis & Strategic Management* 32 (3):256–71. doi:10.1080/09537325.2019.1651263.

Chiatchoua, C., and M. C. Lozano Arizmendi. 2021. Adjustment mechanisms and digital transformation of micro and small companies in the face of COVID-19 in Mexico [English abstract]. *Nova Scientia* 13 (e). Accessed November 16, 2023. https://www.scielo.org.mx/scielo.php?pid=S2007-07052021000300203&script=sci_abstract&tlng=en.

Chin, M. Y., L. P. Foo, and M. Falahat. 2023. Digital free trade zone in facilitating small medium enterprises for globalisation: A perspective from Malaysia small and medium enterprises. *Business and Economic Research* 13 (2):40–52. doi:10.5296/ber.v13i2.20835.

Chow, G. C. 2015. *China's economic transformation*. Chichester, UK: John Wiley & Sons.

Christensen, C. M., E. Ojomo, and K. Dillon. 2019. *The prosperity paradox: How innovation can lift nations out of poverty*. New York: Harper Business.

Couture, V., B. Faber, Y. Gu, and L. Liu. 2021. Connecting the countryside via e-commerce: Evidence from China. *American Economic Review: Insights* 3 (1):35–50.

Curtis, M. 2016. Supporting small businesses in developing countries: Which programmes work and why? Accessed November 26, 2023. https://curtisresearch.org/wp-content/uploads/SupportingSmallBusinessesReport.pd

Ding, Y., A. McQuoid, and C. Karayalcin. 2019. Fiscal decentralization, fiscal reform, and economic growth in China. *China Economic Review* 53:152–67. doi:10.1016/j.chieco.2018.08.005.

Djan, K. O., and W. A. Owusu-Ansah. 2020. Assessing the impact of the Huawei brand on the information communication technology infrastructure of Ghana. In *Huawei goes global, Vol II: Regional, geopolitical perspectives and crisis management*, eds. W. Zhang, I. Alon and C. Lattemann, 187–205. Cham, Switzerland: Palgrave Macmillan.

Erie, M. S., and T. Streinz. 2021. The Beijing effect: China's Digital Silk Road as transnational data governance. *New York University Journal of International Law and Politics* 54 (1):1–92.

eWTP. 2021. Launch of the 2021 Alibaba global digital challenge for youth. Accessed May 12, 2022. https://www.ewtp.org/news_content?id=101&spm=a2o7pe.23825057

Fan, L. 2019. *Taobao Villages: The emergence of a new pattern of rural ecommerce in China and its social implications*. Jakarta, Indonesia: Friedrich-Ebert-Stiftung.

Fortune. Fortune. 2022. The Electronic World Trade Platform: Making global trade more inclusive, January 26. Accessed June 26, 2023. https://brand-studio.fortune.com/alibaba-group/making-global-trade-more-inclusive/?prx_t=dT8HAzi5SAoPEQA&prx_ro=s&ntv_ht=ProZYgA

Gamage, S. K. N., E. M. S. Ekanayake, G. A. K. N. J. Abeyrathne, R. P. I. R. Prasanna, J. M. S. B. Jayasundara, and P. S. K. Rajapakshe. 2020. A review of global challenges and survival strategies of small and medium enterprises (SMEs). *Economies* 8 (4):79. doi:10.3390/economies8040079.

George, S. 2019. 10 success stories of ecommerce in Mexico 2019. Accessed October 31, 2022. https://appscrip.com/blog/ecommerce-in-mexico/

Geldman, A. 2021. Online marketplaces in Latin America. Accessed September 9, 2022. https://www.webretailer.com/marketplaces-worldwide/online-marketplaces-latin-america/

Gioia, D. A., K. G. Corley, and A. L. Hamilton. 2013. Seeking qualitative rigor in inductive research: Notes on the Gioia methodology. *Organizational Research Methods* 16 (1):15–31. doi:10.1177/1094428112452151.

Hamersma, E. 2021. Rwanda's place on the Digital Silk Road: Discussing Rwanda Vision 2020 from the perspective of Chinese development assistance. Accessed December 2, 2023. https://global-studies.doshisha.ac.jp/attach/page/GLOBAL_STUDIES-PAGE-EN-147/149729/file/271-288.pdf

He, X. 2019. Digital entrepreneurship solution to rural poverty: Theory, practice and policy implications. *Journal of Developmental Entrepreneurship* 24 (01):1950004 1–32. doi:10.1142/S1084946719500043.

Heeks, R., and R. Duncombe. 2001. Information, technology and small enterprise: A handbook for enterprise support agencies in developing countries. Manchester, UK: Institute for Development Policy and Management, University of Manchester.

Hernandez, K. 2019. Achieving complex development goals along China's Digital Silk Road (K4D Emerging Issues Report). Brighton, UK: Institute of Development Studies, University of Sussex.

Hilbert, M. 2001. *From industrial economics to digital economics: An introduction to the transition*. Santiago, Chile: CEPAL.

Hong, Y., and E. Harwit. 2020. China's globalizing Internet: History, power, and governance. *Chinese Journal of Communication* 13 (1):1–7. doi:10.1080/17544750.2020.1722903.

IFAD. 2017. Investing in rural people in Mexico. Accessed December 2, 2023. https://www.ifad.org/en/web/knowledge/-/publication/investing-in-rural-people-in-mexico-2014-

Johnston, L. A. 2021. World trade, e-commerce, and COVID-19: Role of and implications for China's Electronic World Trade Platform (eWTP). *China Review* 21 (2):65–86.

Juarez, C. 2022. Alibaba Group abre su primer centro de distribución en México. Accessed April 28, 2022. https://thelogisticsworld.com/actualidad-logistica/alibaba-group-abre-su-primer-centro-de-distribucion-en-mexico

Kshetri, N. 2018. Rural e-commerce in developing countries. *IT Professional* 20 (2):91–5. doi:10.1109/MITP.2018.021921657.

Lefevre, B., and L. Wiart. 2020. Les hubs eWTP d'Alibaba: Une stratégie globale d'articulation d'écosystèmes locaux (Alibaba's eWTP hubs: A global strategy for articulating local ecosystems). *Les Enjeux de L'Information et de la Communication* 21 (1):71–89.

Leong, C., S. L. Pan, S. Newell, and L. Cui, University of New South Wales. 2016. The emergence of self-organizing e-commerce ecosystems in remote villages of China: A tale of digital empowerment for rural development. *MIS Quarterly* 40 (2):475–84. doi:10.25300/MISQ/2016/40.2.11.

Li, A. H. F. 2017. E-commerce and Taobao Villages: A promise for China's rural development? *China Perspectives* 2017 (3):57–62. doi:10.4000/chinaperspectives.7423.

Li, L., F. Su, W. Zhang, and J.-Y. Mao. 2018. Digital transformation by SME entrepreneurs: A capability perspective. *Information Systems Journal* 28 (6):1129–57. doi:10.1111/isj.12153.

Liu, W., M. Dunford, and B. Gao. 2018. A discursive construction of the Belt and Road Initiative: From neo-liberal to inclusive globalization. *Journal of Geographical Sciences* 28 (9):1199–214. doi:10.1007/s11442-018-1520-y.

Luo, X. 2019. Building China-Latin America Digital Silk Road: Challenges and roadmap. *China International Studies* 77:48–63.

Makundi, H., H. Huyse, and P. Develtere. 2016. Cooperation between China and Tanzania on ICT: Fish, fishing tackle or fishing skills? *Journal of Chinese Economic and Business Studies* 14 (2):129–49. doi:10.1080/14765284.2016.1174459.

Malena, J. 2021. The extension of the Digital Silk Road to Latin America: Advantages and potential risks. Accessed December 2, 2023. https://cdn.cfr.org/sites/default/files/pdf/jorgemalenadsr.pdf

Martínez-Domínguez, M., and J. Mora-Rivera. 2020. Internet adoption and usage patterns in rural Mexico. *Technology in Society* 60:101226. doi:10.1016/j.techsoc.2019.101226.

Meltzer, J. P. 2014. Supporting the Internet as a platform for international trade: Opportunities for small and medium-sized enterprises and developing countries. (Working Paper 69). Washington, DC: Brookings Institution.

Naughton, B. 2020. Chinese industrial policy and the Digital Silk Road: The case of Alibaba in Malaysia. *Asia Policy* 15 (1):23–39. doi:10.1353/asp.2020.0006.

Neilson, B. 2022. Working the Digital Silk Road: Alibaba's digital free trade zone in Malaysia. In *Digital work in the planetary market*, eds. M. Graham and F. Ferrari, 117–36. Cambridge, MA: MIT Press.

OECD. 2001. *Understanding the digital divide*. Paris: OECD.

OECD. 2021a. *The digital transformation of SMEs*. Paris: OECD.

OECD. 2021b. *SME and entrepreneurship outlook*. Paris: OECD.

Pisanty Baruch, A. 2005. Marginación digital y educación (Digital marginalization and education). In *Internet, columna vertebral de la sociedad de la información [Internet, backbone of the information society]*, eds. O. Islas and C. Benassini, 115–64. Mexico City: ITESM CEM.

Rashid, Y., A. Rashid, M. A. Warraich, S. S. Sabir, and A. Waseem. 2019. Case study method: A step-by-step guide for business researchers. *International Journal of Qualitative Methods* 18:160940691986242. doi:10.1177/1609406919862424.

Risley, J. 2023. What are the top online marketplaces? Accessed May 26, 2023. https://www.digitalcommerce360.com/article/infographic-top-online-marketplaces/

Samara, G., and J. Terzian. 2021. Challenges and opportunities for digital entrepreneurship in developing countries. In *Digital entrepreneurship: Impact on business and society*, eds. M. Soltanifar, M. Hughes and L. Gocke, 283–302. Cham, Switzerland: Springer.

Santos-Paulino, A. U. 2013. Country role model of development success: Lessons from China and India. In *Achieving development success: Strategies and lessons from the developing world*, ed. A.K Fosu, 176–84. Oxford, UK: Oxford University Press.

Schia, N. N. 2018. The cyber frontier and digital pitfalls in the Global South. *Third World Quarterly* 39 (5):821–37. doi:10.1080/01436597.2017.1408403.

Shen, H. 2018. Building a Digital Silk Road? Situating the Internet in China's Belt and Road Initiative. *International Journal of Communication* 12 (19):2683–701.

Southwood, R. 2004. ICTs and small enterprise: A motor of economic development in Africa (IICD Research Brief No. 9). Accessed April 12, 2022. http://www.bibalex.org/search4dev/files/287952/118865.pdf

Statista. 2021. Most popular e-commerce websites in Mexico as of September 2021. Accessed April 20, 2022. https://www.statista.com/statistics/434042/mexico-most-visited-retail-websites/

Tang, W., and J. Zhu. 2020. Informality and rural industry: Rethinking the impacts of e-commerce on rural development in China. *Journal of Rural Studies* 75:20–9. doi:10.1016/j.jrurstud.2020.02.010.

Tapscott, D., and A. D. Williams. 2010. *Macrowikinomics: Rebooting Business and the World*. New York: Penguin.

Tec Review. 2021. La alianza entre Alibaba y la Escuela de Negocios del Tec de Monterrey [The alliance between Alibaba and the Monterrey Tech Business School]. *Tec Review,* October 19. Accessed April 10, 2022. https://tecreview.tec.mx/2021/10/19/liderazgo-1/alianza-entre-alibaba-y-la-escuela-de-negocios-del-tec-de-monterrey/

Tugendhat, H., and J. Voo. 2021. China's Digital Silk Road in Africa and the future of Internet governance (Working Paper Series No. 2021/50). Washington, DC: China Africa Research Initiative, School of Advanced International Studies, Johns Hopkins University.

Vanek, M. 2018. Chinese Internet giant Alibaba shares its plans for Africa. *CNBC Africa*, July 9. Accessed October 19, 2022. https://www.cnbcafrica.com/2018/chinese-internet-giant-alibaba-shares-its-plans-for-africa/

Vila Seoane, M. F. V. 2020. Alibaba's discourse for the digital Silk Road: The Electronic World Trade Platform and "inclusive globalization. *Chinese Journal of Communication* 13 (1):68–83. doi:10.1080/17544750.2019.1606838.

Wang, L., and C. Liu. 2021. Critical evaluation of China's universal service policy: Toward a harmonious online nation. *The Information Society* 37 (3):177–89. doi:10.1080/01972243.2021.1897912.

Wang, C. C., J. T. Miao, N. A. Phelps, and J. Zhang. 2021. E-commerce and the transformation of the rural: The Taobao Village phenomenon in Zhejiang province, China. *Journal of Rural Studies* 81:159–69. doi:10.1016/j.jrurstud.2020.10.017.

Wei, Y. D., J. Lin, and L. Zhang. 2020. E-commerce, Taobao Villages and regional development in China. *Geographical Review* 110 (3):380–405. doi:10.1111/gere.12367.

Weidong, L. 2017. Inclusive globalization: New philosophy of China's Belt and Road initiative. *Bulletin of Chinese Academy of Sciences* (Chinese Version) 32 (4):331–9.

World Bank. 2016. *World Development Report 2016: Digital Dividends*. Washington, DC: World Bank.

World Bank and Alibaba Group. 2019. *E-Commerce development: Experience from China*. Washington, DC: World Bank.

Yean, T. S. 2018. *The Digital Free Trade Zone (DFTZ): Putting Malaysia's SMEs onto the Digital Silk Road*. Singapore: ISEAS-Yusof Ishak Institute.

Yin, R. K. 2013. Validity and generalization in future case study evaluations. *Evaluation* 19 (3):321–32. doi:10.1177/1356389013497081.

Yin, R. 2018. *Case study research and applications: Design and methods*. Thousand Oaks, CA: Sage.

Zhou, J., L. Yu, and C. L. Choguill. 2021. Co-evolution of technology and rural society: The blossoming of Taobao Villages in the information era, China. *Journal of Rural Studies* 83:81–7. doi:10.1016/j.jrurstud.2021.02.022.

OPEN ACCESS

Learning along the Digital Silk Road? Technology transfer, power, and Chinese ICT corporations in North Africa

Tin Hinane El-Kadi

ABSTRACT

While much attention has been paid to how China's rise as a digital superpower could threaten US hegemony over cyberspace, much less has been written on what the Digital Silk Road, or the presence of Chinese tech firms in developing countries more broadly, means for technological upgrading and development. This article contributes to filling this gap by investigating the technology spillovers emanating from two Chinese tech giants – Huawei and ZTE – in Algeria and Egypt. Using a political economy framework that combines insights from structuralist economic development and techno-politics and drawing on over 70 semi-structured interviews and field-observations, it argues that despite localizing activities that bear the promise of generating significant linkages, the two Chinese tech firms created no meaningful learning opportunities for domestic entities that contribute to technological upgrading. What could at first seem like developmental connections that promote technology transfers are found to be linkages diffusing Chinese infrastructures, hardware, software, processes, and standards that shape distinct digital systems. Without pro-active policies from host governments, the Digital Silk Road risks creating new technological dependencies; locking local ICT actors into activities and relationships captured and defined by Chinese tech giants.

Introduction

Over 2,200 years ago, the movement of people and goods across the Silk Roads facilitated the diffusion of Chinese inventions and technologies to Eurasia, the Middle East, and North Africa. This trade network constituted a channel for Chinese innovations such as papermaking and woodblock printing, which enabled large-scale printing for the first time and transformed information dissemination in Europe (Hernandez 2019). In the twenty first century, Beijing's Digital Silk Road (DSR), the digital component of the Belt and Road Initiative (BRI), could potentially play a similar role in spreading new technologies and practices.

There is a dearth of empirical studies looking at China's contribution to technology transfer in developing nations' ICT (information and communication technology) sectors. The authors have either argued that Chinese ICT multinational companies (MNCs) create significant opportunities for technology transfer (Tsui 2016; Agbebi 2019) or, conversely, that there is weak evidence of such opportunities (Rwehumbiza 2021; Tugendhat 2021), depending on the cases and methodologies used. Such emerging research has tended to use a simple diffusionist technology transfer lens, focusing more on the quantum of linkages rather than a qualitative investigation of their content. By narrowly focusing on the *existence* or *lack* thereof of spillovers, existing research tends to obscure the bargains made in the actual implementation of technology transfers and training programs. What is perhaps as significant as the question of whether Chinese digital companies engage in technology transfer in host developing countries is the role played by spillovers in diffusing specific technological processes, practices, and standards and what this means for structural transformation.

Using a novel political economy framework that combines insights from structuralist economic development and techno-politics, this article examines the technological spillovers emanating from the interaction of two Chinese telecommunication giants – Huawei and ZTE – with local configurations of power and skills in North Africa and their grounded effects. North Africa is an interesting region to analyze the developmental implications of Chinese digital MNCs. While North African countries have different political economies, they all share middle-income status and have in common growing numbers of tech-savvy young people, a relatively high rate of internet penetration, and proximity to the EU market, making the region a strategic hub for the DSR. One of the first high-level references made to the DSR was in the 13th Five Year Plan published by the Central Committee of the Communist Party of China (CCCPC) in 2016, which stated the aim to "develop an online Silk Road with the Arab countries and others through high-speed fiber optic networks" (CCCPC (Central Committee of the Communist Part of China) 2016, 71). Algeria and Egypt, in particular, have emerged as two significant markets for Chinese original equipment manufacturers (OEMs) like Huawei and ZTE, the most prominent Chinese digital firms in North Africa. The OEM sub-sector is a high-linkage sector that can theoretically generate significant technology spillovers.

Based on extensive and triangulated field data, drawing on over 70 interviews in Algeria and Egypt, this study finds that Huawei and ZTE, like their US and European competitors, limit meaningful technology transfers to protect their knowledge premiums. What could at first seem like developmental connections that promote technological learning and upgrading are found to be linkages diffusing Chinese infrastructure, hardware, software, processes, and standards that shape distinct digital systems designed around the consumption of Chinese technologies. Without pro-active policies from host governments, the DSR risks creating new technological dependencies; locking local ICT actors into activities and relationships captured and defined by Chinese digital giants.

By providing an empirically grounded account of the multifaceted forces shaping technological spillovers from Chinese digital MNCs and their implications, this study aims to contribute to ongoing debates on China's growing role in the global digital economy, the Belt and Road Initiative, foreign direct investment (FDI) and technology transfer, and South-South investments.

The article is structured as follows. After this introduction, the second section starts by reviewing the literature on technology transfer. It suggests an analytical framework that departs from standard diffusionist models of technology transfer which focus on the occurrence of spillovers while marginalizing the *hidden* politics behind seemingly technical linkages. The next section discusses the study's methodology, and this is followed by the findings, which trace the channels of knowledge spillovers from digital MNCs in terms of three types of linkages: horizontal linkages, vertical linkages, and linkages with local universities and research institutions. The final section concludes and provides policy recommendations to help countries maximize gains from Chinese tech firms for their own digital transformations.

Literature review and theoretical framework

FDI and technology transfer

Technology transfer – the dissemination of technical knowledge and know-how embodied in products, processes, and management (Wahab, Rose, and Osman 2011, 62) – through FDI has long been regarded as a major engine of technological upgrading and structural transformation (Globerman 1979; Markusen and Venables 1999; Amsden 2001; Saggi 2002; Blalock and Gertler 2008; Fu, Pietrobelli, and Soete 2011). The basic premise underlying the existence of technology spillovers[1] is that foreign-invested firms are technologically superior to local ones; thus, their interaction with local economies is assumed to lead to technology transfers which, in turn, lead to productivity gains (Saggi 2002). Given the lower technology base within developing economies, these spillovers may help local industries build up their domestic technological capabilities and catch up with the international technology frontier (Lall 1992; Ning and Wang 2018).

The theoretical literature identifies two main channels through which foreign firms can generate technology transfer. Horizontally, skills and knowledge transfer can occur through labor mobility across firms, including when local firms "poach" skilled workers from foreign firms (Iršová and Havránek 2013; Liu 2008). Vertically, backward and forward linkages help the diffusion of skills, knowledge, and technology as they provide demonstration effects and training to local firms (Blomstrom and Kokko 2001; Liu, Wang, and Wei 2009; Rojec and Knell 2017). Based on Albert Hirschman's work, the theory of linkages conceptualizes the way in which a factory generates demand for primary materials like sand mining in a cement factory (backward linkage), while its outputs, cinder blocks, might be an input for the local construction industry downstream (forward linkage) (Hirschman 2013, 103). Backward linkages are the most critical mechanism for learning and achieving productivity gains (Javorcik 2004; Blalock and Gertler 2008; Hirschman 2013).

There are also significant sectoral variations in the potential for technology spillovers. Manufacturing and infrastructure building are recognized as high linkage sectors in the literature (Lean 2001; Hirschman 2013). For instance, building digital infrastructure can foster inter-firm spillovers by encouraging industrial clustering and generating a broader supply chain in equipment and component manufacturing and services. Most fundamentally, installing new ICT infrastructure requires the transfer of know-how and skills to operate and maintain advanced technologies (Ockwell et al. 2008). Digital MNCs can thus theoretically provide technical artifacts and managerial skills transfers that contribute to technological upgrading and the building of competitive ICT industries in host countries.

However, the empirical evidence on the transfer of technology through FDI is, at best, mixed. In their seminal study of technology spillovers in Morocco, Haddad and Harrison (1993) found that if domestic and foreign firms compete to capture the same market, the latter does not have the incentive to promote technology linkages. In some instances, foreign firms operated as enclaves with little connection to the local economy (Aitken and Harrison 1999). Measures adopted by foreign companies to limit technology transfer include protecting their intellectual property and trade secrets, hiring mainly foreign workers, and forestalling labor turnover by offering significantly higher wages than local industry averages (Liu, Wang, and Wei 2009). In other instances, research showed that foreign subsidiaries did more harm than good to the local economy by capturing the domestic market and crowding out local competitors without engaging in any meaningful technology transfer (Amendolagine et al. 2013). Any discussion on the developmental potential of foreign subsidiaries needs to tackle the difficult but pragmatic question of whether it is sound to expect technology transfer to occur in the first place, as corporations would naturally be expected to preserve their technological edge. This being said, instances of technology spillovers have occurred. The development trajectories of East Asia's "dragons" are filled with cases of technological learning from foreign firms in a myriad of sectors. Can the DSR contribute to technological upgrading in host countries or does the initiative strictly serve Beijing's interests?

Chinese digital firms and the techno-politics of linkages

With the world's largest online population and a booming digital industry, China has expanded its global digital footprint. Chinese digital MNCs have built the backbone infrastructure used by billions of internet users across the developing world. One estimate suggests that Huawei built 70% of Africa's 4G network (Mackinnon 2019). While the internationalization of Chinese tech firms in developing countries has undoubtedly promoted local economies' catch-up efforts in terms of ICT infrastructure, the role played by these corporations in diffusing knowledge and technology remains under researched.

Two of the few fieldwork-based works looking at technology transfer from Chinese tech corporations are Agbebi's (2018, 2019) studies on Huawei's presence in Nigeria. Based on 29 interviews with staff and beneficiaries of Huawei's training programs in Nigeria, Agbebi points to the existence of dynamic horizontal linkages, finding several instances of trained Huawei staff leaving the firm to join other ventures. She also indicates "considerable backward vertical linkages with local suppliers" (Agbebi 2019, 201), with Huawei Nigeria counting over 500 local partners in its supply chain, many of which receive training from the Chinese tech giant. In a similar vein, Li and Cheong (2017, 764) argue that ZTE and Huawei contribute to technology transfer in Malaysia through partnerships established with Malaysian universities and research centers, through which the Chinese firms have been found to provide courses for local students that led to ZTE and Huawei certifications.

A somewhat different take emerges from the more critical work of Tugendhat (2020), who finds from his fieldwork in Kenya and Nigeria that Huawei, like Ericsson, Nokia, Cisco, and other competitors, treads a fine line between training local engineers and keeping control of its intellectual property. In a subsequent publication, he argues that the Chinese tech giant offers no significant opportunity for technology transfers that could contribute to technological upgrading and stresses that the firm has a "limited impact on knowledge transfer by design" (Tugendhat 2021, 19). Likewise, based on fieldwork in Tanzania, Rwehumbiza (2021) finds that while there is some evidence of local staff and suppliers' training, Huawei Tanzania does not seem to build significant backward linkages with local firms.

These studies provide valuable insights for understanding the developmental implications of Chinese investments in the ICT sector of developing countries.

Yet, the emerging literature adopts a simple diffusionist technology transfer model, which measures technology transfer by the existence or absence of linkages. This framework conceals the idiosyncratic norms, standards, and politics conveyed in the transferred technologies and training programs. Analyzing technology spillovers requires not only observing their occurrence through vertical and horizontal linkages but also scrutinizing what these linkages actually *do* on the ground. In the same way that we cannot expect high-tech firms to willingly share their cutting-edge technology with poorer countries, neither can we assume that the transfer of technology is devoid of political content and consequences. To date, however, there is still a need for a more effective theorization of technology transfer processes to untangle both its technical and political aspects.

In this regard, the techno-politics framework can bring valuable insights into the analysis. From a conceptual perspective, techno-politics unpacks the oftentimes *hidden* political work of technological artifacts and infrastructures (Mitchell 2002; Larkin 2013; Anand 2015). One strand of this intellectual tradition goes back to the work of Langdon Winner (1980), who argued that all technologies, from forks to nuclear power stations, have "politics" embedded into them. In its basic form, techno-politics refers to "the strategic practice of designing or using technology to constitute, embody, or enact political goals" (Hecht 2001, 256). Here technology is defined as both "artefacts and nonphysical, systematic means of making or doing things" (Hecht 2001, 257).

This analytical lens shifts attention from individual innovations to the system of relations in which technology is embedded, emphasizing that the "same" technology can uphold different types of politics as it is negotiated, adopted, and reshaped by various actors to advance their own interests (Edwards and Hecht 2010). Seen from this perspective, power and politics stem from both the social and the technical, with different stakeholders competing over authority by ensuring that some technologies and standards prevail over alternative ones (Hecht 2001). The question of technology standards – the underlying regulations that define how telecommunication networks operate and interwork – is particularly significant in the debate on the role of Chinese digital MNCs in transferring technology to host middle-income countries. Competition over who gets to set technological standards has become intense between China and the US, with China trying to challenge the US-centric cyberspace (Beattie 2019).

Against the backdrop of Chinese tech firms taking a more active role in developing, supplying, and maintaining the physical components upon which future digital infrastructure will rely, a conceivable consequence is that this will speed up the dissemination of Chinese technological standards. Recently, Chinese representatives have been calling for a new standard, which they called "New IP", arguing that the current, US-set protocol of TCP/IP is unable to support the speed of package transfers needed in the upcoming 5G revolution (Smith, Cummins, and Krasodomski-Jones 2021). Underlying this coinage of new technical jargon lies a fierce fight over who gets to set the standards of the next technological wave. The ability to define standards has long been understood as a tool of power, enabling those who set the rules to shape them to their own advantage (Mattli and Büthe 2003; Lee and Oh 2006; Yao, Tan, and Suttmeier 2009). Although international technological standards are approved by multilateral institutions such as the International Telecommunication Union (ITU), the increased number of countries and actors integrated into digital systems built by Chinese tech firms helps amplify China's voice in international standard-setting bodies.

In a study of China's digital presence in Africa, Gagliardone (2019) uses techno-politics to address the question whether China is imposing its internet model on African countries. He finds that China's intervention in Africa's information societies has been driven by the preferences of different African states rather than those of Beijing. This article extends techno-politics to analyze technology spillovers emanating from Chinese tech giants. This opens up a different angle on the transfer of technology from foreign subsidiaries, as the analysis is no longer limited to a binary between the existence or absence of vertical and horizontal spillovers, which diffuse (or not) know-how and technology in ways that are predominantly seen as developmental and unproblematic, but instead questions the more profound and uncertain implications of transferred technologies.

Several possibilities emerge when looking at the issue of technology transfer through this lens. What if horizontal and vertical spillovers are approvingly observed, as argued by Agbebi (2019, 201), but tech firms are building through these linkages markets for staff and subcontractors that revolve around the consumption and use of their products, processes, and standards? In other words, what if emerging linkages are creating "closed-loop systems" that lock local ICT actors into activities and relationships captured and defined by foreign digital giants? As technological latecomers, could it be that Chinese ICT firms are engaging more in training employees, students, and suppliers than their Western counterparts to promote their own brands? Is the technology transferred by Chinese digital firms creating a separate Sino-centric internet among BRI countries?

To address some of these questions and to keep the technical and the political together, this article adopts a conceptual framework that brings together insights from structuralist economic development – to trace the occurrence of vertical and horizontal linkages – as well as from techno-politics – to understand the *hidden* politics conveyed through these channels. This framework recognizes that only a deeper, empirical engagement with technical processes – rather than assumptions based on preconceived ideas – can allow an adequate understanding of the extent and implications of technology transfer. Thus, by zooming in on the actual process of technology transfer through traceable socio-technical linkages, this conceptual lens enables us to go beyond both depoliticized and over-politicized debates about the developmental role of Chinese tech giants.

Methods

How can we capture technology spillovers and their effects, given the complexity and layers that make up the ICT industry? There is a lack of quantitative data on the contribution of Chinese digital firms to technology transfer. But even with rigorous and fine-grained data, quantitative methods fail to capture the nuances and rich insights that can be gathered through fieldwork (Pack 2006). There is a growing recognition that technology transfer is subject to contextual influences and power dynamics, making qualitative tools appropriate (Autio et al. 2014; Auffray and Fu 2015; Cunningham, Menter, and Young 2017; Demena and van Bergeijk 2019). Furthermore, the conceptual framework of this article, which conceptualizes technology transfer as a complex process emerging from power bargains between different actors, calls for thicker descriptions (Denzin 2001).

Algeria and Egypt were selected because, from Mao Zedong's Three World theory to Xi Jinping's Belt and Road Initiative, the two North African countries have developed and sustained strong relations with Beijing rooted in a shared experience of colonial domination (Pairault 2017, 8). Algeria and Egypt are also the two most important recipients of Chinese FDI in the region, and the two most lucrative markets for Chinese OEMs, like Huawei and ZTE, which specialize in building backbone ICT infrastructure. The two firms have played a key role in setting up 3G and 4G networks and will likely continue playing a significant role in the upgrade toward 5G. Furthermore, Algeria is the only African country counting a Huawei manufacturing plant (Agence Ecofin 2019a), and Telecom Egypt signed a rare contract with ZTE to create a joint technology training center and innovation laboratory (Agence Ecofin 2019b).

This study draws on 71 semi-structured interviews conducted in Egypt and Algeria between October 2021 and March 2022. As summarized in Table 1, interviews included employees, subcontractors, customers of Huawei and ZTE, students and startups receiving training and support from Chinese tech-giants, ICT policymakers, government officials, university faculty/researchers, as well as Western ICT equipment manufacturers including Cisco, Ericsson, and Nokia (see Annex 1 for full interview table). The choice of including other foreign firms in data collection and analysis was taken to avoid falling into the trap of "Chinese exceptionalism", which often leads to accounts picturing Chinese firms as unique and somehow detached from broader sectoral practices (Oya and Schaefer 2019).

Interviewees were selected using purposive sampling in the first stage. Having worked in the Algiers office of Huawei Technologies North Africa, regionally headquartered in Egypt the author developed a large network within the ICT industry in the two countries, which facilitated the author's access to key informants during the fieldwork. This work experience allowed the author to gather first-hand observations on the nature and intensity of the training provided to local workers and dynamics between Chinese and

Table 1. Breakdown of respondents by category.

Interviewee Category	Code	Number of Interviewees
Local subcontractors, suppliers, and customers of Huawei and ZTE	S	11
Current and former Huawei and ZTE engineers and managers	W	21
ICT experts and researchers	E	12
Students and instructors of Huawei and ZTE training programmes	U	11
Engineers and managers of Ericsson, Nokia, and Cisco	C	11
Policymakers	G	5
Total		**71**

non-Chinese staff members. LinkedIn further allowed the author to reach out to engineers working for Huawei and ZTE and beneficiaries of training programs offered by the Chinese firms in Algeria and Egypt. Snowballing from different entry points was used to achieve a large enough sample until knowledge saturation was reached. Being a native Arabic and French speaker and an advanced Mandarin speaker, the author was able to conduct interviews with local, Chinese and other foreign actors in Egypt and Algeria.

Data analysis was not separated from data collection but rather conducted simultaneously. A theory-driven coding strategy was used to identify technology spillovers with codes indicating the mechanisms accounting for horizontal and vertical spillovers and linkages between ICT firms and local universities. Codes were later grouped into themes representing different channels of technology transfer. The author followed an inductive approach to analyze the power dynamics between different actors and the content conveyed in linkages. In addition to interviews and field observations, data was collected during and after the fieldwork from financial and business newspapers and the companies' annual reports. Quantitative data was sometimes also collected from interviewees.

Findings and analysis

Overview of the ICT sector in Algeria and Egypt

Before assessing the main channels of technology spillovers from Chinese ICT multinationals in Algeria and Egypt, some remarks are needed to understand the political economies in which Huawei and ZTE are operating. The Algerian and Egyptian economies are concentrated in low-value-added sectors and suffer from sluggish growth. High chronic youth unemployment, estimated at 30 per cent as of 2020, is a distinctive feature of the Middle East and North Africa region (Statista 2021). Remarkably, about 40% of the region's university graduates are unemployed (World Economic Forum 2017). More than ten years after the mass revolt against authoritarianism, poverty, and lack of economic opportunities, no notable change has materialized in the region. For countries in the region to produce and sustain economic growth and create high-quality jobs for the millions of unemployed workers, they need to undergo structural transformation, the process of moving from low-productivity, labor-intensive economic activities to high-productivity, technology-intensive activities that require advanced skills.

At the same time, the two countries have different political economies. Algeria is a state-dominated economy where hydrocarbons represent 95% of export revenues, constituting the largest source of government income (Elliot and Sahar 2020). Algeria is one of the last remaining countries that are not members of the World Trade Organization (WTO) and it imposes strict control over foreign capital, with joint ventures required in strategic sectors (Laouisset 2021). Historically, Algeria has pursued protectionist industrial policies to encourage the development of local industry, including import substitution policies, and local content requirements. In recent years, the Algerian government has tried to welcome more FDI, but investors' appetite has been limited outside of the hydrocarbon sector (Beladi 2023). The country relies on its public funds to ensure infrastructural catch up including in telecommunications.

In contrast, Egypt has a more market-friendly economy and is more open to foreign capital. Major economic liberalization reforms were introduced as early as 1974 with the implementation of the Open Door Policy (Infitah) (Waterbury 1985). In 2017, Egypt passed an investment law[2] that promotes inbound FDI by easing barriers to entry, offering investors more incentives, and supporting foreign multinational firms' localization efforts. Cairo aims to capitalize on its strategic location bridging three continents, and its market of over 100 million consumers, the largest market in the MENA region, to become a regional trade and investment gateway. The government also intends to attract investment in several mega-projects including the construction of a new national administrative capital for which China is a leading funder (McGregor 2022).

Recognizing the potential of the digital economy to help their structural transition, both countries adopted national ICT plans designed to expand internet connectivity, upgrade workers' skills, and create flourishing knowledge economies. Egypt's ICT 2030 plan prioritizes developing ICT infrastructure, fostering digital inclusion, building domestic capacity, and encouraging innovation (MCIT (Ministry of Communications and Information Technology) 2016). Egypt has positioned itself as a regional leader in exporting information technology services and is home to a vibrant startup scene. Algeria was slower to start its digital transformation but has made significant strides in terms of ICT infrastructure, with bandwidth capacity increasing more than twenty times since 2014 (APS (Algeria Press Service) 2021). By creating the Ministry of Microenterprise, Knowledge-Economy, and Startups in 2020, the government is attempting to break away from the current hydrocarbon-dependent model toward a knowledge-based model.

The two North African governments are investing heavily in upgrading network infrastructure. Egypt witnessed significant growth in internet usage, increasing from 29 per cent of the population in 2009 to 72% as of January 2020. In Algeria, internet penetration rates were estimated at 63% by the same year (World Bank 2022a). Growth in mobile broadband access is correlated with a surge in mobile-cellular subscriptions and the expansion of 3G and 4G network coverage. Mobile penetration in Egypt stands at 110 per cent and is covered by four operators, Orange, Vodafone, Etisalat, and Telecom Egypt. Algeria's mobile penetration reached 105.8%, distributed between three core operators, Mobilis, Djezzy and Ooredoo (World Bank 2022b). While these rates represent an important growth, the region's internet penetration remains just slightly above the world's average, estimated at 60% (World Bank 2022a). This creates significant demand for ICT infrastructure provided by equipment manufacturers like ZTE and Huawei.

Chinese tech firms and technology transfer

> "Information technology advances rapidly. I hope that Chinese enterprises not only observe local laws, operate credibly, and have sound management but also disseminate their advanced technologies and experience to the local enterprises and employees. We always say that give a man a fish, and you feed him for a day; teach a man to fish, and you feed him for a lifetime. Do you agree with me?"
>
> —Premier Wen Jiabao on a visit to Huawei's Training Center in Cairo in 2009 (MFA 2009)

The above quote of Premier Wen encapsulates well the importance attributed to technology transfer in the localization strategy of Chinese tech firms abroad before and after the launch of the DSR in 2015[3]. But do Chinese ICT firms contribute to bridging the digital divide by providing opportunities for technology transfer? Guided by the theoretical framework discussed above, this section identifies and assesses the intensity and grounded effects of three core types of linkages: horizontal linkages, vertical linkages, and linkages with universities and research institutes (see Figure 1). It argues that while Huawei and ZTE have localized activities that can theoretically generate significant linkages, the two Chinese tech firms created no meaningful learning opportunities that contribute to technological upgrading. Instead, emerging linkages are creating a distinct techno-political regime that risks locking local ICT actors into new forms of dependencies as they reconfigure ICT ecosystems around the use and consumption of Chinese infrastructures, processes, and standards.

Notably, the Chinese state was not explicitly included in the framework. Dominant accounts tend to assume that the Chinese state holds a tight rein over its tech champions, which, in turn, strictly align with large policy plans such as the DSR (Chen 2021; Hillman 2021). Fieldwork data indicated that the presence of Huawei and ZTE, including their engagement in knowledge transfer initiatives, is shaped by a much wider variety of Chinese and non-Chinese economic

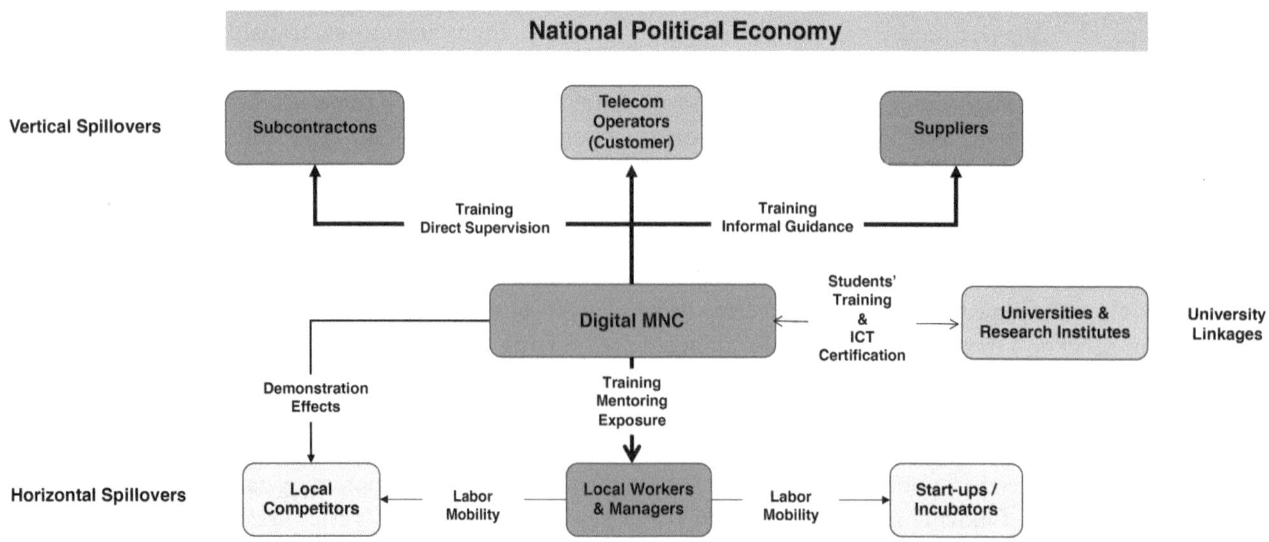

Figure 1. Channels of technology spillovers in the ICT sector.
Source: Author's elaboration.

and political forces. Although the Chinese state, through the DSR, has supported the presence of Chinese tech firms *via* access to preferential loans (Shen 2017), the need to meet commercial imperatives was guiding firms much more strongly than Chinese state political priorities. In terms of policy, Algerian and Egyptian government ICT agendas were more important in shaping Huawei and ZTE strategies to capture markets and increase profits.

Horizontal linkages

As trained workers and managers at multinationals move to domestic firms or start their own businesses, knowledge may be disseminated from MNCs to other firms within the same industry (Iršová and Havránek 2013; Kneller and Pisu 2007). Due to growing labor costs in China, ZTE and Huawei have in recent years localized a bigger share of their labor in North Africa. Huawei employs an estimated 1,000 workers in Egypt, counting both in-house and outsourced contracts and about half as many in Algeria, with about 70% of the staff made up of local employees and the remaining 30% consisting of Chinese and other foreign engineers. ZTE Algeria counts about 200 employees in-house, 70 per cent of whom are locals and 500 outsourced workers, most of whom are local Algerians (W6).[4]

Local engineers and managers at the two Chinese firms, both on in-house and leased contracts, reported going through training programs when they were first hired. The training covered technical and soft skills and continued throughout their employment period, with mandatory tests administered at different stages of their careers. International OEMs also send their local employees abroad for further training. A key motive driving many young engineers to work with Chinese MNCs, and Huawei in particular, is the learning opportunities provided by the companies (W1, W3, W4, W19, W20). When asked to assign a grade from 1 to 5 assessing the quality of the training received by the Chinese tech firms, with 1 indicating low levels of satisfaction and 5 indicating high levels of satisfaction, respondents converged toward a grade of 4. One possible explanation accounting for this high level of workers' satisfaction could be the nature of the ICT industry, a knowledge-intensive sector in which training staff is paramount for firms' operations and profits (Te Velde 2002; King 2013).

The distribution of local managers followed a pyramidal structure in both countries, with local employees well represented at the bottom of the pyramid and Chinese nationals dominating top managerial positions. Similarly to other studies (Auffray and Fu 2015; Oya and Schaefer 2019), this study's findings suggest the existence of a glass ceiling for local employees. At the time fieldwork was conducted, acting CEOs of Huawei and ZTE in Egypt and Algeria were Chinese nationals, while CEOs of Ericsson, Cisco, and Nokia were host country nationals. When questioned about the lack of locals in top-managerial positions, Chinese managers explained that Chinese nationals were more familiar with the firm's work culture, ethos, and processes, giving them an edge in operating projects effectively and in short timeframes (W16).

In the two countries, limited evidence of horizontal spillovers emerged. While, as highlighted by Agbebi (2019), the ICT sector is characterized by high turnover rates, labor mobility tends to occur between foreign multinationals and not toward local firms and institutions. Like Tugendhat (2021), this study found that Algerian and Egyptian OEMs' employees were more likely to move around between Huawei, Nokia, ZTE, Ericsson, and Cisco, among others (C2, C4, C7, W4, W10, W12). About 80 per cent of local workers and managers at Huawei and ZTE responded that they would leave the company for another foreign competitor or to go work abroad. The high salaries offered by international OEMs created a disincentive for local engineers to join local firms or set up their own ventures and constrained the capacity of most local companies to poach talent working for multinationals. This finding is in line with studies that show that MNCs use high wages as a mechanism for labor (and knowledge) retention (Aitken and Harrison 1999; Liu, Wang, and Wei 2009). Most of the younger respondents at Chinese and non-Chinese tech multinationals said that they would go abroad if they were to take up another employment opportunity. Policymakers in both countries expressed concerns about the high rate of locally trained ICT engineers being poached by big tech firms in Europe and the US (G1, G2, G4).

There were few instances of horizontal spillovers, i.e., of respondents indicating the possibility of leaving multinationals to join local firms in the same sector or launch their own firms. In the limited cases found, two main factors account for labor turnover toward national companies: local employees at OEM multinationals leaving to take up higher responsibilities in large national telecommunication firms such as Mobilis in Algeria and Etissalet in Egypt, and those who join smaller local firms and institutions to break away from the hectic workload of international OEMs, especially Chinese ones which are renowned for operating long hours. Additionally, the small number of surveyed subcontractors operating in ICTs were established by former employees of foreign OEMs, including Huawei and ZTE. Managers of these subcontractor firms reported taking with them useful Chinese work culture and management ethos that helped them better operate their businesses (S1).

Vertical linkages

Technology transfer occurs *via* backward linkages from foreign firms to local suppliers and forward linkages from foreign firms to local buyers (Javorcik 2004; Liu, Wang, and Wei 2009). In Algeria and Egypt, foreign companies undertake the biggest ICT infrastructure contracts. In doing so, they often rely on local subcontractors – to install fiber optic cables, towers, and other infrastructure across various regions of the country, and local suppliers – who provide subsidiary equipment, components, administrative and management services, technical assistance and expertise, logistics, etc. This creates potential for backward linkages, alongside potential forward linkages to the customers who use this ICT infrastructure.

Fieldwork findings in Algeria and Egypt suggest this potential was realized, with the existence of both backward and forward linkages emerging from the two firms' operations in building backbone infrastructure. For instance, interviewed suppliers, subcontractors, and customers indicated that Huawei and ZTE provided them with training similarly to other foreign ICT OEMs (S1-S11). The training covered a few different areas, including the operation of machinery and equipment, technical training on the technologies used, and health and safety measures. Local subcontractors, suppliers, and customers also reported having well-established and long-term relations with the two Chinese tech firms and highlighted no notable differences between foreign companies. The length and intensity of the business relationship are important for technology spillovers because frequent and lasting links create greater training and supervision opportunities and pressure the supplier or subcontractor to learn and upgrade to preserve the business relationship (Auffray and Fu 2015, 293). However, there is a need to look beyond the quantum of linkages to scrutinize their actual content and deeper effects, and here two cases will be analyzed: Huawei's mobile phone factory in Algeria and the provision of digital infrastructure by ZTE and Huawei in the two countries.

The case of Huawei's phone factory in Algiers, one of the flagship Digital Silk Road initiatives in North Africa, illustrates how even linkage-intensive activities like manufacturing can be scarce in knowledge transfer opportunities. The factory opened in the Algiers neighborhood of Oued Smar in 2019 after lengthy negotiations between the Algerian government and mobile phone manufacturers for the localization of production, following the rapid decline in the country's foreign reserves due to declining oil prices. The manufacturing plant was the first of its sort in Africa and one of the few outside of China and was set up as a joint venture between Huawei and Algerian firm AFGO-Tech (Agence Ecofin 2019b). The plant has a monthly production capacity of 15,000 smartphones and started operating with about 40 workers, among which 18 local engineers were sent to China to observe Huawei's factories and learn about production processes. Later the factory expanded to 140 workers as extra production lines were added (W7). Commenting on Huawei's manufacturing endeavors in Algeria, one of the Chinese firm's representatives stated that: "The Oued Smar plant is equipped with the latest generation equipment and uses the most innovative technologies and all of Huawei's know-how" (Djazairess 2019).

This rhetoric tied to developmental imaginaries of seamless spillovers and unhindered knowledge flows tells us little about how mechanisms of technology transfer operate on the ground. A closer examination of the factory's embeddedness with local production networks raises concerns about its rate of technological integration. Strong backward linkages would involve important supply inputs from local firms, a mechanism that would help upgrade local suppliers' technical and managerial capabilities (Javorcik 2004; Rojec and Knell 2018). Yet, Huawei's phone production relied on imported SKD (Semi Knocked Down) and CKD (Completely Knocked Down) kits, which are built in China and then exported to Algeria for the final stages of assembly. According to an Algerian line manager working at the factory: "Every component of the phone was imported from China. Even the phones' boxes and the tape used to close the boxes were purchased directly from China" (W7). The supposed local suppliers, Algerian firms, turned into import companies focusing on the purchase of Chinese electronic and non-electronic components. Forward linkages, in this case, consisted of phone distribution and retail companies, which were tasked with boosting the sales of Huawei devices.

While manufacturing activities are assumed to generate considerable spillovers, the nature of the emerging linkages around Huawei's factory resulted in the flooding of the market with Chinese artifacts without much technology transfer. When asked about the reasons behind the factory's low rate of local integration, a manager at Huawei Device explained that the firm had the plan to increase local integration to 40% by localizing the supply of the phone's batteries and chargers, but that they had challenges finding suitable firms and startups to partner with (W11). Low levels of local supply seem to be a pattern in Chinese investments in Africa, with other research indicating that Chinese investors tended to prefer having Chinese suppliers along the value chain rather than sourcing locally (Rwehumbiza 2021; Tang 2021). The Algerian government described the practice, which had become the norm across manufacturers from different countries, as "fictitious production" and "disguised import." In January 2021, the factory's activities were suspended due to the government's ban on the import of CKD and SKD kits, and its workers were laid off for an undetermined period (W7).

The picture is similar when analyzing spillovers emanating from digital infrastructure building, Huawei and ZTE's core activity. Effective forward linkages, in this case, would involve the transfer of knowledge to enable customers (e.g., mobile operators) to learn how to use the technologies and to operate them independently, ultimately allowing technological appropriation and customization. While contracts between mobile carriers and foreign ICT equipment producers in Algeria and Egypt include clauses stating that the equipment's seller transfers know-how on how to operate and maintain the equipment, local engineers working for Huawei and ZTE highlighted that they *intentionally* provided minimal levels of details to customers. As explained by a ZTE engineer in the Algiers office: "We probably give our customers just about 50 or 60 per cent of information. ZTE wants to keep control over its technology and sustain the customers' need for its maintenance services" (W10). Customers of Chinese ICT equipment highlighted that the user guide accompanying the purchased technologies would often come in Mandarin only to constrain the extent of knowledge diffusion.

Likewise, effective backward linkages promoting technology transfer would entail significant local provision of infrastructure components, training, and involvement in equipment installation. But, as with the phone factory, fieldwork interviews and observations indicated that the bulk of components used in digital infrastructure built by Chinese OEMs were imported from China. This practice was also observed among non-Chinese OEMs. Unlike Auffray and Fu (2015), who find that the weak absorptive capacity of Ghanian firms plays a major role in hindering knowledge transfer from Chinese firms, Egyptian and Algerian subcontracting firms responded that the training received by Chinese OEMs fell short of meeting their perceived absorptive capacity. The lion's share of training focused on health and safety procedures, while the more technical content entailed learning how to install, maintain, and troubleshoot the equipment of specific ICT equipment manufacturers (S3, S4, S5, S11). In this sense, training provided by Chinese tech MNCs could not be the basis for effective local appropriation or of movement up the value chain. Instead, it primarily serves as socio-technical links creating ecosystems of identifiable local firms that support value retention by the Chinese firms.

Chinese technology companies are emerging as important infrastructure agents with the power to shape digital ecosystems and keep a tight rein over their maintenance, undermining other actors in the process. Local ICT firms reported being marginalized from public infrastructural bids and highlighted that even when they had the technical capacity to conduct the work (e.g., providing and installing data centers, fiber optic cables, antennas, etc.), governments would issue public bids with such high requirements that only large foreign ICT OEMs could bid. These OEMs would win large, attractive contracts, and then subcontract only limited parts of them to local firms, keeping most of the value (S1, S7, S11).

With developing countries like Algeria and Egypt showing an appetite for digital infrastructure provided by Huawei and ZTE, these companies are increasingly defining the conditions under which countries transition toward digital economies. The rapid construction of digital infrastructure without concurrently establishing meaningful backward and forward linkages with the local economy raises serious concerns about a new kind of technological dependency. While Chinese tech firms are helping developing countries catch up in terms of infrastructure for digital connectivity (Cisse 2012; Rwehumbiza 2021), they are concurrently capturing lucrative markets, excluding potential local competitors, and consolidating dominant positions, and conditioning emerging digital ecosystems. Without effective learning opportunities that could lead to technology and skill transfers and ultimately usher in structural transformation, the DSR may only strengthen the global position of Chinese tech multinationals while exacerbating cross-country inequalities.

Far from Beijing's description of the BRI and the DSR as developmental and knowledge diffusion initiatives, empirical evidence suggests that Chinese OEMs primarily try to protect their intellectual property and profits. This finding echoes the conclusions of Yujia He's study in this special issue on Chinese platforms in Indonesia. The author finds that privately-owned Chinese digital platforms operated overseas largely according to commercial interests, and that China's high-level policy framework had a limited impact on the expansion of these platforms (He 2024).

Linkages with universities

If there is limited evidence of vertical and horizontal linkages emanating from Huawei and ZTE in Egypt and Algeria that are leading to technological upgrading, what about the emerging linkages between these two firms and local universities? University-FDI linkages can support the cross-fertilization of ideas and develop the national innovation base by embedding the existing R&D activity of MNC subsidiaries (Heidenreich 2012; Guimón et al. 2018). Through partnerships with universities, foreign firms can provide training, internships, and certifications to local students, exposing them to cutting-edge technologies and helping them improve their technical and managerial capabilities to match industry practices (Vaaland and Ishengoma 2016).

Although ZTE has several partnerships with educational and research institutions in the region, no other foreign OEM's engagement with universities compares with Huawei. In 2019, the tech firm signed an extensive partnership with the Egyptian government to launch the ICT Talent Bank, its flagship capacity-building program to boost university-industry linkages. The program's ambitions are to create 100 Huawei ICT academies in Egypt, train 200 instructors and 1200 ICT engineers and certify over 4000 trainees (Huawei ICT Academy 2019). Huawei certifications cover several themes like 5G, cloud, artificial intelligence, big data, switches, and routers. Trainees are selected on a competitive basis from a dozen Egyptian universities, such as Port Said University and the University of Suez, among others. Interviewed Egyptian graduates from Huawei's ICT academy who obtained the training stated that it covered high-quality technical and theoretical content that would facilitate their job hunt after graduating (U9, U10, U11).

While university-FDI linkages are often perceived to be beneficial *per se*, shifting to a techno-politics framework, these training initiatives stop being benevolent capacity-building endeavors but become politically charged projects embodying power and creating winners and losers on the way. Traditionally, the ICT OEM enterprise subsector has been dominated by Cisco certifications. Cisco Systems' technologies have been the standard taught in university curriculums worldwide. Until today, most Cisco certifications remain the gold standard among ICT engineers who recognize that Huawei's certifications are a copy of Cisco's with different codes and nominations. As a technological latecomer, Huawei has been actively trying to reverse Cisco's hegemony through its ICT academies. The Shenzhen-headquartered firm created several incentives to raise the rate of students certified in Huawei technologies, one of which consisted of gifting costly technological equipment to universities that succeed in achieving a significant number of Huawei-certified students per year (U1, U9).

Another strategy to promote the number of ICT engineers certified in Huawei technologies involved providing significant discounts on the certification fees, which tend to be paid directly by students. These certifications can cost between 200 and 600 USD for Cisco certifications and 100 to 500 USD for Huawei certifications (U3, U4, U9). During the COVID-19 pandemic, Huawei made all its certifications free, while Cisco only introduced a 50 per cent discount. With free certifications, many interviewed students in Algeria and Egypt opted for Huawei certifications instead of Cisco's. The director of an ICT department in Algeria explained that OEM certifications are not mandatory in the curriculum but that they are highly recommended electives that make graduates more employable. She highlighted the tense competition between big ICT manufacturers on campus and noted that Algerian curriculums avoid training students on a unique system to avoid creating dependencies (U1, U2). Nonetheless, the fee waivers provided by Huawei to students, along with the free training in its ICT academies, made it an easy choice for university students.

In the race to dominate the ICT enterprise business, Huawei has reached out to local channel partners that are already Cisco qualified and financed their conversion to become Huawei partners (S5, S11). Due to the interrelated and interlocking nature of technological regimes, more engineers trained to install, maintain, and troubleshoot Huawei technologies, and more channel partners selling Huawei products, means that governments, mobile carriers, and local companies increasingly decide to buy Huawei equipment. Chinese firms have thus adjusted national visions for the development of the ICT industry while mapping out and structuring digital communities revolving around the consumption of their artifacts and standards. This finding corroborates Tugendhat (2021), who finds that Huawei's training centers in Kenya and Nigeria serve to establish a network of trained technicians, distributors, and salespeople qualified in Huawei technologies.

Yet Tugendhat's analysis neglects the important macro ramifications of these micro-level restructurings. Training programs, digital infrastructure projects, and the emanating linkages at the micro-level are closely intertwined with digital technology standard-setting at the macro-level. China's strategy of increasing its weight in digital technology standardization relies on the use and diffusion of its own technical and industrial standards in the physical infrastructure it builds overseas (Peyrat 2012). In practice, technology standards spread from the top through adoption in international standard-setting bodies and from the bottom when MNCs build infrastructures that gravitate toward a common standard to ensure interoperability (Erie and Streinz 2021). Access to and use of digital infrastructures, and the applications that run over them, are regulated by frameworks that are, in turn, shaped by those who design and operate these infrastructures on the ground (Triolo and Sherlock 2020).

Against the backdrop of the technological competition between the United States and China, emerging linkages from Chinese tech firms are diffusing a mixture of infrastructures, hardware, software, certifications, and processes that are reordering digital systems on various scales and shaping new digital geographies. The experience of a final year student in ICT engineering sums up the situation well: "During my first year's internship at a large Algerian state-owned company, there was equipment from different vendors. But during my final year's internship at the same firm, I realized that most of the equipment had changed to become Huawei's" (U7). Thus, what may seem to be developmental endeavors are found to be connections that end up merely diversifying sources of technological dependency.

Conclusion and policy recommendations

Conclusion

If some attention has been paid to the political, geopolitical, and security implications of China's global digital expansion (Fannin 2019; Gagliardone 2019; Feldstein 2021; Ma 2021), what this expansion means for technological upgrading in other developing countries has been underexplored. This study contributes to filling this gap by investigating the technology spillovers emanating from Chinese tech firms through the cases of Huawei and ZTE in Algeria and Egypt. To do so, this article assessed three different types of linkages: horizontal linkages, vertical linkages, and linkages with local universities, through a conceptual framework that combines insights from development economics and techno-politics to examine the quality of linkages and their deeper effects – what linkages *do* on the ground, *how* they work and for *whom.*

The study finds that despite localizing seemingly developmental activities that can produce considerable linkages, the two Chinese tech firms created no meaningful learning opportunities that contribute to technological upgrading. Instead, the technologies disseminated by Chinese digital corporations, from codes to the hardware making up network infrastructures, as well as the know-how embedded in training programs provided to local employees, suppliers, and students, are reconfiguring ICT ecosystems in ways that render the use of Chinese firms' products, processes, and standards ubiquitous. In this sense, Chinese ICT giants are diffusing, both intentionally and non-intentionally, a distinct techno-political regime that risks locking local ICT actors into new dependencies that resemble those with Western powers. Future research ought to respond to recent calls in development studies for redeploying dependency theory to analyze how certain sectors and countries are conditioned by the development and expansion of other firms and countries (see Kvangraven 2021).

The comparison between tech firms headquartered in different countries reveals that keeping a tight rein over intellectual property is by no means a Chinese specificity. In Algeria and Egypt, both Chinese and non-Chinese firms are found to limit knowledge transfer by design to protect their technological edge (Tugendhat 2021). This being said, as technological latecomers, Chinese ICT firms, and Huawei in particular, have been particularly dynamic in public relations activities and training for employees, students, and suppliers in order to promote their own brands and take market space that was previously occupied by US and European firms. Although not yet conclusive, the preliminary findings suggest that with its energetic efforts in organizing ICT competitions, providing scholarships to students and grants to promising start-ups, Huawei may have a greater footprint in skill building than its competitors.

By highlighting the salience of power in technology transfer and connecting micro-processes with broader geopolitical struggles over global digital infrastructure, this article echoes findings made by communication, development, political economy, and internet governance scholars, among others, and responds to calls to examine China's global digital presence in the Global South from an interdisciplinary perspective. This study provides further evidence that on-the-ground field-based research is critical for grasping the complex dynamics shaping the internationalization of Chinese digital capital (Li and Cheong 2017; Agbebi 2018, 2019; Gagliardone 2019; Erie and Streinz 2021; Tugendhat 2021). The combination of theoretical and empirical work is significant because "global digital China" is notoriously difficult to study due to the inaccessibility of key documents, including memorandums of understanding, contracts, and loan agreements.

It is important to note that this study's findings are limited by the scope of the research and the fieldwork undertaken. It has focused on specific types of knowledge spillovers that may have marginalized more tacit and informal channels of transmission, such as the interpersonal relationships between Chinese and local workers and managers. Another important limitation has to do with the restricted access to private tech MNCs (both Chinese and non-Chinese), which made it challenging to collect more high-level management data and systematically compare practices across firms. Ultimately, further research is needed to better grasp the opportunities and challenges created by localization strategies of Chinese MNCs in different regions and settings. One potential future research direction would look at the question of digital data control in Chinese engagement with other developing countries. While technology transfer that could promote structural transformation is constrained by ICT MNCs, knowledge transfer from North African internet users to these firms may be booming, with Chinese MNCs building much of the region's data centers and cloud systems.

Policy recommendations

This study has a number of policy implications that could be applicable to other countries beyond Algeria and Egypt. The increasingly intricate linkages *via* which knowledge is diffused and absorbed raise concerns regarding the distributive effects of these linkages. Without pro-active policies, the DSR risks exacerbating existing digital inequalities. To reverse current trends, BRI countries ought to adopt a set of digital industrial policies that support technology localization and productive linkages. What follows provides some policy recommendations to improve the three types of linkages assessed in the paper:

First, as the wage premiums offered by MNCs were found to hinder labor turnover, strengthening horizontal linkages may require host governments to introduce financial incentives to help local private and public tech firms align with the salaries and remuneration packages offered by tech MNCs. Such policies would promote labor turnover and poaching, especially of managers, a mechanism long recognized as powerful in promoting domestic innovation and increasing productivity (Beaudry and Francois 2009). Learning from China's own development experience, policies could ensure that emerging tech champions have sufficient financial resources to hire top talents and adopt cutting-edge technical and managerial practices.

Second, to promote vertical linkages – and backward linkages in particular – policies should seek to include local firms in large ICT infrastructure projects to boost learning from foreign digital firms. One way of achieving this would be by requiring consortium bidding between local and foreign firms. Tender winners would have to divide the tasks between them with well-defined compensations for each party and clearly set terms for technology transfers. Furthermore, while joint venture requirements, when feasible, have proven to be powerful vehicles for technology transfer (Blomström and Sjöholm 1999), the case of Huawei's factory in Algiers indicates that without broader local content requirements, these are unlikely to yield significant learning opportunities.

Third, governments ought to move beyond the idea that business-university linkages are inherently valuable, and create dedicated bodies to examine and improve the quality of business-university partnerships. These bodies would ensure that cooperation is leading to effective knowledge transfer and that traineeships and certifications provided to students by tech-MNCs do not simply serve to create future users and repairers of the firms' technologies. Importantly, policies should support universities to improve their internal scientific base, develop indigenous R&D capabilities and adopt curricula that are in phase with technological innovations, rather than leaving them to become fighting grounds between large foreign tech firms.

Ultimately, greater regional collaboration could help smaller economies maximize the gains from global digital initiatives like the Digital Silk Road. The idea of a regional digital policy, such as the one regulating the European Digital Single Market, may be useful for smaller developing countries (Azmeh, Foster, and Echavarri 2020). Moving beyond fragmented bilateral commercial agreements with China and its tech giants would help to level the playing field for all African nations and ultimately enhance opportunities for local agencies to sculpt structures that support inclusive digital development.

Notes

1. Technology spillovers reflect the unintended transfer of technology, while technology transfer has a more intentional/deliberate connotation (Smeets 2008). Similarly, knowledge transfer implies a broader, more general type of knowledge, while technology transfer is narrower and more targeted (Holm et al. 2020).
2. Law No. 72 of 2017. Accessed December 3, 2023. https://www.gafi.gov.eg/english/startabusiness/laws-and-regulations/publishingimages/pages/businesslaws/investment%20law%20english%20ban.pdf.
3. Following China's adoption of its "going out" policy in the late 1990s, Chinese ICT OEMs started venturing out. Both Huawei and ZTE set up subsidiaries in Cairo and Algiers by the early 2000s.
4. The exact number of employees at ZTE Egypt remains unknown. A senior ZTE manager refused to divulge the number of employees in the Egyptian subsidiary, stating that the information was confidential (W12).

Disclosure statement

No potential conflict of interest was reported by the author(s).

Funding

This paper is part of a series from the project, "China's Digital Expansion in the Global South", funded by the Faculty of Humanities, University of Manchester, UK. Richard Heeks and Qingna Zhou of the Global Development Institute, University of Manchester, and Xia Han of the Alliance Manchester Business School, University of Manchester, were the facilitating editors.

References

Agbebi, M. 2018. China in Africa's telecom sector: Opportunities for human capital development? A case of Huawei in Nigeria. *Human Resource Development International* 21 (5):532–51. doi: 10.1080/13678868.2018.1512232.

Agbebi, M. 2019. Exploring the human capital development dimensions of Chinese investments in Africa: Opportunities, implications and directions for further research. *Journal of Asian and African Studies* 54 (2):189–210. doi: 10.1177/0021909618801381.

Agence Ecofin. 2019a. Telecom Egypt signs new deal with Huawei, ZTE and China Telecom. Accessed December 3, 2023. https://www.ecofinagency.com/telecom/0908-40385-telecom-egypt-signs-new-deal-with-huawei-zte-and-china-telecom

Agence Ecofin. 2019b. L'Algérie abrite la toute première usine africaine de Huawei, opérationnelle depuis le 22 janvier 2019 (Algeria hosts Huawei's very first African factory, operational since January 22, 2019). Accessed December 3, 2023. https://www.agenceecofin.com/investissement/2801-63550-l-algerie-abrite-la-toute-premiere-usine-africaine-de-huawei-operationnelle-depuis-le-22-janvier-2019

Aitken, B. J., and A. E. Harrison. 1999. Do domestic firms benefit from direct foreign investment? Evidence from Venezuela. *American Economic Review* 89 (3):605–18. doi: 10.1257/aer.89.3.605.

Amendolagine, V., A. Boly, N. D. Coniglio, F. Prota, and A. Seric. 2013. FDI and local linkages in developing countries: Evidence from Sub-Saharan Africa. *World Development* 50:41–56. doi: 10.1016/j.worlddev.2013.05.001.

Amsden, A. H. 2001. *The rise of "the rest": Challenges to the West from late-industrializing economies*. New York: Oxford University Press.

Anand, N. 2015. Leaky states: Water audits, ignorance, and the politics of infrastructure. *Public Culture* 27 (2):305–30. doi: 10.1215/08992363-2841880.

APS (Algeria Press Service). 2021. L'augmentation du débit internet minimum réalisée grâce à d'"enormes' investissements" (The increase in the minimum internet speed achieved thanks to "huge" investments). Accessed December 3, 2023. https://www.aps.dz/sante-science-technologie/128654-l-augmentation-du-debit-internet-minimum-realisee-grace-a-d-enormes-investissements

Auffray, C., and X. Fu. 2015. Chinese MNEs and managerial knowledge transfer in Africa: The case of the construction sector in Ghana. *Journal of Chinese Economic and Business Studies* 13 (4):285–310. doi: 10.1080/14765284.2015.1092415.

Autio, E., M. Kenney, P. Mustar, D. Siegel, and M. Wright. 2014. Entrepreneurial innovation: The importance of context. *Research Policy* 43 (7):1097–108. doi: 10.1016/j.respol.2014.01.015.

Azmeh, S., C. Foster, and J. Echavarri. 2020. The International Trade Regime and the Quest for free digital trade. *International Studies Review* 22 (3):671–92. doi: 10.1093/isr/viz033.

Beattie, A. 2019. July 24. Technology: How the US, EU and China compete to set industry standards. *Financial Times,* July 24. Accessed December 3, 2023. https://www.ft.com/content/0c91b884-92bb-11e9-aea1-2b1d33ac3271

Beaudry, P., and P. Francois. 2009. Managerial skills acquisition and the theory of economic development. *Review of Economic Studies* 77 (1):90–126. doi: 10.1111/j.1467-937X.2009.00571.x.

Beladi, R. 2023. Algeria.The abolition of the 49/51% law alone is not sufficient to attract significant investment. Accessed December 6, 2023. https://internationalsupermarketnews.com/algeria-the-abolition-of-the-49-51-law-alone-is-not-sufficient-to-attract-significant-investment/.

Blalock, G., and P. J. Gertler. 2008. Welfare gains from Foreign Direct Investment through technology transfer to local suppliers. *Journal of International Economics* 74 (2):402–21. doi: 10.1016/j.jinteco.2007.05.011.

Blomstrom, M., and A. Kokko. 2001. Foreign direct investment and spillovers of technology. *International Journal of Technology Management* 22 (5/6):435–54. doi: 10.1504/IJTM.2001.002972.

Blomström, M., and F. Sjöholm. 1999. Technology transfer and spillovers: Does local participation with multinationals matter? *European Economic Review* 43 (4–6):915–23. doi: 10.1016/S0014-2921(98)00104-4.

CCCPC (Central Committee of the Communist Part of China). 2016. The 13th five-year plan for economic and social development of the People's Republic of China (2016-2020). Accessed December 3, 2023. https://en.ndrc.gov.cn/policies/202105/P020210527785800103339.pdf.

Chen, B.-M. 2021. Digital Leninism: The complex, dangerous relationship between tech giants and the Chinese communist party. Washington, DC: Center for International Private Enterprise. Accessed December 3, 2023. https://www.cipe.org/resources/digital-leninism-the-complex-dangerous-relationship-between-tech-giants-and-the-chinese-communist-party/.

Cunningham, J. A., M. Menter, and C. Young. 2017. A review of qualitative case methods trends and themes used in technology transfer research. *The Journal of Technology Transfer* 42 (4):923–56. doi: 10.1007/s10961-016-9491-6.

Demena, B. A., and P. A. G. van Bergeijk. 2019. Observing FDI spillover transmission channels: Evidence from firms in Uganda. *Third World Quarterly* 40 (9):1708–29. doi: 10.1080/01436597.2019.1596022.

Denzin, N. K. 2001. *Interpretive interactionism*. London: SAGE.

Djazairess 2019. Huawei se lance dans le "Made in bladi". Le numéro deux de la téléphonie mondiale ouvre une usine en Algérie. [Huawei is launching into "Made in bladi". The number two player in the world's telephony industry opens a factory in Algeria]. Accessed 02 December 2023. https://www.djazairess.com/fr/lexpression/308334

Edwards, P. N., and G. Hecht. 2010. History and the technopolitics of identity: The case of apartheid South Africa. *Journal of Southern African Studies* 36 (3):619–39. doi: 10.1080/03057070.2010.507568.

Elliot, S., and I. Sahar. 2020. Algeria's new hydrocarbon law comes into force amid output slump. Accessed December 9, 2023. https://www.spglobal.com/commodityinsights/en/market-insights/latest-news/natural-gas/010620-algerias-new-hydrocarbon-law-comes-into-force-amid-output-slump

Erie, M. S., and T. Streinz. 2021. The Beijing effect: China's "Digital Silk Road" as transnational data governance (SSRN Scholarly Paper No. 3810256). Accessed December 3, 2023. https://papers.ssrn.com/abstract=3810256

Fannin, R. A. 2019. *Tech titans of China: How China's tech sector is challenging the world by innovating faster, working harder, and going global*. Boston, MA: Nicholas Brealey.

Feldstein, S. 2021. *The rise of digital repression: How technology is reshaping power, politics, and resistance*. New York: Oxford University Press.

Fu, X., C. Pietrobelli, and L. Soete. 2011. The role of foreign technology and indigenous innovation in the emerging economies: Technological change and catching-up. *World Development* 39 (7):1204–12. doi: 10.1016/j.worlddev.2010.05.009.

Gagliardone, I. 2019. China, Africa, and the Future of the Internet: New Media, New Politics. 1st edition. Zed Books.

Globerman, S. 1979. Foreign direct investment and "spillover" efficiency benefits in Canadian manufacturing industries. *The Canadian Journal of Economics* 12 (1):42–56. doi: 10.2307/134570.

Guimón, J., C. Chaminade, C. Maggi, and J. C. Salazar-Elena. 2018. Policies to attract R&D-related FDI in small emerging countries: Aligning incentives with local linkages and absorptive capacities in Chile. *Journal of International Management* 24 (2):165–78. doi: 10.1016/j.intman.2017.09.005.

Haddad, M., and A. Harrison. 1993. Are there positive spillovers from direct foreign investment? Evidence from panel data for Morocco. *Journal of Development Economics* 42 (1):51–74. doi: 10.1016/0304-3878(93)90072-U.

He, Y. 2024. Chinese digital platform companies' expansion in the Belt and Road countries. *The Information Society* 40 (2):96–119.

Hecht, G. 2001. Technology, politics, and national identity in France. In *Technologies of power: Essays in honor of Thomas Parke Hughes and Agatha Chipley Hughes*, eds. M. T. Allen and G. Hecht, 253–94. Cambridge, MA: MIT Press.

Heidenreich, M. (ed.). 2012. *Innovation and institutional embeddedness of multinational companies*. Cheltenham, UK: Edward Elgar.

Hernandez, K. 2019. Achieving complex development goals along China's Digital Silk Road. (K4D Emerging Issues Report). Brighton, UK: Institute of Development Studies, University of Sussex. Accessed December3, 2023. https://opendocs.ids.ac.uk/opendocs/handle/20.500.12413/14396.

Hillman, J. E. 2021. *The Digital Silk Road: China's quest to wire the world and win the future*. New York: Harper Business.

Hirschman, A. O. 2013. A generalized linkage approach to development, with special reference to staples. In *The essential Hirschman*, ed. J. Adelman, 155–94. Princeton, NJ: Princeton University Press.

Holm, J. R., B. Timmermans, C. R. Østergaard, A. Coad, N. Grassano, and A. Vezzani. 2020. Labor mobility from R&D-intensive multinational companies: Implications for knowledge and technology transfer. *The Journal of Technology Transfer* 45 (5):1562–84. doi: 10.1007/s10961-020-09776-8.

Huawei. 2017. Huawei announces new OpenLab in Cairo to build ICT ecosystem in Northern Africa. Accessed December 6, 2023. https://www.huawei.com/en/news/2017/12/Huawei-New-OpenLab-Cairo

Iršová, Z., and T. Havránek. 2013. Determinants of horizontal spillovers from FDI: Evidence from a large meta-analysis. *World Development* 42:1–15. doi: 10.1016/j.worlddev.2012.07.001.

Javorcik, B. S. 2004. Does foreign direct investment increase the productivity of domestic firms? In search of spillovers through backward linkages. *American Economic Review* 94 (3):605–27. doi: 10.1257/0002828041464605.

King, K. 2013. *China's aid and soft power in Africa: The case of education and training*. Martlesham, UK: Boydell & Brewer.

Kneller, R., and M. Pisu. 2007. Industrial linkages and export spillovers from FDI. *The World Economy* 30 (1):105–34. doi: 10.1111/j.1467-9701.2007.00874.x.

Kvangraven, I. H. 2021. Beyond the stereotype: Restating the relevance of the dependency research programme. *Development and Change* 52 (1):76–112. doi: 10.1111/dech.12593.

Lall, S. 1992. Technological capabilities and industrialization. *World Development* 20 (2):165–86. doi: 10.1016/0305-750X(92)90097-F.

Laouisset, D. E. 2021. Algeria import substitution policy: The case of the pharmaceutical industry. *Les Cahiers Du Cread* 37 (1):5–39.

Larkin, B. 2013. The politics and poetics of infrastructure. *Annual Review of Anthropology* 42 (1):327–43. doi: 10.1146/annurev-anthro-092412-155522.

Lean, C. S. 2001. Empirical tests to discern linkages between construction and other economic sectors in Singapore. *Construction Management and Economics* 19 (4):355–63. doi: 10.1080/01446190010022686.

Lee, H., and S. Oh. 2006. A standards war waged by a developing country: Understanding international standard setting from the actor-network perspective. *The Journal of Strategic Information Systems* 15 (3):177–95. doi: 10.1016/j.jsis.2005.10.002.

Li, R., and K.-C. Cheong. 2017. Huawei and ZTE in Malaysia: The localisation of Chinese transnational enterprises. *Journal of Contemporary Asia* 47 (5):752–73. doi: 10.1080/00472336.2017.1346697.

Liu, Z. 2008. Foreign direct investment and technology spillovers: Theory and evidence. *Journal of Development Economics* 85 (1–2):176–93. doi: 10.1016/j.jdeveco.2006.07.001.

Liu, X., C. Wang, and Y. Wei. 2009. Do local manufacturing firms benefit from transactional linkages with multinational enterprises in China? *Journal of International Business Studies* 40 (7):1113–30. doi: 10.1057/jibs.2008.97.

Ma, W. 2021. *The digital war: How China's tech power shapes the future of AI, blockchain and cyberspace*. New York: Wiley.

Mackinnon, A. 2019. For Africa, Chinese-built internet is better than no internet at all. *ForeignPolicy.com*, March 19. Accessed December 8, 2023. https://foreignpolicy.com/2019/03/19/for-africa-chinese-built-internet-is-better-than-no-internet-at-all/.

Markusen, J., and A. Venables. 1999. Foreign direct investment as a catalyst for industrial development. *European Economic Review* 43 (2):335–56. doi: 10.1016/S0014-2921(98)00048-8.

Mattli, W., and T. Büthe. 2003. Setting international standards: Technological rationality or primacy of power? *World Politics* 56 (1):1–42. doi: 10.1353/wp.2004.0006.

McGregor, G. 2022. China emerges as lead funder for Egypt's new administrative city. Accessed December 8, 2023. https://www.al-monitor.com/originals/2022/12/china-emerges-lead-funder-egypts-new-administrative-city.

MCIT (Ministry of Communications and Information Technology). 2016. Egypt's ICT 2030 Strategy. Accessed December 8, 2023. https://mcit.gov.eg/en/ICT_Strategy.

MFA (Ministry of Foreign Affairs of the PRC). 2009. Premier Wen Jiabao Talks with Trainees of Huawei Training Center in Egypt. Accessed December 8, 2023. http://nl.china-embassy.gov.cn/eng/zgyw/200911/t20091111_2641062.htm.

Mitchell, T. 2002. *Rule of experts: Egypt, techno-politics, modernity*. Berkeley, CA: University of California Press.

Ning, L., and F. Wang. 2018. Does FDI bring environmental knowledge spillovers to developing countries? The role of the local industrial structure. *Environmental and Resource Economics* 71 (2):381–405. doi: 10.1007/s10640-017-0159-y.

Ockwell, D. G., J. Watson, G. MacKerron, P. Pal, and F. Yamin. 2008. Key policy considerations for facilitating low carbon technology transfer to developing countries. *Energy Policy* 36 (11):4104–15. doi: 10.1016/j.enpol.2008.06.019.

Oya, C., and F. Schaefer. 2019. Chinese firms and employment dynamics in Africa: A comparative analysis (Synthesis report). London: SOAS, University of London. Accessed December 8, 2023. https://www.almendron.com/tribuna/wp-content/uploads/2021/04/file141857.pdf.

Pairault, T. 2017. La Chine au Maghreb: De l'esprit de Bandung à l'esprit du capitalisme. *Revue de la Régulation* 21 (21). doi: 10.4000/regulation.12230.

Peyrat, O. 2012. Normes: Un outil caché de la stratégie économique chinoise (Standards: A hidden tool of Chinese economic Strategy). *Le Journal de L'École de Paris du Management* 6:30–7. Accessed December 9, 2023. https://www.ecole.org/fr/seance/961-normes-un-outil-cache-de-la-strategie-economique-chinoise.

Rojec, M., and M. Knell. 2018. Why is there a lack of evidence on knowledge spillovers from foreign direct investment? *Journal of Economic Surveys* 32 (3):579–612. doi: 10.1111/joes.12207.

Rwehumbiza, D. A. 2021. Huawei's linkages with local firms in Tanzania: Idiosyncratic benefits and risks. *Global Business and Organizational Excellence* 40 (3):20–35. doi: 10.1002/joe.22076.

Saggi, K. 2002. Trade, foreign direct investment, and international technology transfer: A survey. *The World Bank Research Observer* 17 (2):191–235. doi: 10.1093/wbro/17.2.191.

Shen, H. 2017. Across the Great (Fire) Wall: China and the global internet. Doctoral Dissertation, University of Illinois.

Smeets, R. 2008. Collecting the Pieces of the FDI Knowledge Spillovers Puzzle. *The World Bank Research Observer* 23 (2):107–138. doi: 10.1093/wbro/lkn003.

Smith, J., C. Cummins, and A. Krasodomski-Jones. 2021. Good foundations: Why Democracies should care about the wiring of the internet. Accessed December 9, 2023. https://demos.co.uk/wp-content/uploads/2021/03/Good-Foundations-Report-.pdf

Statista, 2021. Share of youth unemployment in the Middle East and North Africa region in 2020, by country. https://www.statista.com/statistics/1259020/menayouth-unemployment-by-country/

Tang, X. 2021. Adaptation, innovation, and industrialization: The impact of Chinese investments on skill development in the Zambian and Malawian cotton sectors. *Journal of Chinese Economic and Business Studies* 19 (4):295–313. doi: 10.1080/14765284.2021.1943734.

Te Velde, D. W. 2002. Government policies for inward foreign direct investment in developing countries: Implications for human capital formation and income inequality. (OECD Development Centre Working Paper No. 193). Paris: OECD.

Triolo, P., and A. Sherlock. 2020. "New infrastructure": China's race for 5G and networked everything has a new catchphrase. Accessed December 9, 2023. https://supchina.com/2020/07/01/new-infrastructure-chinas-race-for-5g-and-networked-everything-has-a-new-catchphrase/.

Tsui, B. 2016. Do Huawei's training programs and centers transfer skills to Africa?. (Policy Brief No. 14). Washington, DC: China-Africa Research Initiative, School of Advanced International Studies, Johns Hopkins University.

Tugendhat, H. 2021. Connection issues: A study on the limitations of knowledge transfer in Huawei's African training centres. *Journal of Chinese Economic and Business Studies* 19 (4):359–85. doi: 10.1080/14765284.2021.1943194.

Tugendhat, H. 2020. How Huawei succeeds in Africa: Training and knowledge transfers in Kenya and Nigeria. (Policy Brief No. 14). Washington, DC: China-Africa Research Initiative, School of Advanced International Studies, Johns Hopkins University.

UNCTAD. 2012. *Technology and innovation report 2012: Innovation, technology and South–South collaboration*. New York: United Nations.

Vaaland, T. I., and E. Ishengoma. 2016. University-industry linkages in developing countries: Perceived effect on innovation. *Education + Training* 58 (9):1014–40. doi: 10.1108/ET-07-2015-0067.

Wahab, S. A., R. C. Rose, and S. I. W. Osman. 2011. Defining the concepts of technology and technology transfer: A literature analysis. *International Business Research* 5 (1):61–71. doi: 10.5539/ibr.v5n1p61.

Waterbury, J. 1985. The "soft state" and the open door: Egypt's experience with economic liberalization, 1974–1984. *Comparative Politics* 18 (1):65–83. doi: 10.2307/421658.

Winner, L. 1980. Do artifacts have politics? *Daedalus* 109 (1):121–36.

World Bank. 2022a. Individuals using the internet (% of population). February 16, 2024. https://data.worldbank.org/indicator/IT.NET.USER.ZS?locations=DZ.

World Bank. 2022b. Mobile penetration per country. Accessed April 12, 2023. https://data.worldbank.org/indicator/IT.CEL.SETS.P2.

World Economic Forum. 2017. The future of jobs and skills in the Middle East and North Africa: Preparing the region for the fourth industrial revolution (Executive briefing). Accessed December 9, 2023. https://www3.weforum.org/docs/WEF_EGW_FOJ_MENA.pdf.

Yao, X., A. Tan, and R. Suttmeier. 2009. Standards of power? Technology, institutions, and politics in the development of China's national standards strategy. *Geopolitics, History, and International Relations* 1 (1):46–84.

Annex 1: List of interviewees

Affiliation	Code	Date	Place
Subcontractors, Suppliers, and Customers of Huawei and ZTE			
CEO of subcontracting firm for major ICT OEM	S1	17/10/2021	Algiers
CEO of subcontracting firm for major ICT OEM	S2	18/10/2021	Algiers
CEO of subcontracting firm for major ICT OEM	S3	22/10/2021	Algiers
CEO of subcontracting firm for major ICT OEM	S4	13/12/2021	Algiers
CEO of subcontracting firm for major ICT OEM	S5	20/12/2021	Algiers
Startup	S6	09/12/2021	Algiers
CEO of subcontracting firm for major ICT OEM	S7	13/12/2021	Algiers
Mobile operator	S8	08/01/2022	Algiers
CEO of subcontracting firm for major ICT OEM	S9	02/03/2022	Cairo
Startup	S10	02/03/2022	Cairo
Subcontractor to Major ICT vendors	S11	15/03/2022	Cairo
Huawei and ZTE Engineers and Managers			
ICT engineer at ZTE	W1	28/10/2021	Algiers
ICT engineer at ZTE	W2	06/11/2021	Algiers
Engineer at Ooredoo with Huawei certification	W3	28/11/2021	Zoom call
Former Huawei engineer	W4	05/12/2021	Algiers
Engineer at Huawei	W5	07/12/2021	Algiers
ZTE manager	W6	22/12/2021	Algiers
Assembly line manager at Afgotech (Algerian Huawei's partner for the factory)	W7	20/01/2022	Phone call
Former Huawei engineer who set up his own business	W8	03/01/2022	Algiers
Engineer at Huawei, the Oran Institute of Telecommunication	W9	06/01/2022	Zoom call
Engineer at ZTE	W10	18/01/2022	Algiers
Manager at Huawei Device – coordinator of phone manufacturing	W11	01/02/2022	Algiers
A senior manager at ZTE Egypt	W12	16/02/2022	Cairo
Junior network engineer at Huawei	W13	17/02/2022	Zoom call
Senior network engineer at Huawei	W14	21/02/2022	Cairo
Training and development manager at Huawei customer	W15	24/02/2022	Phone call
Huawei public relations manager	W16	27/02/2022	Zoom call
Telecom engineer at Huawei	W17	02/03/2022	Cairo
Telecom engineer at Huawei	W18	02/03/2022	Cairo
Telecom engineer at Huawei	W19	02/03/2022	Cairo
Computer engineer at ZTE Egypt	W20	04/03/2022	Phone call
Computer engineer at Huawei's OpenLab	W21	16/03/2022	Cairo
Experts and Researchers			
Economic expert	E1	30/11/2021	Algiers
IT engineer and digital economy expert	E2	30/11/2021	Algiers
Professor of ICTs at the University of Bab Ezzouar	E3	17/11/2021	Algiers
Official responsible for the US-Algeria Trade Chamber	E4	20/11/2021	Algiers
Digital economy expert	E5	15/12/2021	Algiers
Digital economy Expert	E6	19/01/2022	Algiers
Professor of economic innovation at the University of Lille	E7	07/02/2022	Oran
Engineer of digital devices	E8	23/02/2022	Cairo
Researcher focusing on China-Egypt Relations	E9	27/02/2022	Zoom call
Professor of political economy at the American University in Cairo	E10	28/02/2022	Cairo
Professor of economics at the University of Cairo	E11	01/03/2022	Cairo
Senior digital development specialist at the World Bank	E12	10/03/2022	Cairo
Students and Instructors of Huawei and ZTE Training Programmes			
Senior official of the national institute of ICTs, Ucalypthus, Algiers	U1	07/12/2021	Algiers
Pedagogical coordinator at the national institute of ICTs, Ucalypthus, Algiers	U2	07/12/2021	Algiers
Student at the national institute of ICTs	U3	07/12/2021	Algiers
Student at the national institute of ICTs	U4	07/12/2021	Algiers
Student at the national institute of ICTs	U5	07/12/2021	Algiers
Student at the national institute of ICTs	U6	07/12/2021	Algiers
ICT student and coordinator of Huawei ICT academies at the University of Saad Dahleb, Blida	U7	12/21/2021	Zoom call
Senior official at the National School of Computer Science (ESI)	U8	27/12/2021	Algiers
University student and graduate of Huawei ICT Academy	U9	27/02/2022	Cairo
ICT Academy graduate	U10	09/03/2022	Cairo
ICT Academy graduate	U11	04/03/2022	Cairo
Engineers and Managers of Western Competitors			
Senior manager at Ericsson Algeria	C1	21/12/2021	Zoom call
Ericsson engineer	C2	23/12/2021	Algiers
Senior manager at Cisco Algeria	C3	17/01/2022	Algiers
Engineer at Ericsson	C4	29/01/2022	Zoom call
Foreign tech incubator	C5	28/02/2022	Cairo
Foreign tech incubator	C6	28/02/2022	Cairo
ICT engineer at Nokia	C7	08/03/2022	Cairo
Engineer at the Orange Innovation Lab	C8	08/03/2022	Cairo
Engineer at the Orange Innovation Lab	C9	08/03/2022	Cairo
Senior manager at the Orange Innovation Lab	C10	08/03/2022	Cairo
ICT engineer at Ericsson	C11	15/03/2022	Cairo
Policymakers			
Algerian minister with responsibilities for the knowledge economy and startups	G1	28/11/2021	Algiers
Adviser to the Algerian minister of the knowledge economy	G2	28/11/2021	Algiers
Manager at the Egyptian Agency of Investment and Free Zones	G3	22/02/2022	Cairo
Policy Maker at ITIDA – Egyptian agency for informatics and telecommunication development	G4	01/03/2022	Phone call
Former finance minister of Egypt	G5	09/03/2022	Cairo

The Chinese surveillance state in Latin America? Evidence from Argentina and Ecuador

Maximiliano Facundo Vila Seoane and Carla Morena Álvarez Velasco

ABSTRACT
Western authors fear that Chinese exports of surveillance technologies to Global South countries may lead to reproduction of the problematic surveillance practices that the Chinese state practices within its borders. However, much of this literature is not based on empirically-grounded research. To examine such concerns, we investigated two surveillance projects built in Argentina and Ecuador in cooperation with Chinese enterprises—JSeI in Argentina and ECU 911 in Ecuador. Based on empirical evidence, we argue for a more situated and differentiated approach for examining such projects that considers the distributed agency among local and Chinese actors, as well as the economic, social, and political factors that led to their deployment.

Introduction

The internationalization of Chinese companies selling surveillance technologies in the Global South is a matter of pressing academic and policy concern. Western academics, policy analysts, and pundits fear that the export of such technologies may lead to reproduction of the problematic surveillance practices that the Chinese state practices within its borders. Thereby, it is argued that China is at the forefront of spreading what Freedom House has termed "digital authoritarianism" (Shabhaz 2018); a model of governance *via* digital technologies that is believed to further embed autocracies, and degrade democracies. In specific relation to Latin America, US academics, policy makers, and media outlets have advanced similar arguments regarding the threats posed by the deployment of Chinese surveillance systems in the region (Berg 2021; Democratic Staff Report 2020; Ellis 2021, 2022; Garrison 2019; Mozur, Kessel, and Chan 2019). However, much of this literature is not based on empirically-grounded research. Therefore, there is little knowledge about the veracity of such claims, about why states in the Global South initiated such surveillance projects with Chinese companies, and how were they really implemented.

We contribute to this literature by investigating two prominent cases of surveillance systems built by Chinese state-owned enterprises in Latin America: the ECU 911 project in Ecuador (2012–2021) and Jujuy Seguro e Interconectado (JSeI) project in Argentina (2016–2022). These cases matter because they were portrayed as representing the menacing expansion of Chinese surveillance systems into the region (Garrison 2019; Mozur, Kessel, and Chan 2019). Further, if China seeks to expand its problematic surveillance practices into Latin American states, it is reasonable to assume this will be more visible in these cases, where the state influence is direct. Specifically, in this article we investigate the reasons why both states cooperated with their Chinese counterparts, detailing the features of the so-called surveillance projects. Furthermore, we analyze the implementation of the projects, including an examination of the criticisms and opposition they faced.

We argue for a situated and differentiated approach for examining the implementation of Chinese surveillance projects in the Global South. First, although foreign critics have portrayed these projects as surveillance systems, actually they involve more dimensions, e.g. increased the connectivity of government organizations, enhanced emergency response systems.

Second, as our case studies indicate, the agency in these projects is distributed, rather than limited to Chinese actors. In fact, different combinations of Chinese, local, and even foreign actors have participated in the initiation, definition of requirements, technological design, implementation, management and operation, and upgrade of the projects. Third, much of the criticisms against the expansion of Chinese firms selling surveillance technologies is ahistorical, since it disregards the fact that the deployment of such systems had been well under way before the procurement from Chinese companies. Fourth, the procurement of Chinese surveillance technologies does not depend on the political leaning of the Latin American political parties in power. Policy makers chose Chinese systems mainly due to economic reasons. Finally, we found a divergence between the local criticisms of the projects and the widely-distributed foreign ones. The former focused on technological dependence, alleged corruption in the procurement of the systems, and the need for more accountability in the implementation of the systems, whilst the latter reproduced the view of US government sources about the threat posed by Chinese firms.

The rest of the present article has five sections. The first one synthesizes the literature about the expansion of China's surveillance systems in the Global South. The second explains the methods used to collect and analyze data. The third section presents the results of the analysis of both case studies. The final two sections discuss and then conclude with a synthesis of the main findings.

China's surveillance systems in the Global South

During the last decade, Chinese companies selling surveillance technologies have been quite successful in their internationalization in the Global South. Video surveillance cameras, smart city, and safe city solutions provided by firms such as Dahua, Hikvision, and Huawei, among others, can be found in many cities of the developing world. This is an offshoot of the boom in smart cities in China (Hu 2019), which has led to the accumulation of technological capabilities and solutions for urban management. Since then, Chinese firms have sought to export surveillance technologies to other markets, competing with Western firms offering similar products and solutions, such as Bosch, Cisco, IBM, and Siemens.

However, this expansion of Chinese surveillance companies in the Global South has become a persistent issue in policy and media circles in the US and other Western countries (Cheney 2019; Democratic Staff Report 2020; Gravett 2020; Polyakova and Meserole 2019; Shabhaz 2018). These commentators denounce the very problematic practices of surveillance implemented within China. For example, China has deployed the largest video surveillance system in the world, the SkyNet project, which has over 200 million cameras, and can identify a citizen in less than 10 min thanks to advanced facial recognition technology. Likewise, they generally make reference to the controversial use of AI-enabled surveillance technologies against Uyghurs in Xinjiang. Similarly, they condemn China's censorship practiced through digital technologies, such as the Golden Shield Project (also known as the Great Firewall), that blocks Chinese internet users' access to banned foreign websites and services.

Furthermore, they are equally concerned about China's exports of surveillance technologies into the Global South, because it may propagate China's practices of digital authoritarianism (Cheney 2019; Democratic Staff Report 2020; Gravett 2020; Hemmings 2020; Polyakova and Meserole 2019; Shabhaz 2018). Although their criticism targets the digital expansion of Chinese firms in general, the sale of surveillance technologies, often branded as "safe city" projects, has especially attracted scrutiny. They fear that these projects may lead to the violation of human rights in recipient states as in China, because they provide video surveillance cameras and advanced facial recognition technologies that can be used to infringe citizens' rights. For some commentators, these concerns are especially problematic in states they classify as autocracies (Shabhaz 2018). Others consider the export of Chinese surveillance technologies equally dangerous in both autocracies and democracies, because they spread political illiberalism (Cheney 2019; Democratic Staff Report 2020; Feldstein 2019). In fact, they claim that, in the former, surveillance technologies may further entrench the state's power over civil society, whilst in the latter, the use of such technologies may cause democracies to backslide into autocracies.

American academics and policy analysts specializing in China-Latin America relations have expressed worries about Chinese companies selling surveillance technologies to Latin America in articles and public statements, especially at the US-China Economic and Security Review Commission (Berg 2021; Ellis 2021, 2022). For example, Ryan Berg, senior fellow at the Center for Strategic and International Studies, while acknowledging surveillance technology may be used for addressing physical security challenges in Latin

America, claimed that "Chinese surveillance technology could play a key role in assisting democratic backsliding in the region" (Berg 2021, 6). Likewise, Evan Ellis (2021), an American professor at the US Army War College, accused China of cultivating "anti-US leftist populism". In his view, leftist regimes have opened the door to Chinese surveillance systems in the region, and potentially to the expansion of digital authoritarianism. Ellis (2022, 27) considers Bolivia, Ecuador, and Venezuela among China's "authoritarian friends" that have received funding and surveillance systems to remain in power.

In this vein, the projects we studied—JSeI in Argentina and ECU 911 in Ecuador—also received critical coverage in the literature (e.g. Gravett 2022; Kassenova and Duprey 2021). In the case of Ecuador, the *New York Times* published an article titled "Made in China, exported to the world: The surveillance state" (Mozur, Kessel, and Chan 2019), which argued that the ECU 911 system is part of the expansion of the Chinese surveillance state into the country. Its authors stated that Ecuador's "feared domestic intelligence agency" may have abused its access to ECU 911's video feed for domestic espionage. They based their allegation on the testimony of a critic of former President Correa, who said that the government installed a camera in front of his house to spy on him. They concluded that "It was a move out of the police playbook in China, where cameras are positioned outside the doors of high-profile activists" (Mozur, Kessel, and Chan 2019). Likewise, the JSeI project attracted international and national attention due to an article by an American journalist, Cassandra Garrison, working for Reuters wrote an article entitled "'Safe like China': In Argentina, ZTE finds eager buyer for surveillance tech" (Garrison 2019). Garrison asserted that "Chinese telecoms giant ZTE is installing a little slice of the Asian nation's vast surveillance state—security cameras that the local government says will help to curb street crime" (Garrison 2019), prioritizing a US government sources, who said that "China gathers and exploits data on an unrivalled scale, and uses the information to promote corruption, support arbitrary surveillance, and silence dissent" (Garrison 2019). Garrison added that ZTE had been involved in the procurement of technologies for the problematic Chinese surveillance practices in Xinjiang (Garrison 2019).

In contrast, there are few research or other articles that challenge these criticisms. For instance, Gagliardone (2019) points out that the preoccupation with the supposed export of China's digital authoritarianism model underestimates the similar role that Western models have played in justifying repressive surveillance practices. Indeed, numerous African countries have drawn on the US War on Terror to justify the procurement of surveillance equipment and software from foreign providers—including Western ones—to prevent internal and foreign terrorist threats. Similarly, Woodhams (2020) questions the claim that China is entirely to blame for the global spread of surveillance technologies, since many Western firms and governments have also been selling surveillance technologies in the Global South.

A general limitation of this literature is that much of the criticism as well as the few instances of counter-criticism are based on secondary sources and limited reporting, or are speculative claims that extrapolate the surveillance practices within China to all the countries in the Global South. All in all, there is a general lack of empirically-grounded research that supports such claims or even refutes them. In this article we seek to help fill this gap *via* an empirical analysis of how two such surveillance projects were implemented in states of the Global South.

Methodology

We chose projects in Argentina and Ecuador for our case studies—JSeI in Argentina and ECU 911 in Ecuador, because they illustrate the intensifying and broadening relations with China in the region, which has been historically under the influence of the US. Indeed, since 2007 China has displaced the US as Argentina's second most important trading partner after Brazil. Politically, although the bilateral relationship between Argentina and China was not exempt from frictions (Saguier and Vila Seoane 2022), ties have strengthened with the signing of a comprehensive strategic partnership in 2014, and Argentina's joining China's Belt and Road Initiative in 2022. In the case of Ecuador, under the presidency of Rafael Correa (2007–2017), the country established closer ties with China (Herrera-Vinelli and Bonilla 2019). In terms of economic ties, since 2011, China has its second biggest trading partner after the US. With regard to political ties, in 2015, the China and Ecuador signed a comprehensive strategic partnership, and, in 2018, Ecuador joined China's Belt and Road Initiative. Since the presidency of Lenin Moreno (2017–2021) there was a realignment of Ecuador's foreign policy toward the US (Jepson 2022) but China's economic relevance remains. In both countries we find similar criticisms of the increased political and economic ties with China, namely, the emergence of a new and asymmetrical core-periphery relationship, a growth in low added-value natural resource exports that undermines national industrialization strategies, and concerns about the environmental impacts of infrastructure projects, among others (Bernal-Meza and Xing 2020; Gonzalez-Vicente 2017; Herrera-Vinelli and Bonilla 2019; Jepson 2022; Saguier and Vila Seoane 2022). In this context, both states have been subject to US pressure and criticisms against Chinese infrastructure projects and investments.

For our case studies, in 2022, we collected documents, made on-site observations, and conducted in-depth interviews. Specifically, we conducted a web search of policy, media, and government public documents, plus a search of academic articles and books discussing the two surveillance systems. Furthermore, we made on-site visits to the cities of Quito in Ecuador and San Salvador de Jujuy in Argentina, where the main components of each system were installed. In these visits we observed the systems in operation and we visited the management centers. Moreover, we complemented these sources with primary data collected through in-person and online interviews. We contacted local actors involved in the design and implementation of the systems, and other stakeholders who had conveyed both support and criticisms of the projects; conducting 14 interviews in total (see Appendix 1 for details including the interviewee codes used in the Findings section). We prepared an interview guide that we slightly adapted according to the profile of each interviewee. The interview questions sought to explore who were the actors involved in the initiation and implementation of the projects, the partnerships established with Chinese firms, if there were local adaptations of Chinese technologies, opinions of interviewees about the coverage by media outlets of both projects, and criticisms of the projects. We triangulated these different sources to trace the actors involved in the different phases of the projects.

Table 1. Main actors involved in ECU 911 and JSel projects.

	ECU 911	JSel
Initiated by	Coordinating Ministry of Security	Jujuy's Ministry of Security
Requirements defined by	Coordinating Ministry of Security	Jujuy's Ministry of Security
Designed by	CEIEC (technical)	ZTE (technical)
Implemented by	Local firms and CEIEC	Local firms and ZTE
Managed and operated by	ECU 911	Jujuy's Ministry of Security
Maintained and upgraded by	Until 2018: CEIEC From 2018 onwards: still under negotiation	ZTE for 3 years

Findings

Table 1 provides a summary of the various local and foreign actors involved in the different phases of the projects. The next subsections examine each of the case studies in more detail.

ECU 911

The installation of ECU 911 in Ecuador must be contextualized in the broader political transformations that the country experienced during the presidencies of Rafael Correa (2007–2017). In 2007, the center-left political coalition Alianza PAIS led by President Correa started a process of profound political and institutional reform in various areas of the country, which led the passing of a new national constitution in 2008. The reorientation of Ecuador's foreign policy and changes in its security sector are the reforms that matter most for our present discussion.

In terms of foreign policies, the Correa administration strengthened political and trade alliances with different countries, both within and outside Latin America. One of the administration's goals was to weaken Ecuador's economic and political dependence on the US. In this context, the government sought a strategic rapprochement with China with the aim of increasing exports to it, as well as accessing its funding sources. Furthermore, in 2008, the new national constitution prohibited the installation of military bases within Ecuador. Consequently, President Correa refused to renew the 10-year agreement that Ecuador had with the US military which, in 2009, had to close its Forward Operating Location base in the coastal city of Manta (Álvarez Velasco 2014).

As for the security sector, the new constitution introduced the "integral security" concept, which would thereafter become the guiding precept to rethink the national security architecture of Ecuador (Cabrera 2019; Lucio Vásquez 2020). It called for the updating of the National Security Law, enacted in 1979 during the transition from military dictatorship to a democratic regime, during the Cold War, when it was influenced by the US counterinsurgency strategy against communism in the region (Lucio Vásquez 2020). The 1979 law was especially criticized for its focus on military actions against external threats. Instead, the integral security precept called for broadening the areas falling within the security sphere, less linked to the field of defense and closer to the notion of human security formulated by UNDP (1994) as well as extending security concerns to nature (EC1). Although the specificities of the actualization of the integral security concept evolved during the Correa administration (Cabrera 2019), it led to a planning process whose outcomes were two national plans for Integral Security for the periods 2011–2013 and 2014–2017 respectively.

ECU 911 implementation under the Correa administrations (2011–2017)

After the 2010 police strike that caused a national political crisis and a local insecurity crisis in Quito (EC5), in 2011, the National Integral Security Plan for 2011–2013 announced the creation of an Integrated Security System (SIS), named ECU 911. This project aimed to materialize integral security by articulating all related institutions with responsibilities within this broader framework, such as the National Police, the Secretariat of Risk Management, local governments, the Red Cross, the Ministry of Public Health, the Ecuadorian Social Security Institute, the National Transit Agency, the Fire Department, and the Ministry of National Defense. In particular it established a comprehensive response system for citizens' emergencies *via* a national 911 number (Ministerio de Coordinación de Seguridad 2011, 34), which the country lacked (Corral-De-Witt et al. 2018). Moreover, the main specificity of this project is that it sought to build a network of centers of national, regional, and local scope. Each of them would have video surveillance capabilities to reduce violence in public spaces and to respond to emergencies. Furthermore, these centers would generate other data of public interest. Most importantly, these ECU 911 centers would all be interconnected, creating a network. Thereby, this system, ECU 911, would have national reach.

Although announced in 2011, the government had been planning ECU 911 since 2008. In that year, the Correa administration organized a technical commission comprising public officials of the Coordinating Ministry of Security and Ecuador's navy (EC8), which studied smart city projects in other countries, such as Argentina, Brazil, China, Spain, the UK and the US, (EC2, EC3). It sought to learn from the strengths and weaknesses of other preexisting projects to design a system for Ecuador that went beyond the surveillance function (EC1). During the 2008 Beijing Olympics, Ecuadorean public officials saw the smart city solution employed in China's capital (EC3). This led to a contact with the Chinese government *via* its embassy in Ecuador, which offered funding for a project tailored to Ecuador's needs on the condition that it was implemented by a Chinese state-owned enterprise: the China National Electronics Import & Export Corporation (CEIEC). Based in Beijing and founded in 1980, CEIEC had an overseas division with experience in integration engineering in numerous sectors in African and Asian countries, and it also had a division of defense electronics system integration (CEIEC 2011). On February 2011, the Coordinating Ministry of Security signed an agreement with CEIEC to develop the project in Ecuador (Secretaría Nacional de Riesgos 2011). China funded the project *via* an estimated USD 240 million loan (Aid Data n.d.).

Although CEIEC was the firm integrating and deploying the project, interviewees noted that the design of the system was based on the knowledge Ecuador's public officials had acquired during their visits to smart city projects of other countries. According to a former ECU manager, "the ECU-911 has the best of each of these places we visited" (EC3). For example, the video surveillance system copied the practices in the UK, whilst the 911 system was copied from the US system (EC3). Other norms and procedures for operation of the system were developed in a participatory manner by different stakeholders involved in the actualization of the integral security concept (EC1). According to ECU 911's management, this is the reason the project has received prestigious certifications from different Western organizations related to public security (EC3). For instance, the ECU 911 established measures to safeguard the information captured by the ECU 911 nodes, such as video surveillance, audio, and other data types, for the purpose of analysis and evaluation by the judicial institutions in accordance with national legislation (ECU 911 2015, 21). These local guidelines could reduce the concerns about how data from a Chinese-installed system is used, though there have still been criticisms by some human rights organizations that, at the time, Ecuador still lacked a data protection law that could effectively underpin such guidelines (Access Now 2021, 53).

In terms of technology, ECU 911 used components from suppliers from countries other than just China; for example, the data storage devices were supplied by HP, a US company (EC3, EC5). Therefore, it is inaccurate to present the ECU 911 as solely Chinese in origin or design (EC3). The main part developed entirely by CEIEC was the software platform that integrates components and coordinates the ECU 911 system. The source code was given to ECU 911's public officials, who could, in principle, keep on developing it afterwards (EC3). However, Ecuadorian technicians never modified the source code by themselves (EC5). Instead, the changes were implemented by Chinese technicians upon the request and supervision of Ecuadorian technicians (EC3). Overall, then, the cooperation with CEIEC did not involve any process of technology or knowledge transfer that would allow Ecuadorians locally to maintain or update the software or hardware. In case of malfunctions or upgrades, CEIEC offered technical support until December 2018 (EC5).

Local Ecuadorian actors have always been in charge of the overall management and operation of ECU 911. To facilitate this and to learn about the operation of the system, a small group of Ecuadorian technicians were trained in China, who then replicated the training in Ecuador. Our sources stressed that the training was technical, not ideological, with the purpose of developing local capabilities to operate ECU 911's technologies, as indeed happened (EC2, EC3). ECU 911 operators received training from other states as well. For instance, ECU 911 signed a cooperation agreement with the UK Government, which sent specialists from the College of Policing to train local operators in video surveillance (British Embassy Quito 2014). There has also been some degree of transparency about the operation of the system with resolutions and other administrative documents made available on ECU 911's web page. This somewhat rebuts the presumption that Chinese-installed systems are implemented in an opaque way, though it is notable that, despite this transparency by ECU 911 and its public officials, CEIEC representatives did not reply to our interview requests.

On February 6, 2012, President Correa inaugurated the first national center of ECU 911 in the city of Samborondón, neighboring Guayaquil. From then onwards, numerous other centers were installed across the country until the network of centers was completed. Each of these centers articulates the services provided by different institutions in charge of operationalizing the concept of integral security. By 2016, ECU 911 had two national centers, five zonal centers, and nine local centers, managing a total of approximately 4,600 cameras that would increase in the following years. From 2012 to 2016, ECU 911 received around 62 million calls, out of which 10 million were emergencies that required response from the involved institutions (Corral-De-Witt et al. 2018).

Due to its scale and achievements, ECU 911 became an emblematic project in the cooperation between China and Ecuador. In November 2016, President Xi visited ECU 911's center at Quito, where he heard workers' testimonies about the key role the system had played in coordinating the response to the earthquake that Ecuador suffered in April of that year (Xinhua Español 2016). This leading case helped CEIEC to project its technological prowess, which led it to offer similar projects to other countries in the region, such as Argentina, Bolivia, Peru, and Venezuela.

ECU 911 under the Moreno administration (2017–2021) and beyond

In 2017, the results of the presidential elections that took place in Ecuador would affect the development trajectory of ECU 911. Although former President Correa supported Lenin Moreno, who won the election and governed during the period 2017–2021, soon after his inauguration, Moreno broke with his mentor. This cleavage significantly modified numerous policies in Ecuador. President Moreno denounced his predecessor as authoritarian, corrupt, and initiated a process of persecution of his former allies. These tensions aggravated the political polarization in the country. Economically, President Moreno distanced his administration from the "Socialism of the twenty first Century" of Correa, and brought back again policies characterized by critics as neoliberal. This involved a steep adjustment of the public budget, which reduced funds for the security sector. On top of that, the COVID-19 pandemic forced the government to prioritize health care above other sectors, which led to further cuts for security. In terms of foreign policies, President Moreno realigned Ecuador with the US (Jepson 2022). For example, Ecuador returned as a debtor to the IMF. In 2018, the country accepted once again US military operations in its territory. The concept of integral security was downgraded to prioritize more militarized security strategies.

These dramatic twists in Ecuador's politics led to a decline of ECU 911. This was caused partly due to the neoliberal policies of budget constraints, which meant that ECU 911 could not replace outdated technologies on time (ECU 911 2019). For instance, in 2022, ECU public officials estimated 50% of their cameras required replacement by 2023, while they stated 1,081 cameras were no longer working (Sanchez 2022). The deterioration was further accentuated by both domestic and international criticisms voiced against ECU 911. Domestically, the most important one was the presumed overpricing involved in Ecuador's dealings with CEIEC during the construction of ECU 911 (El Comercio 2018). Internationally, the *New York Times* published the article referenced above claiming that ECU 911 was part of the Chinese surveillance state's expansion into Ecuador (Mozur, Kessel, and Chan 2019). This article has been highly influential: cited 93 times at the time of writing according to Google Scholar and referenced by numerous Western policy documents as evidence that the Chinese surveillance state is dangerously expanding into Latin America (Access Now 2021; Berg 2021; Ellis 2022). The Moreno administration echoed this reporting to further accuse his previous mentor, former President Correa, of authoritarianism. Finally, US politicians have used this reporting to criticize ECU 911, and more broadly, to oppose the cooperation between Ecuador and China (Democratic Staff Report 2020; Menendez 2022).

The allegations in the *New York Times* are problematic for three main reasons. First, the reporting was done and published during Moreno's administration, without consulting sources linked to the previous Correa administration, although the latter was the target of the criticisms. Hence, the article reproduced the Moreno administration's view about his predecessor, which was unsurprisingly negative, and rather overblown, amidst the public political struggle between them. Second, the alleged danger posed by the expansion of Chinese surveillance technologies into Ecuador disregarded the broader local factors driving the procurement of the system, such as the concept of integral security. Similarly, these sources overlooked that the system was managed and operated mainly by local actors. Finally, it overlooked the view of officials from Ecuador's intelligence agency, who rejected claims that the ECU 911 system was used for surveillance of citizens (EC7). Although they recognize they had access to video feeds, they stressed these were rarely used, and definitely not useful for the generation of strategic intelligence, which is the main mission of the agency (EC7). In fact, for their daily analysis of strategic data they use IBM Watson artificial intelligence technology (EC7).

In this context, the technical support that CEIEC offered was not renewed from January 2019 onwards (EC5). Although Ecuador and CEIEC initiated a discussion for a new contract, they did not reach a new agreement for two reasons. First, Ecuador's public officials found that the price CEIEC demanded was unreasonable (EC5). This indicates that the tailored platform that CEIEC developed for ECU 911 brought with it the danger of technological dependence on the Chinese provider, which could arbitrarily increase its price over time. Second, in November 2020 the US sanctioned CEIEC over alleged cooperation with the Venezuelan government to undermine democracy. Consequently, since then, CEIEC cannot trade with Ecuador (EC5), a challenge that is compounded by the fact that Ecuador's economy is dollarized.

The situation has not changed much since the presidency of Guillermo Lasso, who took office in mid-2021. Since then, ECU 911 public officials have been planning and budgeting a major upgrade of the system to replace the hardware and software that passed its life expectancy (EC5). Although this has not been accomplished yet, the sources we consulted said they will be open to all providers, irrespective of nationality. However, the pressures from US government officials against the project have continued. For example, in March 2022, the US Senate introduced the United States-Ecuador Partnership Act, which pledges to combat the negative Chinese influence in the country, and portrays ECU 911 as a threat to Ecuador's democratic governance (Menendez 2022). Despite these allegations, neither the Moreno nor the Lasso administration closed ECU 911 because of any alleged misuse for authoritarian surveillance practices. By contrast, it has continued operating basically for the public service it offers to citizens, though with economic and technological difficulties to fulfill its work. However, the trend suggests Western actors are increasingly becoming involved either as financers or technology suppliers, in replacement of previous Chinese counterparts. For instance, the US-led Inter-American Development Bank (IADB) has been granting credits to upgrade parts of the system. Likewise, during the pandemic, ECU 911 incorporated machine learning software developed by the IADB to detect patterns in the video surveillance images of people that were not respecting a 1-meter social distancing. To conclude, how the system may unfold in the future remains open, and shaped by local and international politics.

Argentina: Jujuy Seguro e Interconectado (JSeI)

During the last two decades, Chinese surveillance firms have been expanding significantly in Argentina. A market study by the Argentine Chamber of Electronic Security shows that in 2018 national firms commercializing surveillance technologies imported them mostly from China (62%), followed far behind by Canada (5.7%), Brazil (5.2%), México (5%), and the US (4.7%) (CASEL 2019, 35). Indeed, any pedestrian of Argentine cities can easily find video cameras supplied by Chinese private firms in shops and as part of public safety systems. Among Chinese state-owned enterprises, ZTE is the most prominent one selling surveillance equipment to the Argentine state. This company, which has been at the forefront of the internationalization of Chinese telecommunication firms across the globe, has been operating in Argentina since 2005, mainly providing equipment and services to telecommunication carriers, governments, and selling smartphones to consumers.

Our particular focus here is a public safety system sold by ZTE to the northwestern province of Jujuy. To understand the origins of this project, we need to contextualize the security and political situation of the province. Jujuy's crime statistics are not as dramatic as in other parts of the country. In fact, whilst during 2017–2020 the average national homicide rate was 5.35 victims per 100,000 inhabitants, Jujuy had 3.4 victims per 100,000 inhabitants (Ministerio de Seguridad de Argentina 2022). If we consider citizens' perception of insecurity, the last available statistics from 2017 show that 40.2% of Jujuy' citizens thought that security was a very serious problem, slightly below the national average which was 41.7% (INDEC 2018). In this context, security policies are usually at the top of politicians' agendas. This was the case of candidate Gerardo Morales who, in 2015, was running for Governor of Jujuy as part of Cambiemos (Let's Change), a national center-right political coalition. On the campaign trail, Morales made several promises to fight crime, such as creating a Ministry of Security, which the province lacked, and upgrading video surveillance capabilities. The preexisting system was deployed in 2013 by the left-wing ruling party. It consisted of a 911 emergency response number and a video surveillance system supplied by a German company (TodoJujuy 2015). They were under the management and operation of the provincial police. However, during the campaign, deputies of Morales' party denounced these systems as dysfunctional, because the number of working cameras (44) was insufficient and the police force was under-resourced to respond to emergencies (Jujuy al Día 2015).

Once elected, Governor Morales' team at the brand-new Ministry of Security began working on the update of the 911 response and video surveillance system. The first option they considered was following a similar model to that of the municipality of Tigre. This touristic city near Buenos Aires, inspired by the models in New York and Washington, DC, was one of the first in the country to implement a cutting-edge surveillance system in cooperation with NEC, a Japanese company. However, this model involved the procurement of cameras under a commodatum agreement, which meant the devices would not be owned by the province. Therefore, Jujuy's policy makers did not favor this model (AR1). The other safe city model that Jujuy's policy makers visited was deployed in the neighboring province of Salta by Claro, a Mexican telecommunications firm, in partnership with Chinese companies, initially Huawei and later updated by ZTE (AR1). Jujuy's policy makers were not convinced by this model either, because the fiber optic network needed for the surveillance system remained owned by the Mexican firm (AR1). Despite this, the visit to Salta led to a contact with ZTE, which proposed a tailored solution to Jujuy's needs, in which the provincial government would own both the cameras and the fiber optic network (AR1). Therefore, the policy makers were persuaded by this provider's offer due to the advantages of ownership over the equipment and network.

In July 2016, the Government of Jujuy and ZTE signed a Memorandum of Understanding to advance the project. ZTE sought to use direct contracting procurement without the need for public tender, which was possible through a state-to-state agreement that Argentina had signed with China. However, Jujuy public officials preferred an international public procurement process to ensure transparency (AR1). In November 2016, the public tender for the project was launched, and it was titled Jujuy Seguro e Interconectado (JSeI) (Ministerio de Seguridad de Jujuy 2016), describing the technical requirements of the project defined by the Government of Jujuy. It involved deploying a video surveillance system composed of 600 cameras, a monitoring center for 24 operators, and a TV wall. In addition, the tender required the installation of a telecommunications network connecting 310 points of government, such as government offices, hospitals, police stations, schools. The tender included the list of government-defined geolocations of video cameras and points of government. The budget was estimated at US$24 million plus taxes. The government called this first tender phase 1 of the project, because it was focused on the city of San Salvador of Jujuy, though the authorities envisioned its extension to the rest of the province in subsequent phases of the project. In comparison to Ecuador's case, this was therefore a relatively small turnkey project.

ZTE was the only company that presented a proposal and it won the tender. It proposed that 85% of the project's cost be paid *via* an 8-year term loan granted by the Chinese Exim Bank to the province of Jujuy. The result of the tender was questioned by opposition politicians, who disputed the decision to borrow in dollars, since it endangered the fragile finances of the province (AR2). Furthermore, they alleged that the video cameras were overpriced, suggesting that there was corruption in the procurement process (AR2). Although these accusations were not proven, and debt-related worries were dismissed by Jujuy's government, it is important to note that the surveillance capabilities of the system were not questioned, but rather how it was procured.

In May 2017, in the presence of President Xi, Jujuy's Minister of Security signed the contract with ZTE in Beijing. The project was then delayed for two years due to contractual issues that were finally solved on March 2019, though the Chinese funding was finally channeled *via* a different bank (BBVA Hong Kong) but under the same initial funding conditions agreed with the Exim Bank (AR1, AR3). In May 2019, the government of Jujuy and ZTE officially launched the project. The ZTE executive in charge of the presentation pledged to finish it in 18 months. He also presented the company's special task force for implementing the project, composed of Chinese, local, and other foreign workers (Morales 2019). The Chinese executive closed the presentation promising to turn Jujuy into a "safe, interconnected and intelligent city" (Morales 2019, 1:05).

Six weeks after this official launch, Reuters published an article asserting that the project represented the expansion of the Chinese surveillance state into Argentina (Garrison 2019). Although the reporting prioritized US government sources, in contrast to the *New York Times's* article about Ecuador, this one did include views of Argentine and Chinese actors dismissing such criticisms. However, rather than analyzing in depth what the project actually consisted of and what were the reasons for its implementation, the article framed the project as part of the so-called "US-China tech war" (Garrison 2019). As in Ecuador's case, the importance of the Reuters article resides in the broader ramifications it had in Argentina. For example, Argentine national newspapers reproduced the US critical views about ZTE's project that the Reuters article conveyed, without any further local reporting. Similarly, the Reuters article has been cited in reports by Access Now that criticize the spread of surveillance technologies into the region (e.g. Access Now 2021).

However, the fears of US government sources about expansion of the so-called Chinese surveillance state conveyed *via* the Reuters article seem overstated when we take into account several features of the project. First, the supposed "Chinese surveillance system" is in fact the work of many actors, including local firms. For instance, the installation of the cameras was done by local firms in cooperation with the provincial state-owned electric company (EJESA) (AR1). Likewise, the fiber optic network connecting the points of government, once finished, will be managed by a provincial state-owned enterprise, Jujuy Digital SAPEM (AR1). Second, the capital city of Jujuy already had a 911 and a video surveillance system, which was deployed during the previous administration of the current left-wing opposition party, mainly using surveillance technologies from a German supplier. In effect, the cooperation project with ZTE upgraded this earlier system rather than introduce entirely new surveillance capabilities into Jujuy. Third, ZTE won the tender because it could offer the tailored solution that Jujuy needed in a cost-effective way, in particular the ownership of both the cameras and the fiber optic network (AR1, AR4). Chinese state funding was important in tipping the balance in favor of ZTE, but there was no a priori reason why non-Chinese foreign suppliers could not have bid and provided similar technological capabilities. Finally, the project is under the management and operation of Jujuy's Ministry of Security. Although ZTE did offer training, this was solely technical and related to the operation of the telecom infrastructure and the cameras; it did not involve wider political or ideological content (AR4). For all these reasons, it seems that ZTE's motivations were commercial, rather than political—exporting Chinese surveillance practices.

Nevertheless, opposition politicians do fear that the video surveillance system may strengthen what they characterize as a punitive state in the province (AR2). Indeed, since Governor Morales came to power, there have been numerous cases of persecution of his critics, though not *via* the use of video surveillance. The most salient case was the incarceration of the indigenous leader Milagro Sala who, in 2016, was imprisoned by the Jujuy courts due to alleged incitement to commit crimes, organize riots, and sedition. The Inter-American Court of Human Rights and the UN Human Rights Council have denounced this decision as arbitrary and demanded that the province release her, with no results so far. A researcher from an Argentine human rights organization shared these worries about the potential misuse of the system by Morales' administration, but also extended the concerns to the opposition center-left party, which similarly had problematic cases of police abuse while in power (AR5). These concerns are based on the lack of independent accountability mechanisms for the use of such systems by security forces (AR5). Furthermore, the researcher criticized the lack of public documents assessing the human rights impact of the JSeI (AR5). In this context, these critics fear that the video surveillance part of JSeI might be misused for political purposes (AR2, AR5).

During fieldwork in 2022, these were speculative concerns, however, at the moment of writing this article (July 2023), the situation looks far more problematic. The reason for this assessment is that in June 2023, the police of Jujuy used excessive force against indigenous protestors who resisted a reform of the provincial constitution. Several human rights organizations condemned the provincial state violence (Buenos Aires Herald 2023). Although the manner in which JSeI was employed in these incidents is not public, this context of violence supports the apprehensions posited by the aforementioned sources.

Discussion

The empirical data we gathered from Argentina and Ecuador challenges several claims of the authors criticizing the expansion of Chinese surveillance systems into the Global South (Berg 2021; Cheney 2019; Democratic Staff Report 2020; Ellis 2021, 2022; Garrison 2019; Gravett 2020; Hemmings 2020; Mozur, Kessel, and Chan 2019; Polyakova and Meserole 2019; Shabhaz 2018), at least in relation to democratic countries. Thereby, our research supports and extends the counterarguments advanced by Gagliardone (2019) and Woodhams (2020) regarding the export of Chinese surveillance technologies.

Although video surveillance is a central component of the projects we studied, naming them just as surveillance systems is inaccurate, because it is not the locally-used term nor does it cover all the other dimensions involved in the projects. Indeed, their main aim has been to tackle citizens' concerns about security; hence, they are locally presented as public safety or citizens security systems. Likewise, they are not limited to video surveillance capabilities. Take the case of Ecuador, where the name of the system, ECU 911, plainly conveys the number that allows citizens to contact the public authorities in case of emergencies. In the case of Jujuy, the project also includes connectivity in its name, since it deployed a fiber optic network to connect different arms of the provincial government.

Likewise, our cases indicate that the projects are not entirely Chinese. They comprised different combinations of Chinese, local, and even foreign actors at different phases of the project. For instance, in both cases, local actors led the initiation of the projects and defined the requirements for their technical design, which was then undertaken by the Chinese firms. In the case of Ecuador, the requirements were based on smart city models from Western countries, and part of the equipment was sourced from Western firms (e.g. HP), whilst in JSeI the technical design was implemented by ZTE in response to requirements of the provincial government. Regarding the deployment of the systems, apart from the Chinese companies, in both cases local firms were involved. The management and operation of the systems is undertaken by local actors, with no Chinese actors involved. For contractual reasons, the maintenance and update of the systems depends on the Chinese companies, but they can be replaced by other providers (EC5, AR1).

Furthermore, much of the criticism against the spread of surveillance technologies in the Global South is ahistorical, assuming they began with the export of Chinese technologies. In fact, in both cases the spread of surveillance technologies had been well underway, and provided by other foreign providers, including Western ones. Prior to the timeframe of our study, the city of Quito initiated its surveillance system in 2002 in partnership with a Colombian firm (Löfberg 2008), whilst as noted in our case, the video surveillance system in Jujuy had been initiated with German technologies. For the same reasons, both systems could potentially have been sourced from non-Chinese foreign providers, offering technologies with similar capabilities. In fact, Ecuador's public officials consulted several others before choosing the Chinese company. Likewise, Jujuy's public officials were first interested in the offer of a Japanese company.

US-based critics accuse leftist parties of introducing Chinese surveillance technology in Latin America (Berg 2021; Ellis 2021, 2022). However, in the Jujuy case, it was the governing center-right political coalition that closed the deal with Chinese firms. Indeed, even though the source we consulted in Jujuy's government expressed apprehension about China's political system, in their view, that is unrelated to the attractive financing and technology offer made by ZTE (AR1). Our empirical data therefore contradicts the idea that only anti-US leftist political parties procure surveillance technologies from Chinese firms.

Be that as it may, the cases indicate that the Chinese state is supporting the internationalization of companies involved in the provision of citizen security equipment, who compete with other foreign firms selling similar technologies in Latin America. Actually, the access to Chinese state funding alongside low price was the key factor according to decision makers in Argentina and Ecuador that inclined them to choose Chinese providers over others, rather than technological superiority or an ideological affinity with the problematic surveillance practices within China.

In both cases, the documents by Western academics, policy makers, and media were more concerned to show the malign influence that China had in the projects (Berg 2021; Democratic Staff Report 2020; Ellis 2021, 2022; Garrison 2019; Mozur, Kessel, and

Chan 2019), rather than to explore why they were started, how they were implemented, and any achievements they may have had. Notwithstanding these limitations, these examples do demonstrate the power of Western media portrayals of Chinese projects, and the associated narrative they follow, which have had an impact both in the West and in Latin America. Local policy makers accused such sources of defaming their projects with Chinese actors; something seen as originating due to the geopolitical threat that China represents to US influence in Latin America (EC2, EC3, AR1).

Nonetheless, there have been local criticisms of these projects, but not focused on the presumed authoritarian practices that the partnership with Chinese companies may trigger, as denounced by foreign critics. First, local media reports focused on the shadowy practices in the procurement processes that favored Chinese companies. Second, policy makers were concerned with the issue of technological dependence. In our particular cases, this related to Chinese suppliers because, even though the management and operation of the systems is done by local actors, in neither case did we find a transfer of technological capabilities for repurposing the software platform at the core of both systems. However, this reflects a wider issue not solely linked to China, as seen in the concerns expressed about technological ownership by the Japanese and Mexican companies in existing Argentine surveillance systems. Third, human rights organizations have been questioning the deployment of surveillance technologies in general: not just the specific projects with Chinese companies but thus also including those in both countries where the suppliers are firms from Western countries, such as Germany, Japan and Israel. Finally, although opposition politicians and civil society sources that we spoke to expressed concerns about the potential abuse of video surveillance technologies (EC6, AR5), during fieldwork, such worries remained in the speculative plane, and did not attract much national media coverage. However, the potential misuse of these systems should not be underestimated.

We think there are at least two reasons that explain this divergence between the foreign criticisms and the local ones. First, Western critics reproduced a dominant narrative within Western, particularly US, sources that portrays whatever is linked to China as a threat. In doing this, these authors assume a simplistic model, in which legitimate concerns about the use of Chinese surveillance technologies in some contexts have been over-extrapolated, and supposed to apply in the same way in all countries of the Global South. But, as this article suggests, a differentiated approach is needed that takes into account of each individual context the particular history, actors, motivations, processes, technologies, etc. Second, surveillance technologies are perceived differently across the world. In contrast to many other Chinese infrastructure projects in extractive industries of Latin America, which are seriously questioned by the citizens due to their environmental impacts, these citizen security projects were demand-driven. Indeed, among the many reasons for the acceptance of such technologies in Latin American countries (Arteaga Botello 2012; Lio 2015), it is worth noting the widely shared belief—even if not evidence-based—that surveillance technologies contribute to address the pressing security challenges faced by citizens on a daily basis. Accordingly, citizen security projects are demanded both by politicians and citizens, regardless of the country of origin of the suppliers.

Conclusions

The empirical data collected in Argentina and Ecuador suggests the need for a differentiated and situated approach to the study of citizen security projects built in cooperation with Chinese firms. Indeed, we showed that it is inaccurate to present such projects just as surveillance systems, when in fact they cover other dimensions, such as emergency response, or increasing the connectivity of public institutions. Furthermore, our data also challenges the claim that these systems are Chinese. Not only are the technologies within them sometimes of multiple origins but we found that the agency in these projects is distributed among Chinese, local and other foreign actors, varying with the phase of the project: initiation, requirements, technical design, implementation, management and operation, and maintenance and update. Similarly, the criticisms against Chinese providers are ahistorical, since they overlook the fact that surveillance processes were already well underway in both states due to the sale of surveillance technologies by non-Chinese foreign firms, including Western ones. In fact, they could have provided a similar solution as the chosen Chinese firms. Additionally, our results showed that the procurement of Chinese surveillance technologies did not depend on the political leaning of the Latin American political parties in power. Policy makers from both right- and left-leaning political parties chose Chinese providers mainly due to their lower costs and state financing, rather than an ideological affinity to emulate Chinese surveillance practices. Finally, the local criticisms of the projects did not overlap with those made by Western sources, which have too often fitted a US-generated narrative about the presumed threat posed by Chinese companies.

For all these reasons, we conclude that the incorporation of surveillance technologies from Chinese providers did not transfer the problematic authoritarian surveillance practices criticized in China to Argentina and Ecuador. However, our contextualized and differentiated approach does not exclude such an outcome in other conditions of deployment, where local actors may actively seek to emulate such practices, or where preexisting authoritarian practices may be enhanced by the procurement of such technologies. If Chinese companies are only trying to compete against Western companies for market share, then to avoid getting entangled in such cases, it is important that they conduct thorough due diligence of who their clients are.

Acknowledgements

We thank Richard Heeks, Nick Jepson and Seth Schindler of the Global Development Institute, University of Manchester, for the constructive feedback that we received in previous versions of this manuscript. We also thank the comments and suggestions from two anonymous reviewers. All remaining errors are the authors' own responsibility.

Disclosure statement

No potential conflict of interest was reported by the author(s).

Funding

This article was supported by the project, "China's Digital Expansion in the Global South," funded by the Faculty of Humanities, University of Manchester, UK. Vila Seoane also thanks the support received from the National Scientific and Research Council (CONICET) of Argentina *via* a postdoctoral scholarship grant.

ORCID

Maximiliano Facundo Vila Seoane http://orcid.org/0000-0002-0134-7714
Carla Morena Álvarez Velasco http://orcid.org/0000-0002-3372-5273

References

Access Now. 2021. Surveillance tech in Latin America: Made abroad, deployed at home. https://www.accessnow.org/cms/assets/uploads/2021/08/Surveillance-Tech-Latam-Report.pdf (accessed June 12, 2023).

Aid Data. n.d. China commits a loan of $240 million to Ecuador to set up security service ECU 911. https://china.aiddata.org/projects/39281/ (accessed August 10, 2022).

Álvarez Velasco, C. 2014. *Reforms and contradictions in Ecuador's drug policy*. Washington, DC: Washington Office on Latin America (WOLA). https://www.wola.org/sites/default/files/Drug%20Policy/Ecuador%20memo%20English_FINAL.pdf (accessed June 12, 2023).

Arteaga Botello, N. 2012. Surveillance studies: An agenda for Latin America. *Surveillance & Society* 10 (1):5–17. doi: 10.24908/ss.v10i1.4282.

Berg, R. C. 2021. *China in Latin America and the Caribbean*. Washington, DC: Center for Strategic and International Studies (CSIS). http://www.jstor.org/stable/resrep37529 (accessed June 12, 2023).

Bernal-Meza, R., and L. Xing, eds. 2020. *China-Latin America relations in the 21st century: The dual complexities of opportunities and challenges*. Cham: Springer. doi: 10.1007/978-3-030-35614-9.

British Embassy Quito. 2014. Especialistas ingleses del College of Policing entrenan personal del ECU 911 – Ecuador [English specialists from the College of Policing train ECU 911 personnel – Ecuador]. https://www.gov.uk/government/news/254304.es-419 (accessed June 12, 2023).

Buenos Aires Herald. 2023. Jujuy: International human rights organizations express concern. *Buenos Aires Herald*, June 21. https://buenosairesherald.com/human-rights/jujuy-international-human-rights- organizations-express-concern (accessed July 17, 2023).

Cabrera, L. 2019. La seguridad integral en Ecuador: Una visión crítica del concepto a una década de su concepción [Integral security in Ecuador: A critical view of the concept a decade after its conception]. *UNISCI Journal* 17 (51):397–416. doi: 10.31439/UNISCI-69.

CASEL. 2019. Estudio de mercado de la seguridad electrónica de la República Argentina [Market study of electronic security in the Argentine Republic]. *Innovación: Seguridad Electrónica* 17 (115):6–69. https://www.revistainnovacion.com/uploads/revista/pdf/INNOVACION_115_Estudio_de_Mercado.pdf (accessed June 12, 2023).

CEIEC. 2011. Corporate profile (September 1). https://web.archive.org/web/20110901021720/http://www.ceiec.com.cn/english/type/Info.aspx?code=01002 (accessed June 12, 2023).

Cheney, C. 2019. China's digital silk road: Strategic technological competition and exporting political illiberalism. [Issues & Insights Working Paper 19 (WP8)]. Honolulu, HI: Pacific Forum. https://pacforum.org/wp-content/uploads/2019/08/issuesinsights_Vol19-WP8FINAL.pdf (accessed November 5, 2023).

Corral-De-Witt, D., E. V. Carrera, J. A. Matamoros-Vargas, S. Munoz-Romero, J. L. Rojo-Alvarez, and K. Tepe. 2018. From E-911 to NG-911: Overview and challenges in Ecuador. *IEEE Access*. 6:42578–91. doi: 10.1109/ACCESS.2018.2858751.

Democratic Staff Report. 2020. The new big brother: China and digital authoritarianism (A Democratic staff report prepared for the use of the Committee on Foreign Relations

United States Senate). https://www.foreign.senate.gov/imo/media/doc/The%20New%20Big%20Brother%20-%20China%20and%20Digital%20Authoritarianism%20-%20SFRC%20Dem%20Staff%20Report.pdf (accessed June 12, 2023).

ECU 911. 2015. Informe: Gestión anual del servicio integrado de seguridad ECU 911 (Report: Annual management of the integral security service ECU 911). https://issuu.com/ecu911/docs/informe_de_gestion2015 (accessed June 12, 2023).

ECU 911. 2019. Plan estratégico institucional 2020-2023 (Strategic institutional plan 2020-2023). https://www.ecu911.gob.ec/wp-content/uploads/2022/02/Plan-Estrat%C3%A9gico-SIS-ECU-911-2019-2023.pdf (accessed June 12, 2023).

El Comercio. 2018. Ministro Navas negó que haya un informe de la contraloría en su contra [Minister Navas denied that there is a report from the comptroller against him]. El Comercio, January 9. https://www.elcomercio.com/actualidad/seguridad/ministro-cesarnavas-niega-informe-contraloria.html (accessed June 12, 2023).

Ellis, R. E. 2021. China's diplomatic and political approach in Latin America and the Caribbean (Testimony before the US-China Economic and Security Review Commission). https://www.uscc.gov/sites/default/files/2021-05/Evan_Ellis_Testimony.pdf (accessed June 12, 2023).

Ellis, R. E. 2022. El avance digital de China en América Latina [The digital advance of China in Latin America]. *Revista Seguridad y Poder Terrestre* 1 (1):15–39. doi: 10.56221/spt.v1i1.5.

Feldstein, S. 2019. The road to digital unfreedom: How artificial intelligence is reshaping repression. *Journal of Democracy* 30 (1):40–52. doi: 10.1353/jod.2019.0003.

Gagliardone, I. 2019. *China, Africa, and the future of the Internet*. London: Zed.

Garrison, C. 2019. "Safe like China": In Argentina, ZTE finds eager buyer for surveillance tech. *Reuters*, May 7. https://www.reuters.com/article/us-argentina-china-zte-insight-idUSKCN1U00ZG (accessed June 12, 2023).

Gonzalez-Vicente, R. 2017. South-South relations under world market capitalism: The state and the elusive promise of national development in the China-Ecuador resource-development nexus. *Review of International Political Economy* 24 (5):881–903. doi: 10.1080/09692290.2017.1357646.

Gravett, W. H. 2020. Digital coloniser? China and artificial intelligence in Africa. *Survival* 62 (6):153–78. doi: 10.1080/00396338.2020.1851098.

Gravett, W. H. 2022. Digital neocolonialism: The Chinese surveillance state in Africa. *African Journal of International and Comparative Law* 30 (1):39–58. doi: 10.3366/ajicl.2022.0393.

Hemmings, J. 2020. Reconstructing order: The geopolitical risks in China's digital silk road. *Asia Policy* 15 (1):5–21. doi: 10.1353/asp.2020.0002.

Herrera-Vinelli, L., and M. Bonilla. 2019. Ecuador-China relations: The growing effect of Chinese investment on Ecuadorian domestic politics, 2007–2016. *Journal of Chinese Political Science* 24 (4):623–41. doi: 10.1007/s11366-018-09588-6.

Hu, R. 2019. The state of smart cities in China: The case of Shenzhen. *Energies* 12 (22):4375. doi: 10.3390/en12224375.

INDEC. 2018. Encuesta nacional de victimización 2017 [National victimization survey 2017]. https://www.indec.gob.ar/uploads/informesdeprensa/env_2017_02_18.pdf (accessed June 12, 2023).

Jepson, N. 2022. Infrastructure-led development with post-neoliberal characteristics: Buen Vivir, China, and extractivism in Ecuador. In *The Rise of the infrastructure state: How US-China rivalry shapes politics and place worldwide*, eds. by S. Schindler and J. DiCarlo, 106–21. Bristol, UK: Bristol University Press. doi: 10.51952/9781529220803.ch008.

Jujuy al Día. 2015. *El gobierno no tiene política de seguridad* [El gobierno no tiene política de seguridad]. *Jujuy al Día*, May 19. https://www.jujuyaldia.com.ar/2015/05/19/el-gobierno-no-tiene-politica-de-seguridad/ (accessed June 12, 2023).

Kassenova, N., and B. Duprey, eds. 2021. *Digital silk road in Central Asia: Present and future*. Cambridge, MA: Davis Center for Russian and Eurasian Studies, Harvard University.

Lio, V. 2015. Ciudades, cámaras de seguridad y video-vigilancia: Estado del arte y perspectivas de investigación [Cities, security cameras and video surveillance: State of the art and research perspectives]. *Astrolabio* 15:273–302. doi: 10.55441/1668.7515.n15.9903.

Löfberg, S. 2008. *Ojos de Águila: Una primera aproximación al sistema de video vigilancia en Quito* [Eagle Eyes: A first approximation to the video surveillance system in Quito]. *Ciudad Segura. Programa Estudios de La Ciudad*. https://www.flacso.org.ec/biblio/catalog/resGet.php?resId=20859 (accessed June 12, 2023).

Lucio Vásquez, A. G. 2020. Evolución del concepto de seguridad en la República del Ecuador: Desde una perspectiva de seguridad nacional hacia la seguridad integral [Evolution of the concept of security in the Republic of Ecuador: From a national security perspective towards integral security]. *Relaciones Internacionales* 43 (43):171–88. doi: 10.15366/relacionesinternacionales2020.43.009.

Menendez, R. 2022. S.3591 - United States-Ecuador Partnership Act of 2022. https://www.congress.gov/bill/117th-congress/senate-bill/3591 (accessed November 5, 2023).

Ministerio de Coordinación de Seguridad. 2011. Plan nacional de seguridad integral (National integral security plan). https://issuu.com/micsecuador/docs/plan_nacional_seguridad_integral (accessed June 12, 2023).

Ministerio de Seguridad de Jujuy. 2016. Proyecto integral Jujuy Seguro e Interconectado [Integral project Jujuy Seguro e Interconectado]. http://seguridad.jujuy.gob.ar/wp-content/uploads/sites/27/2016/11/LICITACION-JUJUY-SEGURO-E-INTERCONECTADO-FINAL.pdf (accessed June 12, 2023.

Ministerio de Seguridad de Argentina. 2022. Homicidios dolosos 2017-2020 [Intentional homicides 2017-2020]. https://estadisticascriminales.minseg.gob.ar/reports/Informe_Homicidios_Dolosos.pdf (accessed June 12, 2023).

Morales, G. 2019. Presentación del plan de trabajo de Jujuy Seguro e Interconectado [Presentation of the work plan for Jujuy Seguro e Interconectado]. https://www.youtube.com/watch?v=Jb9ORPUxva4 (accessed June 12, 2023).

Mozur, P., J. M. Kessel, and M. Chan. 2019. Made in China, exported to the world: The surveillance state. New York

Times, April 24. https://www.nytimes.com/2019/04/24/technology/ecuador-surveillance-cameras-police-government.html (accessed June 12, 2023).

Polyakova, A., and C. Meserole. 2019. *Exporting digital authoritarianism: The Russian and Chinese models.* Washington, DC: Brookings Institution. https://www.brookings.edu/research/exporting-digital-authoritarianism/ (accessed June 12, 2023).

Saguier, M., and M. F. Vila Seoane. 2022. Argentina and the spatial politics of extractive infrastructures under US-China tensions. In *The rise of the infrastructure state: How US-China rivalry shapes politics and place worldwide*, eds. S. Schindler and J. DiCarlo, 153–66. Bristol, UK: Bristol University Press. doi: 10.51952/9781529220803.ch011.

Sanchez, E. 2022. El 60% de los equipos del ECU 911 necesita renovación [60% of the ECU 911 equipment needs renewal]. *Expreso,* June 3. https://www.expreso.ec/actualidad/60-equipos-ecu-911-necesita-renovacion-128805.html (accessed June 12, 2023).

Secretaría Nacional de Riesgos. 2011. Sistema nacional de comando y control para la seguridad ciudadana SIS911 [National command and control system for citizen security SIS911]. http://app.sni.gob.ec/sni-link/sni/PDOT/SNRG/GALAPAGOS/GALAPAGOS/VARIOS/AUTOCAD/Isla%20San%20Cristobal/PresSIS%20Galapagos.pdf (accessed June 12, 2023).

Shabhaz, A. 2018. The rise of digital authoritarianism (Report: Freedom on the net 2018). Washington, DC: Freedom House. https://freedomhouse.org/sites/default/files/2020-02/10192018_FOTN_2018_Final_Booklet.pdf (accessed June 12, 2023).

TodoJujuy. 2015. Capacitan a operadores del 911. *Todo Jujuy,* March 26. https://www.todojujuy.com/jujuy/capacitan-operadores-del-911-n32613 (accessed June 12, 2023).

UNDP. 1994. Human development report 1994: New dimensions of human security. New York: Oxford University Press. https://hdr.undp.org/sites/default/files/reports/255/hdr_1994_en_complete_nostats.pdf.

Woodhams, S. 2020. China, Africa, and the private surveillance industry. *Georgetown Journal of International Affairs* 21 (1):158–65. doi: 10.1353/gia.2020.0002.

Xinhua Español. 2016. Presidente Chino promete a Ecuador más apoyo para reconstrucción tras sismo [Chinese President promises Ecuador more support for reconstruction after earthquake]. *Xinhua Español*, November 19. http://spanish.xinhuanet.com/2016-11/19/c_135841469.htm (accessed June 12, 2023).

Appendix 1. Interviews

Code	Interviewee
EC1	Former ECU 911 director
EC2	Former vice-minister of the Defense Ministry
EC3	Former ECU 911 director and former Minister of Coordination of Internal and External Security
EC4	Ecuadorian academic who investigated ECU 911
EC5	Current technical manager of ECU 911
EC6	Senior communications and advocacy specialist at Access Now Ecuador
EC7	Former official of Ecuador's intelligence agency during Correa's administration
EC8	Former vice-minister of the Coordinating Ministry of Security
AR1	Public official at Ministry of Security of Jujuy in charge of JSeI
AR2	Representative of opposition political party of Jujuy
AR3	Public official within national government in charge of international funding
AR4	ZTE manager
AR5	ADC researcher (Argentine human rights organization)
AR6	Argentine academic who investigates surveillance

China's expansion into Brazilian digital surveillance markets

Esther Majerowicz and Miguel Henriques de Carvalho

ABSTRACT
A number of countries in the Global South have adopted anti-China rhetoric in recent years. Here, we seek to assess the relation of such rhetoric to procurement of Chinese digital systems. We use the example of Brazil during the Bolsonaro government, examining whether Bolsonaro's anti-China stance impacted procurement of Chinese surveillance technologies by sub-national (state/city) governments, which are the main bodies responsible for public security. We find that there has been broad and sustained procurement of Chinese surveillance technologies across the political spectrum; both among local governments politically allied to Bolsonaro and those from the opposition. Combined with acquisition at federal level, this suggests anti-China rhetoric does not feed through into procurement realities. Nor can China be singularly associated with diffusion of surveillance technologies as Western democracies have also been suppliers.

Introduction

In 2019, Brazil witnessed the rise to power of far-right, authoritarian-leaning political leaders both to the presidency, with Jair Bolsonaro, and some of its local (state- and city-level) governments. Just 15 days after the beginning of Bolsonaro's government, an entourage of parliamentarians, all of them at the time members of Bolsonaro's then political party (Partido Social Liberal, PSL), arrived in China by invitation of the Chinese embassy in Brazil. The objective of the visit was for the lawmakers to learn about China's facial recognition-based surveillance system (Rebello 2019). During the visit, the parliamentarians expressed the intention to present a bill on their return to Brazil that would make facial recognition mandatory in public spaces to support public security.

These events foreground the intersection of the Brazilian far-right's eagerness for surveillance technologies and China's capacity and eagerness to export such technologies. This conjunction has been increasingly interpreted by US think tanks and foreign policy establishment as China's export of "digital authoritarianism" (Minority Staff, US Senate Committee on Foreign Relations 2020; Polyakova and Meserole 2019). This visit, however, did not unfold as one might imagine on the grounds of some sort of supposed "authoritarian affinity" of the political forces in question: the visit was met with criticisms from Bolsonaro's close allies, while the President said he was "surprised" about the visit (Sadi 2019).

Bolsonaro, who was elected with an anti-China platform (Spring 2018), tended to automatically align with the Trump administration (2017–2021), which condemned Chinese surveillance hardware and software companies, banned US companies and nationals from doing business with these enterprises without governmental approval, and pressurized allies to do the same (BIS 2019a, BIS 2019b). Bolsonaro was not alone in this, with leaders in a number of Global South countries adopting anti-China rhetoric of varying degrees and particularly during elections; for example, in Ghana, Indonesia, Kenya, Malaysia, Zambia, and Zimbabwe, among others in recent years (Sibiri 2022, 2021; Schipani 2022). Such rhetoric necessarily comes into contact with China's sizeable and growing digital presence in the Global South. In Brazil, for example, China already had a significant foothold with the supply of generations of surveillance cameras for public security, dating from when Brazil started implementing these technologies at scale in 2013–2014 for the Confederations Cup and the FIFA

World Cup during Dilma Rousseff's presidency (Worker's Party). It is important to note here that Chinese companies were not the only suppliers, as Brazil procured technologies from diverse suppliers, including IBM, which installed the Rio Operations Center (Gaffney and Robertson 2018; Venturini and Stepanovich 2016).

Even though these systems are not exactly new in Brazil, the country – like many others in the Global South – has recently witnessed the accelerated proliferation of high-tech digital surveillance systems, particularly those based on facial recognition. This proliferation occurred in a context wherein the pursuit of austerity policies by the federal government rapidly worsened Brazil's social and economic indicators, provoking a major economic and social crisis (Carvalho and Carneiro 2022) and thereby aggravating the country's extreme wealth and income inequality, which gives rise to violence, among the highest in the world. Since in Brazil's urban violence has been treated as a matter of public security, the ground has been fertile for these systems to spread. Hence, digital surveillance markets in Brazil were booming under a government with authoritarian inclinations, whose head of state held that "the enemy is not external, but internal … in a fight between good and evil" (Bolsonaro quoted in Casado 2022). For foreign enterprises in countries with surveillance-related technological capabilities, this situation presented a great opportunity for profits.

For China, however, the opportunity could be stunted if Bolsonaro's government and its anti-China position posed political obstacles for China's digital expansion. In this context, the present article aims to study China's expansion in digital surveillance technologies in Brazil, particularly but not exclusively in surveillance cameras with facial recognition, during Bolsonaro's government (2019–2022). In doing so, it helps illuminate a topic little-researched to date: the relation between anti-China rhetoric and digital expansion realities in the Global South. It also makes two further contributions to the existing literature on China and its export of digital surveillance technologies. This literature has to date mainly focused on national governments, neglecting local governments, even though for public security systems, local governments are the relevant level of policy decision, as "it is especially important to note that the officials who make the initial decisions on platform adoption are often subnational officials—typically municipal mayors, provincial governors, or the heads of public safety departments for various jurisdictions" (Greitens 2020, 8). Because of this, we here expose and analyze the role of sub-national (state- and city-level) governments, of varying political inclinations, in procurement of Chinese surveillance technology. In addition, we join the body of emerging literature that challenges viewpoints that associate supply of digital surveillance technologies to regimes in the Global South solely with China.

To achieve these goals, the present article is divided into five other sections. The next section is dedicated to reviewing the existing literature, which sees China playing an exceptional role in the export of digital surveillance. Analyzing "digital authoritarianism," the section highlights how this concept has been operationalized by the US and its close allies with a view to containing China's digital expansion in foreign markets, and how this echoed in Bolsonaro's government. The following section discusses the analytical methodology used in the article (i) to assess whether this echo affected Brazil's procurement of Chinese surveillance technology at the local level, through Bolsonaro's political alliances with local governments, and (ii) to characterize the political status of both demand and supply in Brazilian governmental surveillance markets in order to verify if China has been single-handedly propagating "digital authoritarianism." Findings relating to these aims are next discussed and the article ends with discussion and conclusions sections.

Digital authoritarianism: A rhetoric of China's digital surveillance export exceptionalism

Over the last decade, a new geopolitical rivalry has emerged in the world economy centered on technological contestation, particularly in digital technologies. It arose from China's ascension with its impressive economic, technological, and military trajectory, and a shift in the US position in relation to China (Majerowicz 2022, forthcoming; de Medeiros and Majerowicz 2022). China, whose post-reform industrialization occurred alongside deep integration with the world economy, never abandoned its military autonomy and never subordinated itself to the US. Since the Great Financial Crisis, in 2008, China's greater technological convergence with advanced countries, especially in dual-use technologies (civil-military) such as digital technologies, has increasingly shifted its relation of complementarity to a relation of competition with several large US enterprises. This increased competition prompted a change in the political position of large American businesses, whose interests started to oppose those of China; aligning with the national security interests of the hawkish forces that always existed in the US, and altering the configuration of US domestic forces in the making of the China policy.[1] It is in this context that the rhetoric of China's digital authoritarianism emerges in the US, particularly fixated on a set of technologies of dual-use such as 5G, artificial intelligence, facial recognition, digital surveillance cameras, and smart city packages, in which China has either surpassed or emerged as the major US rival in the global market, even though it still depends on critical inputs and machinery from the US and its military allies, that is, semiconductors and semiconductor manufacturing equipment (Majerowicz and de Medeiros 2018; Majerowicz 2022; Majerowicz forthcoming).

According to a Report of the Minority Staff of the US Senate Committee on Foreign Relations entitled "The New Big Brother: China and Digital Authoritarianism," published in July 2020, China's expansion in information and communication technologies (ICTs) is not merely economically-motivated, as it seeks to gain market shares as well as outpace the US technologically (Minority Staff, US Senate Committee on Foreign Relations 2020). China's expansion is "also a push to establish, expand, internationalize, and institutionalize a model for digital governance that this report describes as 'digital authoritarianism'" (Minority Staff, US Senate Committee on Foreign Relations, 6).[2]

What exactly constitutes digital authoritarianism? The report tells us, based on a Brookings' paper (Polyakova and Meserole 2019), that digital authoritarianism is "The use of ICT products and services to surveil, repress, and manipulate domestic and foreign populations" (Minority Staff, US Senate Committee on Foreign Relations 2020, 6). According to an analysis published by the Lowy Institute, an Australian think tank dedicated to international political, strategic, and economic issues, importation of Chinese technology per se would ultimately pose a threat: "The danger for other countries importing Chinese technological solutions is that it will result in a growing acceptance of mass surveillance, habituation to restrictions on liberties, and fewer checks on the collection and use of personal data by the state …" (Khalil 2020, 1). Hence, in this interpretation – shared also by other sources within a tranche of publications that particularly emerges from US think tanks (e.g. Cheney 2019; Hemmings 2020; Shahbaz 2018) – the expansion of China's digital technologies means the expansion of digital authoritarianism.

Ironically, the definition operationalized by the Minority Staff, US Senate Committee on Foreign Relations (2020) stems from the institution of a government that has used ICT products and services along with its allies – including Australia – to massively surveil both domestic and foreign populations, as proven by the Snowden revelations[3] (Greenwald 2014), in a sense making the US sort of the "older" Big Brother. The Brookings' paper (Polyakova and Meserole 2019) gives a slightly different definition of digital authoritarianism, applying it only to authoritarian governments, which means that "democratic" governments can engage in all these activities and still not carry the label. Yet the danger of mass surveillance "and the collection and use of personal data by the state" aiming at social control (Khalil 2020, 1) is very far from being a particularity of China or of authoritarian regimes. All of this significantly reduces the scope for making distinctions between democracy and authoritarianism.

Nation-states across the world – democratic and authoritarian – have been implementing vast apparatuses of digital surveillance cameras across the urban fabric, making it every day more difficult to find a state that does not engage in mass surveillance. Although China seems to be the dominant supplier in surveillance cameras and highly competitive in "safe city" solutions, due to its low prices, it is not the sole supplier of explicit surveillance technology to the capitalist periphery, as Woodhams (2020) and Lugt (2021) have shown in Africa, and Venturini and Garay (2021), Pisanu et al. (2021), and Reis et al. (2021) have shown in Latin America. Enterprises from both democratic countries like the US and authoritarian countries like China are supplying both democratic and authoritarian-leaning political regimes, as they are driven by the profit motive and compete for market share. Western states' singular association of "digital authoritarianism" with China hence does not match reality since those same states: a) implement international mass surveillance systems, b) engage in domestic mass surveillance, and c) export surveillance technology to the capitalist periphery irrespective of regime. Additionally, these countries are also great consumers of Chinese surveillance cameras (Migliano and Woodhams 2021).

What appears to draw so much attention to China for the supply of surveillance technology so as to deserve the accusation of exporting digital authoritarianism, despite the existence of multiple suppliers from democratic countries doing exactly the same, is that Chinese companies are extremely competitive in surveillance hardware and embedded software and can dominate markets, particularly in the Global South. The "concept" of digital authoritarianism has thus been operationalized by the US and its close allies in an attempt to contain China's digital expansion in foreign markets. According to a "Report Prepared on Behalf of the U.S.-China Economic and Security Review Commission," democracy curiously hinges on US market access: "if U.S. market access decreases, then so does the U.S. government's ability to promote democratic values and human rights through smart cities channels …" (Atha et al. 2020, 110). As Greitens (2020, 8) recognizes, another huge problem for those competing with China in policing and public security platforms is that "Chinese companies appear to be outpacing the United States, and other countries, in setting emerging global standards for the use of these technologies." As the capitalist periphery of the Global South becomes a new frontier for technological competition including the export of digital surveillance systems, so too, operationalization of the digital authoritarianism "concept" reaches that periphery to counter China's digital expansion. Brazil presents a pertinent example of a country where these tensions play out.

In Brazil, US foreign policy and rhetoric against China's exports of surveillance technology found an echo in Bolsonaro's government, which was very much in the US sphere of influence during the Trump administration. Bolsonaro's foreign policy of US alignment contrasts with previous Worker's Party's foreign policy (2002–2016) characterized by the pursuit of multilateralism and the strengthening of strategic partnerships, which included the US and China among others (Vidigal and Bernal-Meza 2020). Emblematically, in a debate at the World Economic Forum, Bolsonaro's Minister of Foreign Affairs stated that Brazil was attempting to hinder the "techno-totalitarianism" of countries with "different models of society" through alliances with democratic countries, in a veiled criticism to China, according to Gross et al. (2021). More directly, Bolsonaro himself and those close to him were critical both during his election campaign and after his election of Chinese investment in Brazil, of the effect of trade with China, and joined US criticism of Chinese 5G technology, including accusing China of using 5G as a platform for spying (Magalhães 2022; Spring 2018; Vazquez 2022).

Hence, China's expansion in surveillance technologies might have found political and diplomatic obstacles posed by Bolsonaro's government. Whatever the impact at federal level, one outcome was growing sub-national relations between China and Brazil, involving both state- and city-level governments. According to Belasques et al. (2020), "the aggressive rhetoric directed against China by high-level government officials, as well as the bad management of the bilateral relations by the Minister of Foreign Affairs Ernesto Araújo, have led the management of the interactions between Brazil and China to be in practice transferred from the Foreign Ministry to other actors with more pragmatic view, among them stand out the subnational units, individually or in consortium."

As noted earlier, firstly, we seek to understand whether political tensions arising from the rhetoric of digital authoritarianism – understood as a strategy to contain China's digital expansion that was both echoed and endorsed by Bolsonaro's government – have impacted procurement from China. Consequently, from the above analysis, our focus will be sub-national governments, determining whether China's expansion was facilitated or hampered by their political alignment/opposition to Bolsonaro. Since China is not the sole supplier of digital surveillance technology, sub-national governments in theory have other options for their purchases. Here, as Greitens (2020) argues, in their procurement decisions, local officials might not be as prone to incorporate the values of the US foreign policy such as anti-China views.

Therefore, whatever the rhetorical or real impact of anti-China views and US foreign policy within Brazil's federal government, these tensions might not carry through to the local level, and the expansion of China's surveillance systems might be unaffected by such political tensions at the local level. In order to assess this, we will analyze mainly acquisitions of digital surveillance systems, scrutinizing primarily the deals carried out at state and city level in a set of selected representative localities.

Second, instead of assuming a mechanical and univocal link associating China's exports of digital surveillance systems to authoritarian political systems or to political leaders with authoritarian inclinations – a link that supposedly sustains the thesis that China is single-handedly propagating "digital authoritarianism" across the world through such exports – the present article seeks to shed light on the multiplicity of suppliers and demanders with diverse political statuses that compose digital surveillance markets through the case study of Brazil. Given Brazil's political make-up then, at the relevant level of decision for the acquisition of public security digital systems, we can differentiate democratic and authoritarian-leaning political forces in Brazil; and by focusing on the multiplicity of foreign suppliers, we can differentiate them as coming from democratic and authoritarian countries.

Methodology

The research triangulated evidence from four sources: academic literature; grey literature in the form of trade journals and other outlets; primary documentation in the form of government policy documents, official announcements, and government bid and procurement records; and interviews with state government officials from the Northeast region (chosen, as explained below, because it was the one region largely populated by parties opposed to Bolsonaro). This therefore provided for both data and methodological triangulation (Flick and von Kardoff 2004).

While there is a body of academic literature on digital authoritarianism, there are few academic papers on the implementation of digital surveillance technology in Brazil, particularly with a focus on Chinese technology. Hence, grey literature and primary documentation were fundamental to complement the existing academic literature. Further, we also conducted interviews with local officials who participated in negotiations and/or received technical missions from Chinese tech companies. However, a series of obstacles severely reduced the number of possible interviews:

1. Our research started in late March 2022 and 2022 was an electoral year in Brazil, with all officials running for office required to have left government by April 1. Hence, many of those who participated in the relevant negotiations had left government at the beginning of our research; they were campaigning and were unavailable for interviews.
2. In two states, the local official who had negotiated with the Chinese tech company had been accused of being involved in corruption relating to procurement from China. One of them was removed from office and neither was available for interview.
3. In one state, the official who negotiated with the Chinese tech company was removed from office because he was filmed in the integrated surveillance center, where the feeds of all city cameras are centralized, when the police was brutally repressing a peaceful political demonstration, begging the question if the order for this action came from him.

More generally, there was a lack of willingness of local officials to be interviewed in relation to issues deemed sensitive such as surveillance or relations with Chinese firms. Given these obstacles, despite seeking interviews with eleven officials, we were ultimately only able to interview four local officials: three in bureaus of public security in Pernambuco, Piauí, and Rio Grande do Norte, and one in "Consórcio Nordeste" (Northeast Consortium; see explanation below).

Research design

The research was carried out in two stages:

1. The first stage examined, in general terms, the adoption of surveillance technologies, particularly surveillance cameras with facial recognition, in Brazil, through the analysis of selected politically-representative localities, since the beginning of the presidential term of Jair Bolsonaro in 2019.
2. The second analyzed specifically the relationship between China and the state governments of the Northeast region, stronghold of political opposition to the federal government, in the adoption of these technologies.

In the first stage, we selected local governments based on the following criteria: i) the state or city has had relevant experience with surveillance technology including facial recognition; ii) the combination of states and cities is representative of the political spectrum; iii) the combination of states and cities is representative of the experiences of different macro regions of Brazil (South, Southeast, Midwest, North and Northeast). In enacting the second criterion, we wanted to ensure representation ranging from i) the institutional left[4] opposition to Bolsonaro, passing through ii) the right-wing opposition (or partial opposition – that means, which may agree with several economic points in Bolsonaro's programme but remained part of the political opposition) to iii) local government allies on the far-right.

Our political classification of states and cities was based on the party of the chief of the executive branch, as follows[5]:

1. Partido dos Trabalhadores (PT, Workers' Party), Partido Socialista Brasileiro (PSB, Brazilian Socialist Party), and Partido Comunista do Brasil (PC do B, Communist Party of Brazil) as the institutional left/center-left,
2. Partido Social Democrático (PSD, Social Democratic Party) and Movimento Democrático Brasileiro (MDB, Brazilian Democratic Movement) as center-right,
3. Partido da Social Democracia Brasileira (PSDB, Brazilian Social Democracy Party) as right,
4. Partido Social Liberal (PSL, Social Liberal Party) as far-right.

More important than precisely defining the content of this classification, this scheme indicates how, from a relative point of view, the different parties position themselves. In a simplistic and summarized way, the more to the right the party, the greater its tendency to support punitive policies and to increase ostensive repression in dealing with violence, and to support liberal policies in the economic field. In contrast, the more to the left the party, the greater the tendency to support less repressive policies and to focus on policies aiming at social inclusion, as well as to support a greater role of the state in the promotion of public policies. Such differentiation is common to the experiences of a number of other countries and, as will be seen, the important point highlighted is that adoption of surveillance technologies has been undertaken by governments right across the political spectrum shown above.

Table 1 displays the states and cities selected to represent Brazil's political spectrum in the first stage of the research, namely: a) at the far-right, Rondônia and Roraima, which were Bolsonaro's allies; b) as the partial opposition, São Paulo, which was initially an ally at the right but flipped, plus the city of Aparecida de Goiânia, and Foz do Iguaçu at the center-right; and c) as the opposition, Espírito Santo and the city of Campinas.[6]

The second stage of the research was dedicated to a particular political geometry that seems to be propelling China's digital expansion: the political relations between the Northeastern governments of Brazil and China. The Northeast (Figure 1) is the poorest region of Brazil. During the 2018 presidential elections, it was the only one of the five macro-regions in Brazil where Bolsonaro lost in every single state, and all states elected governments that opposed or partially opposed Bolsonaro's federal government (Table 2). The Northeastern states formed, during Bolsonaro's government, a political forum called "Consórcio Nordeste." Among many other political actions, this forum acted as a way for the Northeastern governments to negotiate directly with China, bypassing the federal government. Hence, in the research's second stage, we analyzed the digital surveillance deals made by the states of the Northeast region and particularly identified those that might be considered a result of political talks and visits to China.

Findings

Overall, the evidence we gathered showed the involvement of Brazilian state and city governments across the political spectrum in the acquisition of Chinese digital surveillance technologies, and not merely those with authoritarian inclinations, while we found not only China as a supplier but also Western democracies.

Stage 1: The adoption of surveillance technologies with facial recognition in states and cities across the political spectrum in Brazil

On the far-right, despite Bolsonaro's political tensions with China, both of the representative states allied with Bolsonaro's government acquired and/or implemented Chinese digital surveillance technologies. In 2021, Rondônia acquired police special vehicles with security cameras with facial and license plate recognition systems through a bid won by a consortium of local enterprises – TB and Tecway – that supplied Dahua products (Ferreira 2021).

The case of Roraima is of particular interest as it was Bolsonaro's government itself, in 2020, through the Brazilian Agency for Industrial Development – a federal agency attached to the Ministry of Economy – which donated Hikvision cameras with facial recognition to the state for the Fronteira Tech project to monitor the frontier between Brazil and Bolivia (g1 2021; Hikvision 2022). Hence, not only did the political tensions with China and the echo of the rhetoric of digital authoritarianism in Bolsonaro's

Table 1. Selected states and cities representative of the Brazilian political spectrum.

Region	State/city	Population Year-end 2022	Governing party (2019-2022)[a]	Political profile	Position relative to Bolsonaro
North	Rondônia [state]	1.6 million	PSL	Far-right	Ally
North	Rorama [state]	0.6 million	PSL[b]	Far-right	Ally
Southeast	São Paulo [state]	46.0 million	PSDB	Right	Partial opposition (flip)
Center-west	Aparecida de Goiânia [city]	0.5 million	MDB	Center-right	Partial opposition
South	Foz do Iguaçu [city]	0.3 million	PSD	Center-right	Partial opposition
Southeast	Espírito Santo [state]	4.0 million	PSB	Center-left	Opposition
Southeast	Campinas [city]	1.1 million	PSB[c]	Center-left	Opposition

Notes: [a]These years refer to Bolsonaro's presidential term. Local governments' terms may differ, so the column specifies the governing parties during Bolsonaro's presidential term. [b]In 2021, the acting governor Denarium changed political party, however, remaining with the same political profile. [c]During these four years, the PSB stayed in office between 2019 and 2020, when the relevant facts discussed in the article occurred.

Source: Population data from Brazilian Institute of Geography and Statistics (Instituto Brasileiro de Geografia e Estatística, IBGE) (2023) and data on the ruling parties from the Superior Electoral Court (TSE) (2023). Elaborated by the authors.

Figure 1. Brazilian states and macro-regions. *Source:* Brazilian Institute of Geography and Statistics (Instituto Brasileiro de Geografia e Estatística, IBGE) (2023), adapted by the authors.

Table 2. Northeast states' political profile.

Northeast states	Population	Governing party (2019-2022)[a]	Political profile	Position relative to Bolsonaro
Bahia	14.7 million	PT	Center-left	Opposition
Pernambuco	9.1 million	PSB	Center-left	Opposition
Ceará	8.9 million	PT	Center-left	Opposition
Maranhão	6.8 million	PCdoB/PSB	Center-left	Opposition
Paraíba	4.0 million	PSB	Center-left	Opposition
Rio Grande do Norte	3.3 million	PT	Center-left	Opposition
Alagoas	3.1 million	MDB	Center-right	Partial opposition
Piauí	2.8 million	PT	Center-left	Opposition
Sergipe	2.2 million	PSD	Center-right	Partial opposition

Notes: [a]These years refer to Bolsonaro's presidential term. Local governments' terms may differ, so the column specifies the governing parties during Bolsonaro's presidential term.
Source: Population data from end of 2022 [Brazilian Institute of Geography and Statistics (Instituto Brasileiro de Geografia e Estatística, IBGE) 2023] and data on the ruling parties from the TSE (2023). Elaborated by the authors.

government not impede his far-right allies in local government from acquiring Chinese surveillance technology, but also his own government made such acquisitions, in blatant contradiction with its discourse. In here we find the same pattern of action as in the 5G case, since after accusing China of using 5G as a platform for spying and claiming its adherence to the US Clean Network Initiative targeted against Huawei and ZTE, Bolsonaro's government ultimately enabled Chinese enterprises to participate in Brazilian networks due to cost reasons, except for the separate network for governmental agencies (Boadle 2020; Kahhat 2022). As a result of these acquisitions, Bolsonaro's government and its local allies in state governments directly contributed to China's digital expansion in surveillance technologies.

The partial opposition includes both the traditional right that initially supported Bolsonaro but flipped due to his denialism of the coronavirus pandemic, represented by São Paulo, and the center-right, represented by Foz do Iguaçu in the state of Paraná and Aparecida de Goiânia in the state of Goiás. In all cases, there was implementation of facial recognition technology for public security. Aparecida de Goiânia contracted from Huawei the implementation of 600 km of fiber optics supporting surveillance cameras with facial recognition – a project for which the city was awarded a Smart City international prize (Cardoso 2019; Tavares 2019). In Foz do Iguaçu, the federal Brazilian Agency for Industrial Development was again responsible for implementing Hikvision cameras with facial recognition in the context of the FronteiraTech project; this time to monitor the frontier with Paraguay (Hikvision 2022).

In the case of São Paulo, facial recognition was introduced as part of an automated biometric identification system (ABIS) for the state's Civil Police (Governo do Estado de São Paulo 2020). The Civil Police acquired the facial recognition system through a bid won in 2019 by the French company Thales Dis (Governo do Estado de São Paulo 2020), whose large database of biometrics can be linked with images extracted from surveillance cameras dispersed throughout the state (Boselli 2020).

It is noteworthy that, in contrast to surveillance cameras in which Chinese providers seem to predominate, in the supply of facial recognition technology in ABIS, French suppliers stand out in Brazil. Not only did Thales Dis provide the São Paulo system, but also Bolsonaro's government acquired through a bid, in 2021, an ABIS for the Brazilian Federal Police from a consortium formed by Iafis Brasil and the French multinational Idemia[7] (Telesíntese 2021). According to Tagiaroli (2021), such a system "will be capable of crossing the biometric data, as fingerprints and images of cameras with facial recognition, of 50 million Brazilians in the next 48 months … it can be expanded to reach 200 million – almost the totality of the Brazilian population"[8]. Hence, in the provision of facial recognition software, we can find enterprises of a democratic country without discrimination supplying surveillance technology for both democratic political forces at the local level and authoritarian-leaning political forces at the federal level.

Regarding the opposition, at the center-left, represented by the state of Espírito Santo and the city of Campinas in the state of São Paulo, both localities were involved with Chinese surveillance technologies. In the case of Campinas, the city received a donation of surveillance cameras with facial recognition from Huawei to be tested in 2019 – in order to become an open-air laboratory – but eventually decided not to invest due to the high rate of misidentification in open spaces with huge flows of people (Reis et al. 2021). This is not the sole instance in which Chinese firms donated surveillance technology to Brazilian cities. For example, in 2017, the former mayor of São Paulo (and at the time governor of São Paulo) visited both Hikvision and Dahua. In each case, he asked for and was given a donation of 1,000 surveillance cameras and one drone for the city (Balloussier 2017). Additionally, in 2019, Mogi das Cruzes, a city in the state of São Paulo, received a donation of surveillance cameras with facial recognition from Dahua for a safe city project (Reis et al. 2021; Secretaria de Segurança de Mogi das Cruzes 2019).

In the case of Espírito Santo, the state implemented a call for the acquisition of surveillance cameras with facial and license plate recognition, and a consortium of two local enterprises – Perkóns and Velsis – along with Dahua, was the winner (Fardin 2022). However, the process was contested, with an accusation of corruption emerging in the Brazilian media through a supposedly leaked pen drive containing internal documents and emails of Dahua. This was said to show Dahua to have been involved in the specifications of the call before it went public in order to guarantee that only its products would fit the call's specifications (Gordon 2021; Rangel 2021). Despite the accusations, Dahua remained part of the contract consortium and has already implemented the first phase of the surveillance project, in which 1,160 surveillance cameras feed into a Dahua big data-based analytics platform (Infor Channel 2022; Tostes 2022). Regardless of the validity of the accusations, this exemplifies the building of ties and expansion of surveillance deals by Chinese firms with democratic political forces in Brazil. This is particularly true in the stronghold of political opposition to the federal government, the Northeast region, as discussed next.

Stage 2: Chinese surveillance technologies in the Northeast region

Chinese firms were already providing surveillance technology to the Northeast region prior to Bolsonaro's government and to the state governments elected during his time in office. In 2018, in the city of Salvador in the state of Bahia, a pilot surveillance project implemented cameras with facial recognition, updating and expanding on previous surveillance technologies implemented since 2014. This surveillance infrastructure involved a Spanish enterprise as distributor: El Corte Inglés; a Swedish camera provider: Axis; and Chinese camera suppliers: Huawei and Hikvision (Secretaria de Segurança Pública do Estado da Bahia 2019; Reis et al. 2021). In Ceará state in 2017, Hikvision provided surveillance cameras without facial recognition through a consortium with two local enterprises, IPQ Tecnologia and Sysdesign (Governo do Estado do Ceará 2017).

During Bolsonaro's government, these states experienced a massive expansion of their surveillance systems. In the case of Bahia, Salvador's pilot program was expanded to 77 other cities (Gonçalves 2021). The winning consortium was led by Brazilian firms, Avante SA and Oi SA, but according to Bahia's governor, the actual camera suppliers are Chinese enterprises (Jornal Grande Bahia 2021). In the case of Ceará, a call for the implementation of surveillance cameras with facial recognition was opened in 2020, and a local enterprise distributing Dahua products, IPQ Tecnologia, emerged as the winner in 2022 (Governo do Estado do Ceará 2022). Similar to the case of Espírito Santo, the bid process was contested and was paralyzed for more than a year due to suspicions of Dahua potentially benefitting through call specifications tailored by the state government to fit its products (Uellner e Silva and Santos 2020). These allegations appear in a context in which Dahua had built close ties with the state government since 2019, when the state governor and local officials visited Hangzhou, where the company is headquartered, and met with Dahua's CEO, Fu Liquan, and the state received a technical mission from the company (Governo do Estado do Ceará 2019).

Several other states introduced facial recognition-enabled surveillance camera systems for public security during the period under scrutiny, for instance, Sergipe, Rio Grande do Norte, and Paraíba. In the case of Paraíba, the initial provider was a British company, Facewatch, whose system was installed in 2019 by a private enterprise for a large popular festival. Nonetheless, when the state entered the scene and opened a call for bids for purposes of public security, Hikvision emerged as the major winner and dominated the market, surpassing Facewatch (Pisanu et al. 2021; Reis et al. 2021). In Rio Grande do Norte, surveillance cameras with facial recognition were first introduced in 2019 (Tribuna do Norte 2019). A local enterprise, Interjato, won the bid and supplied Hikvision's and Huawei's cameras to the state (interview Rio Grande do Norte 2022). However, the facial recognition software was not Chinese; instead, Interjato supplied Intellect, a program developed by the Russian enterprise Axxonsoft (interview Rio Grande do Norte 2022). Other states, such as Pernambuco and Piauí, also sought to introduce these technologies, and opened calls for bids in 2022 (interview Pernambuco; interview Piauí).

Regarding the sources of funding for the acquisition and implementation of these surveillance infrastructures, a multiplicity of sources has been observed. In Rio Grande do Norte, acquisition of the Chinese and Russian facial recognition surveillance technologies (*via* the local enterprise Interjato) was financed with funds from the World Bank (Tribuna do Norte 2019; interview Rio Grande do Norte). In Pelourinho, in Salvador in the state of Bahia, a project to implement facial recognition surveillance technology used resources from the Inter-American Development Bank (Alves 2021). In both instances, surveillance technologies were thus funded by established institutions of development finance dominated by the democracies of the Global North.

Beyond international sources of funding, and those provided by local-level budgets, there have also been national funds allocated for the implementation of surveillance systems. For instance, the Brazilian Development Bank (BNDES), in the city of Teresina in Piauí, funded a "project that has as a focus, regions with high rates of criminality" (BNDES 2020). Alongside its role noted above in other regions, in the Northeast, the Brazilian Agency for Industrial Development funded a smart city project in Petrolina in the state of Pernambuco (Hikvision 2022), as well as a project in the city of Itabaiana in Sergipe (Connected Smart Cities 2022) and the city of Campina Grande in Paraíba – the latter in partnership with the Northeast Development Superintendence (Sudene) (Ministério do Desenvolvimento Regional 2022). Additionally, the National Fund for Public Security was earmarking funds for the implementation of facial recognition since 2019 (Martins 2020) by means of ordinance n°793, through which the federal government regulated financial support for actions to combat violent crime, "fostering the implementation of video surveillance systems with facial recognition solutions, by optical character recognition – OCR, use of artificial intelligence or others" (our translation) (Diário Oficial da União (DOU) 2019). These funds were used to support a pilot project in each region of the country (Peduzzi 2019).

At least in the case of Petrolina – as well as in the initiatives of FronteiraTech discussed in the previous subsection – Brazilian federal funds, through the Brazilian Agency for Industrial Development, were spent on Chinese surveillance technology. In contrast, in none of the surveillance projects researched in this study, and from neither interviews nor documentation, was it possible to identify any Chinese funding, even though we could not rule out the possibility that such funding existed.

As expected in the Northeast, due to the under-development of the region, one of the major constraints for the spread of digital surveillance technologies is the lack of proper infrastructure. Meanwhile, the demand for surveillance technologies itself becomes a vector for the development of such infrastructure. In this context, the operations of Huawei and ZTE in the region should be differentiated from those of Hikvision and Dahua. While these are all providers of surveillance cameras with facial recognition, Hikvision and Dahua have a surveillance-only strategy, i.e., to just provide cameras and facial recognition software, even if adapted to different contexts and users. By contrast, Huawei and ZTE, which operate in multiple layers of the ICT stack, have an integrated approach to expansion in the region and are able to implement both vertical and horizontal integration strategies, as explained next.

According to Bruno Zitnick, the director of Public and Government Relations at Huawei Brazil:

> Huawei has a range of options for smart cities devices such as security cameras and facial recognition and license plate cameras, solutions for city control that bring cost savings to public management, and for that connectivity is essential. We are seeing in the current scenario everyone talking about the arrival of 5G, but we also have to understand that the expansion of fiber optics in the infrastructure of cities and that the implementation of these technologies makes cities smart (Zitnick quoted in Prefeitura de 2021)

As this quote reveals, smart cities are largely conceived of as surveillance technologies, and the development of fiber optics as a means for the development of surveillance infrastructure. In this context, surveillance cameras can be seen as the first (and preferred) application by which these Chinese tech firms seek to expand into the application layer after they have built a foundation in the network equipment and telecommunication infrastructure layers. Hence, their strategy is to vertically integrate from their infrastructural foundations into applications.

These infrastructural foundations, from which both companies have been seeking to expand into surveillance applications, are strong in the Northeast region. It hosts the transatlantic link to Africa built by Huawei in 2018 in the city of Fortaleza, Ceará (Huawei 2018). Meanwhile in Piauí, where a bid was open at the time of research for the acquisition of surveillance cameras with facial recognition (interview Piauí), ZTE – along with Cisco, Gemelo, and Furukawa – provides the fiber optic infrastructure for the public-private partnership program, Connected Piauí (Piauí Conectado), which seeks to connect the whole state (Piauí Hoje 2020). Due to this program, Piauí, despite being one of the poorest states of the country, has the fastest internet in Brazil (Méliuz apud Governo do Estado do Piauí 2021). Piauí's program is a model for a similar program for the whole of the Northeast region that was under discussion by Consórcio Nordeste – Connected Northeast (Nordeste Conectado) – in which both Huawei and ZTE may well be involved (interview Consórcio Nordeste). Furthermore, following the many visits made by Northeastern governors and officials to China in 2019, the state of Alagoas consolidated further investments to double the capacity of the Chinese ZTT Cable fiber optics factory hosted in the state, which serves not only the region but also the whole country (Tribuna do Agreste 2019).

If the surveillance and facial recognition market constitutes the preferred and first application through which Chinese conglomerates Huawei and ZTE target the application layer, this market al.so represents a "bridge" between the telecom infrastructure market and the broader multi-domain application market. The surveillance market is hence the entry point into the application layer from where they seek to expand further to other sectoral applications, in a horizontal integration strategy, particularly to other governmental services. For example, according to Ricardo Mansano, Huawei's solutions manager: "Our suggestion is for governments to start from the setting up of the part of public security and traffic, which can be adapted to other ends" (Mansano quoted in Balago 2021).

The horizontal integration strategy stemming from the surveillance market is particularly evident in the operations of Huawei in Bahia. Here, the state government started by acquiring surveillance technology from the company and, subsequently, moved to buy education and health "solutions." These acquisitions were so large that Huawei decided to open a South America technological demonstration center for government – which includes public security, education, and health – in Bahia to showcase its "solutions" for the continent (Gonçalves 2021).

Huawei's operations in Bahia – a state where, as noted, its surveillance system is being scaled out to 77 cities and where Huawei's horizontal integration strategy has thrived – is arguably the most successful and advanced case of a Chinese tech firm's digital expansion into government at the local level in Brazil.

Such expansion has been built through the development of close political ties between Bahia and China since 2019, when the governor visited China. According to Tian Min, General Consul of China in Rio de Janeiro:

> The State of Bahia has been keeping a friendship and cooperation agreement with the Chinese government. The governor Rui Costa has been personally to China and has promoted even more this pragmatic bilateral partnership, and he has all our support. In this moment, both parts are striving to develop diverse projects, and the Chinese government supports the Chinese enterprises respecting the rules of the market to develop these projects in Bahia. (quoted in Jornal Grande Bahia 2021)

Hence, the political relations between the governments of Bahia and China have not only propelled the digital expansion of Chinese firms into the governmental services of Bahia but have also acted as a point of support for the further expansion of Chinese enterprises in the country and the continent through its demonstration center. Emblematically, Rui Costa, Bahia's governor, in a virtual seminar about digital technology hosted by the Chinese Embassy in Brazil and the Chinese General Consulate in Rio de Janeiro, stated:

> I come here to give my extremely positive testimony about the relationship between Bahia and China, and say that possibilities are very large for the use of technology for the development of health and education, in the advancement of smart cities, in the pursuit of a better public security, using technological tools (quoted in Jornal Grande Bahia 2021).

Discussion

As evidenced in our review above, a significant tranche of publications on China's digital expansion in the Global South is imbricated in a particular US-centric discourse that incorporates a rhetoric identifying China's digital exports as the epicenter of digital authoritarianism (Cheney 2019; Khalil 2020; Shahbaz 2018; Polyakova and Meserole 2019). Both influenced by and influencing this literature, US foreign policy has adopted a position and rhetoric that portrays China as a digital threat and this has found an echo in the politics of some Global South countries particularly, but not solely, during election campaigns, with Brazil being a prime example. Some few papers have emerged challenging the notion of Chinese exceptionalism in export of surveillance systems that can be used for authoritarian purposes (e.g. Lugt 2021; Venturini and Garay 2021), but we found no in-depth investigation assessing whether anti-China rhetoric in the Global South materializes in procurement decisions for digital systems.

Our main contribution to the literature, then, is the finding that there is no such materialization in Brazil. It is beyond the scope of this study to assess whether anti-China rhetoric in Brazil has been deliberately confected solely for public consumption but certainly we can see it has little material substance in terms of impacting procurement. Despite the rhetoric of Jair Bolsonaro and allies against Chinese investment and trade, including specific criticism of Chinese digital exports, we find that there was a broad and sustained procurement of Chinese surveillance technologies in Brazil during his presidency, based on the overwhelming success of Chinese companies in public bids due in part to their capacity for offering the lowest prices. This procurement included those agencies of government specifically aligned to Bolsonaro: the federal government itself and local government allies of the far-right. However, it also included local governments right across the political spectrum, suggesting there is no real connection between rhetoric and procurement.

If "digital authoritarianism" as a concept and rhetoric was conceived as a US strategy to contain China's digital expansion in Global South markets, it does not appear to have worked in Bolsonaro's Brazil. Despite Bolsonaro's anti-China platform, the US foreign policy founda echo in Brazilian foreign policy during the Trump Administration, and the political tensions that were generated with China, at the end of the day, these manifestations mostly remained at the rhetorical level. Not only did any attempted US influence on Brazil's federal government not carry through to the local level, but also the federal government itself did not translate its discourse into practice, as it itself was involved in many acquisitions of Chinese surveillance technologies.

For those Global South countries which are part of China's Belt and Road Initiative (BRI), including its Digital Silk Road components, the literature portrays digital procurement as significantly linked to actions of the Chinese state including Chinese state funding (Erie and Streinz 2021; Tugendhat and Voo 2021). Brazil is not an official member of BRI and, perhaps linked to this, we found no evidence of Chinese state funding, at least from the more-detailed investigation of the Northeast region. Funding has come from local, federal, and international sources. The Chinese embassy in Brazil has been an important actor; for example, facilitating the invitations for local and other government agencies in Brazil to visit

China. But the core activities have been visits by government officials to the headquarters of Chinese tech firms, and counter-visits of technical missions from these firms to Brazilian cities and states. It is thus the relationships between Chinese tech firms and Brazilian government agencies that have underpinned procurement, though sometimes with accusations that the relationships had become too close as in the case of Dahua in the states of Espírito Santo and Ceará. Considering that Dahua, Hikvision, and ZTE are state-owned or partially state-owned companies, this shows that China's digital engagements with Global South countries is more varied than that of activities directed or led solely by the Chinese central government.

US rhetoric and also some strands of the literature on China's digital expansion associate digital authoritarianism with China on the supply side, and with national authoritarian or quasi-authoritarian regimes in the Global South on the demand side (Black 2019; Cheney 2019). Our key contribution in this regard has been to show that, in investigating the spread of China's digital surveillance systems, attention must be paid not merely to national but also to sub-national governments. Given they are the main bodies responsible for public security, it is city and state governments that have been the primary locus for the procurement of Chinese surveillance technologies, their implementation, and all associated issues.

In two ways, our findings here provide support for emergent research that has been critical of surveillance-focused literature about China's expansion in the Global South. First, in supporting research that challenges the notion of a Chinese monopoly of surveillance exports (e.g. Lugt 2021; Venturini and Garay 2021). Our case study has shown that, while Chinese companies have dominated the Brazilian market for facial recognition-enabled surveillance systems, China is by no means the sole source for these technologies. Firms from Western democracies, for example, have provided facial recognition software to both private and public security forces, in the case of France and the United Kingdom; acted as distributors of Chinese surveillance technologies, in the case of Spain; and supplied surveillance cameras in competition with China, in the case of Sweden. It is notable, though, that we only found one example of a Western firm competing head-on with Chinese firms in supply of surveillance cameras; a market in which Chinese firms seem to have a strong competitive edge. Most Western firms were instead competing in complementary market niches such as software, distribution, and systems integration. Building on this, our findings contradict the literature that portrays Chinese surveillance firms as detached entities acting in isolation from other actors (Feldstein 2019; Shahbaz 2018). Chinese firms were part of consortia involving local and, not uncommonly, Western firms, and are thus one part of an ecosystem.

Our findings also support literature seeking to open up the simplistic association of Chinese surveillance technologies with un-democratic, authoritarian regimes of the Global South (Feldstein 2019; Woodhams 2020). This applies in the general sense that Brazil is a democracy that has shown a good appetite for these technologies. It also applies more specifically, given we have shown that, while far-right governments in Brazil have been adopting Chinese surveillance technology, so also have those of the center-right and center-left. Any picture focused solely on Chinese technology supply meeting undemocratic, authoritarian national government demand is shown to be far too simplistic, with multiple sources and levels of both supply and demand emerging from these cases, including some instances of demand in the absence of any Chinese supplier[9].

Conclusions

The installation of digital surveillance cameras across the urban landscape became commonplace in the higher-income countries of the world during the 2000s. From the 2010s, the countries of the Global South became increasingly involved in absorption of these infrastructures and their associated practices. With China's rapid ascent as a supplier of surveillance equipment, the Global South then found itself part of a rush for markets and spheres of influence by the technologically-capable great powers, including US geopolitical and economic interests promoting the idea that China was exporting "digital authoritarianism" and should be blocked from so doing. This was part of a broader US-led attempt to resist the rise of China's engagement in the Global South; an attempt that found echoes in the anti-China rhetoric of some Global South regimes, including that of Jair Bolsonaro in Brazil.

Our findings, though, have found no evidence that the anti-China rhetoric of the Bolsonaro regime impacted procurement of surveillance technologies from China. Chinese firms have been the overwhelming beneficiaries of the active build-up of surveillance infrastructures in Brazil, supplying cameras, software, and the associated infrastructure such as fiber optic cables to buyers across the political spectrum and at federal, state, and city levels. Invitations to visit China and Chinese tech firms and the building of relations with Brazilian political actors have occurred with far-right parliamentarians and sub-national officials, as well as for those of the center-right and center-left, including those from Northeast of Brazil, stronghold of political opposition to Bolsonaro's government. If it is a US device to limit Chinese exports, the construct of "digital authoritarianism" appears not to have worked as intended, at least in this one instance of Brazil. Instead, we found supply of surveillance technologies coming from many countries including a number of Western nations, and demand coming from many different types of government in Brazil including those with both more and less authoritarian leanings.

While the Chinese state has played a role through the local Chinese embassy, it is Chinese tech firms who emerge as the dominant actor on the supply side, albeit, except for Huawei, these are state-owned or partially state-owned. Firms such as Huawei and ZTE may prioritize full-stack, integrated strategies but others such as Hikvision and Dahua supply technologies that form part of an overall multi-source package that often includes Western technologies. However, the lack of evidence of Chinese state funding indicates a more varied model of technology exports to the Global South than is often presented.

Indeed, our findings call for a move away from Sino-centricity toward at least a more balanced view that understands the role of the domestic context in adoption and use of surveillance technologies. One result is that, rather than analyzing just at the national government level as almost all past work has done, there is a need to include the sub-national level in the analysis because it is an important governance level for decision-making about public security.

Just as our broader understanding of demand for surveillance technologies in Brazil should be situated in the domestic context, the country of origin of these technologies is less relevant than other associated factors. The fact that these technologies are Chinese, French, US, etc., is less important than the fact that they are being implemented at all.

Chinese companies such as Dahua and Hikvision have been accused of providing facial recognition cameras that enable police forces to recognize certain population groups, and such capabilities are said to have been employed in the Xinjiang province, contributing to the ethnic segregation of the Uyghurs (Bhuiyan 2021). Even if these accusations are confirmed, this would only be part of a more general trend intrinsic to facial recognition surveillance technologies, which are a current tool to amplify the power of police forces to exercise control in ways that breach privacy, engender racial[10] and gender biases, and undermine freedom of assembly and association. Fundamentally, it is well known that the causes of crime and violence in Brazil are rooted in the extreme income and wealth inequalities of the country (Sachsida et al. 2010). Upgradation of the state's repressive apparatus does not address that root cause. In effect, the bigger issue is surveillance technology and its use and regulation in Brazil, not the country of origin of the technology.

This case also speaks to another much broader and long-standing issue in Brazil, which is its dependency on foreign technology (Goedhuys and Veugelers 2012). Procurement and use of technology should not be mistaken for development. If the productive structures and capabilities remain outside Brazil, then it does not develop its own capabilities and its technological dependency increases. If surveillance technologies – Chinese or otherwise – are just imported, then they will fit this pattern, despite the defense of digital surveillance projects by local governments and federal governmental agencies on the grounds of promoting development. Furthermore, as seen in the strategies of some Chinese firms, digital surveillance technologies are the gateway to the sale of digital "solutions" in other sectors such as health and education. From this perspective, policies would be needed to counter the current approach; ensuring greater technology transfer from all foreign multinationals and greater investment in local research and development (and science and technology more generally) in order to build up local innovation and production capabilities in areas of social and economic interest for the population, instead of focusing on strengthening the repressive apparatuses and associated technological capabilities of the state.

In sum, while the expansion of Chinese surveillance technologies in the Global South is an important issue, we must always recognize the broader domestic context into which these technologies are inserted.

Notes

1. We thank Carlos Aguiar de Medeiros for his contribution in bringing forward these arguments.
2. "China's digital efforts erode democratic values and enable the rise of digital authoritarianism around the world. At best, China is selling digital technology that has remarkable capacity for surveillance and control to authoritarian or authoritarian-leaning countries with no second thought for the consequences. At worst, China is pairing its economic investment with aggressive outreach and training on internet

governance and domestic regulations to further inculcate authoritarian values and methods of social control." (Minority Staff, US Senate Committee on Foreign Relations 2020, 26).

3. If any discussion on digital authoritarianism and the threat of Chinese technologies is to be taken seriously, then one should set the record straight regarding the threats posed by the competing technologies available in the market, for it has been demonstrated that importing US technology has meant mass surveillance and use of personal data by the US government. Snowden revealed that the US international surveillance system, in cooperation with the other Five Eyes members (intelligence agencies of Australia, the UK, New Zealand, and Canada), operated in all the distinct layers of the telecommunication system: from the physical layer, with submarine fibre optic cable taps through collaboration with "intercept partners" (MacAskill et al. 2013), i.e. commercial cable operators such as British BT and Vodafone Cable, and American Verizon Business (Ball, Harding, and Garside 2013); passing through cooperation with telecom operators such as AT&T to couple surveillance equipment to the operator's routers and switches and redirect data to the National Security Agency (Gallagher and Moltke 2016); up to the application layer, in partnership with internet service providers such as Google, Yahoo, Facebook, Skype, Microsoft, Apple, YouTube, AOL and Paltalk, in Prism's framework (NSA 2013).
4. Includes the left and the center-left.
5. Although not necessarily under the same rubric, the relative positioning of the parties presented above is consistent with the new ideological classification of Brazilian political parties presented by Bolognesi, Ribeiro, and Codato (2021).
6. This classification is not strictly rigid and was guided by the position of the states' and cities' governing parties relative to Bolsonaro, even though, in some cases, one might find some statements from the local government chief executive in disagreement with the general line adopted by his/her party. Such are the cases of Campinas and Foz do Iguaçu over the latter years of Bolsonaro's time in office, when the mayors appeared to be more aligned with Bolsonaro and/or his political allies.
7. "Morpho Safran, now called IDEMIA … is a French multinational company dedicated to technology development, mainly focused on the sale of facial recognition products. The company has been criticized by Amnesty International for exporting digital surveillance technology to China, due to the human rights risk involved. IDEMIA was blamed for problems with the general election in Kenya in 2017, which resulted in the National Assembly cancelling its existing contracts and banning it from entering into new ones. The decision was repealed by the country's Supreme Court" (Venturini and Garay 2021, 12).
8. According to Zanatta (cited in Tagiaroli 2021), this system may be used for political persecution, though it would be illicit were it to be used by intelligence agencies and its use not to remain strictly confined to specific investigations for which the data is gathered. Zanatta's worries are plausible, especially after it came to light that an intelligence agency under Bolsonaro started to put together dossiers of antifascist public servants, particularly in public security and universities, and the government contracted an enterprise to monitor journalists according to their published standpoints vis-à-vis the government (Valente 2020a, 2020b).
9. Though we do acknowledge the argument that surveillance systems can introduce authoritarian tendencies into even democratic regimes (Hintz and Milan 2018).
10. In June 2022, a multiparty movement named "sai da minha cara" ("get out of my face") was formed by parliamentarians acting in state and municipal legislatures in 13 different states, seeking to present legal proposals to ban the use of facial recognition in public spaces (Nakagawa 2022).

Acknowledgements

This paper is part of a series from the project, "China's Digital Expansion in the Global South," funded by the Faculty of Humanities, University of Manchester, UK. Richard Heeks and Seth Schindler of the Global Development Institute, University of Manchester, were the facilitating editors.

Disclosure statement

No potential conflict of interest was reported by the author(s).

ORCID

Esther Majerowicz http://orcid.org/0000-0001-6055-2788
Miguel Henriques de Carvalho http://orcid.org/0009-0006-6917-3139

References

Alves, S. 2021. Pelourinho vai ganhar câmeras de reconhecimento facial; isso é bom ou ruim? *Tilt*, March 1st. Accessed December 10, 2023. https://www.uol.com.br/tilt/noticias/redacao/2021/03/01/pelourinho-vai-ganhar-cameras-de-reconhecimento-facial-isso-e-bom-ou-ruim.htm

Atha, K., J. Callahan, J. Chen, J. Drun, K. Green, B. Lafferty, J. McReynolds, J. Mulvenon, B. Rosen, and E. Walz. 2020. China's smart cities development (Research report prepared by SOS International LLC on behalf of the U.S.-China Economic and Security Review Commission) Accessed December 10, 2023. https://www.uscc.gov/sites/default/files/2020-04/China_Smart_Cities_Development.pdf

Balago, R. 2021. Tecnologias de smart cities da China prometem desafogar o trânsito. *Folha e São Paulo*, December 25. Accessed December 10, 2023. https://www1.folha.uol.com.br/mundo/2021/12/tecnologias-de-smart-cities-da-china-prometem-desafogar-o-transito.shtml

Ball, J., L. Harding, and J. Garside. 2013. BT and Vodafone among telecoms companies passing details to GCHQ. *The Guardian*, August 2. Accessed December 17, 2023. https://www.theguardian.com/business/2013/aug/02/telecoms-bt-vodafone-cables-gchq

Balloussier, A. V. 2017. Doria pede e ganha câmeras e drones de empresas Chinesas de segurança. *Folha de São Paulo*, July 25. Accessed December 10, 2023. https://www1.folha.uol.com.br/cotidiano/2017/07/1904096-doria-pede-e-ganha-cameras-e-drones-de-empresas-chinesas-de-seguranca.shtml

Belasques, P. B., B. Castro, G. Carneiro, R. Abrão, V. H. Santos, and A. T. Marra, dos. 2020. Relações subnacionais entre Brasil e China: No combate a pandemia e ao governo federal? *Observatório de Política Externa e da Inserção Internacional do Brasil*, June 26. Accessed December 17, 2023. https://opeb.org/2020/06/26/relacoes-subnacionais-entre-brasil-e-china-no-combate-a-pandemia-e-ao-governo-federal/

BIS (Bureau of Industry and Security, US Department of Commerce). 2019a. Addition of entities to the entity list. *The Federal Register* 84 (98):22961–8. Accessed December 10, 2023. https://www.govinfo.gov/content/pkg/FR-2019-05-21/pdf/2019-10616.pdf.

BIS (Bureau of Industry and Security, US Department of Commerce). 2019b. Addition of certain entities to the entity list. *The Federal Register* 84 (196):54002–9. Accessed December 10, 2023. https://www.govinfo.gov/content/pkg/FR-2019-10-09/pdf/2019-22210.pdf.

Bhuiyan, J. 2021. "There's cameras everywhere": Testimonies detail far-reaching surveillance of Uyghurs in China. *The Guardian*, September 30th. Accessed December 10, 2023. https://www.theguardian.com/world/2021/sep/30/uyghur-tribunal-testimony-surveillance-china

Black, D. 2019. Revitalizing democracy assistance to counter threats to democratization (Policy Paper No. 26). Washington, DC: German Marshall Fund of the United States. Accessed December 10, 2023. https://www.gmfus.org/news/revitalizing-democracy-assistance-counter-threats-democratization

BNDES. 2020. BNDES apoia investimento em tecnologia e inteligência para segurança pública em Teresina (PI). *BNDES.gov.br*, February 5. Accessed December 10, 2023. https://www.bndes.gov.br/wps/portal/site/home/imprensa/noticias/conteudo/bndes-apoia-investimento-em-tecnologia-e-inteligencia-para-seguranca-publica-em-teresina

Boadle, A. 2020. Brazil backs U.S. clean network proposal for transparent 5G technology. *Reuters*, November 11. Accessed December 10, 2023. https://www.reuters.com/article/us-usa-brazil-5g-idUSKBN27R06T

Bolognesi, B., E. Ribeiro, and A. Codato. 2021. A new ideological classification of the Brazilian political parties. *Dados* 66 (2):1–27. Accessed December 10, 2023. https://www.scielo.br/j/dados/a/zzyM3gzHD4P45WWdytXjZWg/?format=pdf&lang=en.

Boselli, A. 2020. Polícia paulista usará reconhecimento facial em investigações. *Consultor Jurídico*, January 29. Accessed December 10, 2023. https://www.conjur.com.br/2020-jan-29/policia-paulista-usara-reconhecimento-facial-investigacoes

Brazilian Institute of Geography and Statistics (Instituto Brasileiro de Geografia e Estatística, IBGE). 2023. Panorama do Censo 2022. Accessed December 20, 2023. https://censo2022.ibge.gov.br/panorama/index.html?localidade=BR&tema=1

Cardoso, M. 2019. Premiação internacional de cidade inteligente para Aparecida de Goiânia. *Diário da Manhã*, July 23. Accessed December 10, 2023. https://www.dm.com.br/cidades/2019/07/premiacao-internacional-de-cidade-inteligente-para-aparecida-de-goiania/

Carvalho, M., and V. Carneiro. 2022. Some remarks on the social and economic backsliding and the foreign sector stability. *Brazilian Keynesian Review* 8 (2):235–47. Accessed December 10, 2023. doi: 10.33834/bkr.v8i2.301.

Casado, L. 2022. Bolsonaro fala como candidato e diz que disputa será do "bem contra o mal." *Revista Veja*, March 27. Accessed December 10, 2023. https://veja.abril.com.br/politica/bolsonaro-fala-como-candidato-e-diz-que-disputa-sera-do-bem-contra-o-mal/

Cheney, C. 2019. China's Digital Silk Road: Strategic technological competition and exporting political illiberalism (Working Paper Vol. 19, WP8). Honolulu, HI: Pacific Forum. Accessed December 10, 2023. https://pacforum.org/wp-content/uploads/2019/08/issuesinsights_Vol19-WP8FINAL.pdf

Connected Smart Cities. 2022. Município sergipano investe em projeto de cidades inteligentes da ABDI. *Conteúdos Cidades*, April 18. Accessed December 10, 2023. https://portal.connectedsmartcities.com.br/2022/04/18/municipio-sergipano-investe-em-projeto-de-cidades-inteligentes-da-abdi/

Diário Oficial da União (DOU). 2019. *Portaria N° 793*, October 24, 55-56. Accessed December 10, 2023 https://dspace.mj.gov.br/bitstream/1/1380/4/PRT_GM_2019_793.pdf

Erie, M. S., and T. Streinz. 2021. The Beijing effect: China's Digital Silk Road as transnational data governance. *New York University Journal of International Law and Politics* 54 (1):1–92.

Fardin, A. 2022. OAB pede na Justiça afastamento e bloqueio dos bens de cúpula governista por suspeita de fraude em licitação de R$140 milhões no Detran/ES. *Opinião ES*, March 18. Accessed December 10, 2023. https://alertaespiritosanto.com.br/noticia/805/oab-pede-na-justica-afastamento-e-bloqueio-dos-bens-de-cupula-governista-por-suspeita-de-fraude-em-licitacao-de-r-140-milhoes-no-detran-es

Feldstein, S. 2019. The global expansion of AI surveillance (Working Paper). Washington, DC: Carnegie Endowment for International Peace. Accessed December 10, 2023. https://carnegieendowment.org/2019/09/17/global-expansion-of-ai-surveillance-pub-79847

Ferreira, F. 2021. Rondônia é o primeiro estado da América Latina a adotar tecnologias para a implantação de IA, reconhecimento facial e placas em viaturas. *Revista Segurança Eletrônica*, March, 18–19. Accessed December 17, 2023. https://issuu.com/revistasegurancaeletronica/docs/revista_capa_ed50_issu

Flick, U., and E. von Kardoff. 2004. Triangulation in qualitative research. In *A companion to qualitative research*, eds. U. Flicki, and I. Steinke, 178–83. London: Sage.

g1. 2021. Roraima instala câmeras de monitoramento na fronteira do Brasil com a Venezuela. *g1*, September 9. Accessed December 10, 2023. https://g1.globo.com/rr/roraima/

noticia/2021/09/09/roraima-instala-cameras-de-monitoramento-na-fronteira-do-brasil-com-a-venezuela.ghtml

Gaffney, C., and C. Robertson. 2018. Smarter than smart: Rio de Janeiro's flawed emergence as a smart city. *Journal of Urban Technology* 25 (3):47–64. doi: 10.1080/10630732.2015.1102423.

Gallagher, R., and H. Moltke. 2016. TITANPOINTE: The NSA's spy hub in New York, hidden in plain sight. *The Intercept*, November 16. Accessed December 10, 2023. https://theintercept.com/2016/11/16/the-nsas-spy-hub-in-new-york-hidden-in-plain-sight/

Goedhuys, M., and R. Veugelers. 2012. Innovation strategies, process and product innovations and growth: Firm-level evidence from Brazil. *Structural Change and Economic Dynamics* 23 (4):516–29. doi: 10.1016/j.strueco.2011.01.004.

Gonçalves, G. 2021. Bahia se torna referência de uso da tecnologia na administração pública. *Acorda Cidade*, September 28. Accessed December 10, 2023. https://www.acordacidade.com.br/noticias/bahia-se-torna-referencia-de-uso-da-tecnologia-na-administracao-publica/

Gordon, R. W. 2021. Massive bid rigging evidence contradicts Dahua denial. *IPVM*, April 20. Accessed December 16, 2023. https://ipvm.com/reports/dahua-evidence-rig

Governo do Estado do Ceará. 2017. *Ata de Registro de Preços n° 0009/2017*. Accessed December 16, 2023. https://www.etice.ce.gov.br/wp-content/uploads/sites/5/2017/11/Ata-de-Registro-de-Pre%C3%A7o-n%C2%BA-0009.2017.pdf

Governo do Estado do Ceará. 2019. China: Governo do Ceará firmará parceria com gigante da tecnologia em segurança. *Portal do Governo*, April 25. Accessed December 16, 2023. https://www.ceara.gov.br/2019/04/25/china-governo-do-ceara-firmara-parceria-com-gigante-da-tecnologia-em-seguranca/

Governo do Estado do Ceará. 2022. *Ata do Registro de Preços, n° 2022/05385* Accessed December 16, 2023 https://www.etice.ce.gov.br/wp-content/uploads/sites/5/2022/03/Ata-de-Registro-de-Preco-202205385.pdf

Governo do Estado do Piauí. 2021. Piauí tem a internet mais rápida do Brasil, aponta estudo. *Imprensa*, November 5. December 16, 2023. https://www.pi.gov.br/noticias/piaui-tem-a-internet-mais-rapida-do-brasil-aponta-estudo/

Governo do Estado de São Paulo. 2020. Governo inaugura laboratório de reconhecimento facial e digital da Polícia Civil. *Portal do Governo*, January 28. Accessed December 16, 2023. https://www.saopaulo.sp.gov.br/spnoticias/governo-inaugura-laboratorio-de-reconhecimento-facial-e-digital-da-policia-civil/

Greenwald, G. 2014. *Sem Lugar para se Esconder*. Rio de Janeiro: GMT Editores.

Greitens, S. C. 2020. Dealing with demand for China's global surveillance exports. Accessed December 16, 2023. https://www.brookings.edu/research/dealing-with-demand-for-chinas-global-surveillance-exports/

Gross, C., R. Zanatta, B. M. dos Santos, and I. V. Scarpelli. 2021. Vigiar e confundir. Quatro Cinco Um, May 1. Accessed December 16, 2023. https://quatrocincoum.folha.uol.com.br/br/artigos/laut/vigiar-e-confundir

Hemmings, J. 2020. Reconstructing order: The geopolitical risks in China's Digital Silk Road. *Asia Policy* 15 (1):5–21. doi: 10.1353/asp.2020.0002.

Hikvision. 2022. Forças de Segurança de Roraima utilizam câmeras da Hikvision para segurança pública em zona de fronteira. Accessed December 16, 2023. https://www.hikvision.com/pt-br/newsroom/latest-news/2022/forcas-de-seguranca-de-roraima-utilizam-cameras-da-hikvision-/

Hintz, A., and S. Milan. 2018. Through a glass, darkly: Everyday acts of authoritarianism in the liberal West. *International Journal of Communication* 12:3939–59.

Huawei. 2018. South Atlantic inter link connecting Cameroon to Brazil fully connected. Accessed December 16, 2023. https://www.huawei.com/en/news/2018/9/south-atlantic-inter-link

Infor Channel. 2022. Dahua Technology emprega IA e Big Data no monitoramento rodoviário do Espírito Santo. *Segurança*, February 7. Accessed December 20, 2023. https://inforchannel.com.br/2022/02/07/dahua-technology-equipa-o-monitoramento-rodoviario-no-espirito-santo/

Jornal Grande Bahia. 2021. Governador participa de seminário virtual sobre tecnologia promovido pela Embaixada da China. *Jornal Grande Bahia*, September 9. Accessed December 22, 2023. https://jornalgrandebahia.com.br/2021/09/governador-rui-costa-participa-de-seminario-virtual-sobre-tecnologia-promovido-pela-embaixada-da-china-no-brasil/

Kahhat, F. 2022. In Brazil, A new gambit in 5G battle between U.S. and China. Accessed December 16, 2023. https://worldcrunch.com/business-finance/china-5g-huawei

Khalil, L. 2020. Digital authoritarianism, China and C0VID. Accessed December 16, 2023. https://www.lowyinstitute.org/publications/digital-authoritarianism-china-covid

Lugt, S. 2021. Exploring the political, economic, and social implications of the Digital Silk Road into East Africa: The case of Ethiopia. In *Global perspectives on China's Belt and Road Initiative: Asserting agency through regional connectivity*, ed. F. Schneider, 315–46. Amsterdam: Amsterdam University Press.

MacAskill, E., J. Borger, N. Hopkins, N. Davies, and J. Ball. 2013. GCHQ taps fibre-optic cables for secret access to world's communications. *The Guardian*, June 21. Accessed December 17, 2023. https://www.theguardian.com/uk/2013/jun/21/gchq-cables-secret-world-communications-nsa

Magalhães, D. T. d Á. 2022. Efeitos do antiglobalismo brasileiro sobre as relações Brasil-China (2018-2020). *Revista de Ciências Humanas* 1 (22):119–38.

Majerowicz, E., and C. A. de Medeiros. 2018. Chinese industrial policy in the geopolitics of the information age: The case of semiconductors. *Revista de Economia Contemporânea* 22 (1):1–28. doi: 10.1590/198055272216.

Majerowicz, E. 2022. A disputa sino-estadunidense nas tecnologias da informação e comunicação. In *A China no capitalismo contemporâneo*, eds. E. Majerowicz and E. Paraná, 319–74. São Paulo: Expressão Popular

Majerowicz, E. forthcoming. The Sino-American dispute in information and communication technologies. In *China in contemporary capitalism*, eds. E. Majerowicz and E. Paraná. Boston: Brill.

Martins, H. 2020. Reconhecimento facial: A banalização de uma tecnologia controversa. *Le Monde Diplomatique Brasil*, April 22. Accessed December 16, 2023. https://diplomatique.org.br/reconhecimento-facial-a-banalizacao-de-uma-tecnologia-controversa/

de Medeiros, C. A., and E. Majerowicz. 2022. Developmentalism with Chinese characteristics. *International Journal of Political Economy* 51 (3):208–28. doi: 10.1080/08911916.2022.2146388.

Migliano, S., and S. Woodhams. 2021. Hikvision and Dahua surveillance cameras: Global locations report. Accessed December 16, 2023. https://www.top10vpn.com/research/hikvision-dahua-surveillance-cameras-global-locations/

Ministério do Desenvolvimento Regional. 2022. Sudene realiza visita técnica guiada ao projeto Cidades Inteligentes de Campina Grande (PB). *Sudene*, Assuntos, Notícias, April 14. Accessed December 17, 2023. https://www.gov.br/sudene/pt-br/assuntos/noticias/sudene-realiza-visita-guiada-ao-projeto-cidades-inteligentes-de-campina-grande-pb

Minority Staff, US Senate Committee on Foreign Relations. 2020. The new big brother: China and digital authoritarianism (A minority staff report). Accessed December 17, 2023. https://www.govinfo.gov/content/pkg/CPRT-116SPRT42356/pdf/CPRT-116SPRT42356.pdf

Nakagawa, L. 2022. #SaiDaMinhaCara: Iniciativa quer banir reconhecimento facial dos espaços públicos; entenda. *Techmasters*, June 21. Accessed December 17, 2023. https://tecmasters.com.br/iniciativa-banir-reconhecimento-facial-publicos/

NSA (National Security Agency). 2013. NSA Prism program slides. *The Guardian*, November 1. Accessed December 1, 2023. https://www.theguardian.com/world/interactive/2013/nov/01/prism-slides-nsa-document

Peduzzi, P. 2019. Moro anuncia 5 cidades para programa de enfrentamento à criminalidade. *Agência Brasil*, May 15. Accessed December 17, 2023. https://agenciabrasil.ebc.com.br/geral/noticia/2019-05/moro-anuncia-cidades-do-programa-de-enfrentamento-criminalidade

Piauí Hoje. 2020. Piauí Conectado finaliza primeira fase com implantação de internet em 96 municípios. *Notícias*, October 10. Accessed December 17, 2023. https://piauihoje.com/noticias/municipios/piaui-conectado-finaliza-primeira-fase-com-implantacao-de-internet-em-96-municipios-353997.html

Pisanu, G., V. Arroyo, L. Ucciferri, E. Ferreyra, T. Moraes, J. R. Laranjeira, E. C. Almeida, F. F. Dourado, C. Reis, F. R. Silva, et al. 2021. Surveillance tech in Latin America made abroad, deployed at home. *Access Now*, August 8. Accessed December 20, 2023. https://www.accessnow.org/surveillance-tech-in-latin-america-made-abroad-deployed-at-home/

Polyakova, A., and C. Meserole. 2019. Exporting digital authoritarianism: The Russian and Chinese models (Policy Brief). Accessed December 17, 2023. https://www.brookings.edu/research/exporting-digital-authoritarianism/

Prefeitura de, A. 2021. Aracaju troca experiência com municípios e empresas sobre cidades inteligentes. *Agência Aracaju de Notícias*, November 25. Accessed December 17, 2023. https://www.aracaju.se.gov.br/noticias/93382/aracaju_troca_experiencia_com_municipios_e_empresas_sobre_cidades_inteligentes.html

Rangel, J. 2021. URGENTE: Nova denúncia conecta governo de Casagrande com DAHUA. *Folha ES*, April 13. Accessed December 17, 2023. https://www.folhadoes.com/noticia/politica-denuncia/77598/urgente-nova-denuncia-conecta-governo-casagrande-com-dahua

Rebello, A. 2019. 2019. Bancada do PSL vai à China conhecer sistema que reconhece rosto de cidadãos. *Folha de São Paulo*, January 16. Accessed December 17 https://www1.folha.uol.com.br/mercado/2019/01/bancada-do-psl-vai-a-china-importar-sistema-que-reconhece-rosto-de-cidadaos.shtml

Reis, C., E. Almeida, F. da Silva, and F. Dourado. 2021. *Relatório sobre o uso de tecnologias de reconhecimento facial e câmeras de vigilância pela administração pública no Brasil*. Brasília: Laboratório de Políticas Públicas e Internet. Accessed December 17, 2023. https://lapin.org.br/2021/07/07/vigilancia-automatizada-uso-de-reconhecimento-facial-pela-administracao-publica-no-brasil/.

Sachsida, A., M. J. C. de Mendonça, P. R. Loureiro, and M. B. S. Gutierrez. 2010. Inequality and criminality revisited: Further evidence from Brazil. *Empirical Economics* 39 (1):93–109. doi: 10.1007/s00181-009-0296-4.

Sadi, A. 2019. Bolsonaro está "surpreso" com viagem de grupo do PSL à China, diz presidente do partido. *g1*, January 17. Accessed December 17, 2023. https://g1.globo.com/politica/blog/andreia-sadi/post/2019/01/17/bolsonaro-esta-surpreso-com-viagem-de-grupo-do-psl-a-china-diz-presidente-do-partido.ghtml

Schipani, A. 2022. China's role at the heart of Kenya's election campaign. *Financial Times*, August 3. Accessed December 17, 2023. https://www.ft.com/content/40ea35ea-b9b2-4c92-b595-e5ab191431df

Secretaria de Segurança de Mogi das Cruzes. 2019. Empresa chinesa doa equipamentos para Mogi das Cruzes e fará projeto de Safe City. *Notícia*, March 14. Accessed December 17, 2023. https://www.mogidascruzes.sp.gov.br/noticia/empresa-chinesa-doa-equipamentos-para-mogi-das-cruzes-e-fara-projeto-de-safe-city

Secretaria de Segurança Pública do Estado da Bahia. 2019. *Projeto vídeo polícia expansão*. Accessed December 20, 2023. https://comprasnet.ba.gov.br/sites/default/files/termo_de_referencia_v1.pdf

Shahbaz, A. 2018. The rise of digital authoritarianism: Fake news, data collection, and the challenge to democracy. Accessed December 17, 2023. https://freedomhouse.org/report/freedom-net/2018/rise-digital-authoritarianism

Sibiri, H. 2021. The emerging phenomenon of anti-Chinese populism in Africa: Evidence from Zambia, Zimbabwe and Ghana. *Insight on Africa* 13 (1):7–27. doi: 10.1177/0975087820971443.

Sibiri, H. 2022. Politicians are taking advantage of anti-Chinese sentiments for electoral purposes. Accessed December 20, 2023. https://hksspr.org/politicians-are-taking-advantage-of-anti-chinese-sentiments-for-electoral-purposes/

Spring, J. 2018. Bolsonaro's anti-China rants have Beijing nervous about Brazil. *Reuters*, October 26. Accessed December 17, 2023. https://www.reuters.com/article/us-brazil-election-china-insight-idUSKCN1MZ0DR/

Superior Electoral Court (TSE). 2023. Elections: Statistics. Accessed December 20, 2023. https://international.tse.jus.br/en/elections/statistics

Tagiaroli, G. 2021. Reconhecimento facial pela PF é considerado "preocupante" e até ilícito. *Tilt*, July 13. Accessed December 17, 2023. https://www.uol.com.br/tilt/noticias/redacao/2021/07/13/abis-como-e-o-novo-sistema-da-pf-que-criara-uma-base-nacional-de-biometria.htm

Tavares, A. 2019. A nova era da "governança digital" em Aparecida de Goiânia. *Diário de Goiás*, August 22. Accessed December 17, 2023. https://diariodegoias.com.br/a-nova-era-da-governanca-digital-em-aparecida-de-goiania/

Telesíntese. 2021. Polícia Federal adquire sistema de identificação biométrica com reconhecimento facial. *Telesíntese*, July 6. Accessed December 17, 2023. https://www.telesintese.com.br/policia-federal-adquire-sistema-de-identificacao-biometrica-com-reconhecimento-facial/

Tostes, F. 2022. "Teve muita disputa empresarial e política para que não ficasse de pé, mas ficou," diz Casagrande sobre Cerco Inteligente. *Folha Vitória*, January 14. Accessed December 17, 2023. https://www.folhavitoria.com.br/politica/colunas/de-olho-no-poder/2022/01/teve-muita-disputa-empresarial-e-politica-para-que-nao-ficasse-de-pe-mas-ficou-diz-casagrande-sobre-cerco-inteligente/

Tribuna do Agreste. 2019. Missão à China candidata Alagoas a novos investimentos. *Tribuna do Agreste*, July 12. Accessed December 22, 2023. https://www.tribunadoagreste.com.br/2019/07/missao-china-candidata-alagoas-novos-investimentos/

Tribuna do Norte. 2019. Região metropolitana de Natal terá mais 184 câmeras de videomonitoramento. *Notícia*, September 12. Accessed December 20, 2023. https://tribunadonorte.com.br/natal/regiao-metropolitana-de-natal-tera-mais-184-cameras-de-videomonitoramento/

Tugendhat, H., and J. Voo. 2021. China's Digital Silk Road in Africa and the future of internet governance (Working Paper No. 50). Washington, DC: China Africa Research Initiative, School of Advanced International Studies, Johns Hopkins University. Accessed December 17, 2023. https://static1.squarespace.com/static/5652847de4b033f56d2bdc29/t/61084a3238e7ff4b666b9ffe/1627933235832/WP+50+-+Tugendhat+and+Voo+-+China+Digital+Silk+Road+Africa.pdf

Uellner e Silva, A., and K. D. Santos. 2020. Representação com requerimento liminar de suspensão do certame. Processo: 01923613/2020. Pregão eletrônico n.° 20200002 - ETICE/DITEC. UASG: 943001. Número Comprasnet: 0390/2020. Accessed December 20, 2023. https://www.etice.ce.gov.br/wp-content/uploads/sites/5/2022/03/Edital.pdf

Valente, R. 2020a. Ação sigilosa do governo mira professores e policiais antifascistas. *UOL Notícias*, July 24. Accessed December 17, 2023. https://noticias.uol.com.br/colunas/rubens-valente/2020/07/24/ministerio-justica-governo-bolsonaro-antifascistas.htm

Valente, R. 2020b. Relações subnacionais entre Brasil e China: No combate a pandemia e ao governo federal? *UOL Notícias*, December 1. Accessed December 17, 2023. https://noticias.uol.com.br/colunas/rubens-valente/2020/12/01/governo-bolsonaro-jornalistas-redes-sociais.amp.htm

Vazquez, K. C. 2022. Brazil-China relations: Contestation, adaptation, or transformation? In *The China question: Contestations and adaptations*, eds. D. Pavlićević and N. Talmacs, 201–22. Singapore: Palgrave Macmillan.

Venturini, J., and V. Garay. 2021. Reconhecimento facial na América Latina: Tendências na implementação de uma tecnologia perversa. Accessed December 17, 2023. https://www.alsur.lat/sites/default/files/2021-10/ALSUR_Reconocimiento%20facial%20en%20Latam_PR_Final.pdf

Venturini, J., and A. Stepanovich. 2016. Brazil's Olympic surveillance legacy. *Access Now*, August 24. Accessed December 17, 2023. https://www.accessnow.org/brazils-olympic-surveillance-legacy/

Vidigal, C. E., and R. Bernal-Meza. 2020. Bolsonaro *versus* Rio Branco: Transição hegemônica, América do Sul e política externa. *Revista de Relaciones Internacionales, Estrategia y Seguridad* 15 (2):11–26. doi: 10.18359/ries.4673.

Woodhams, S. 2020. China, Africa, and the private surveillance industry. *Georgetown Journal of International Affairs* 21 (1):158–65. doi: 10.1353/gia.2020.0002.

Index

Note: **Bold** page numbers refer to tables; *italic* page numbers refer to figures and page numbers followed by "n" denote endnotes.

advanced technologies 74, 78; facial recognition 91
Africa/African countries 2, 6–8, 10, 12, 13, 15, 36, 40, 60, 64, 67, 74–5, 80–1, 106
African Union (AU) 15
Agbebi, M. 75, 79
Algeria/Algerian/Algiers 2, 76–80, 82, 84; and Egypt 73, 76–7, 80–4; government 77, 80–1
Alibaba Group 2, 14, 24, 35, 37, 40, 49, 56–68, 71; activities in Latin America 59, 67; investments 9, 37; in Mexico 2, 56, 61–2; platforms 58–9, 62, 67; and Tencent 49
American Enterprise Institute 36, 40
anti-China rhetoric 3, 104–5, 114–15
Araújo, Ernesto 107
Argentina 90, 92–8; and Ecuador 3, 90, 92, 99–101
Association of Southeast Asian Nations (ASEAN) 32
Atomic88 2, 57, 59–63, 65
Auffray, C. 81
authoritarian: affinity 104; countries 106–7; inclinations 105, 107, 109; -leaning political forces 107, 111
automated biometric identification system (ABIS) 111
Azmeh, S. 50n6

backward linkages 73–4, 80, 84
Bahia 111–14; and China 114
Belasques, P. B. 107
Belt and Road Initiative (BRI) 5, 7–8, 10, 17, 21, 23, 32–3, 35–9, 41–2, 48, 72–3, 81, 114; announcement 37–8; countries 2, 12, 20–1, 32–5, 37–9, 48, 50, 76, 84; DSR 33–4, 37, 39–41, 48; participating countries 37–8, 40, 44
Bolsonaro 104–5, 107–9, 114; government 104–5, 107, 109–11, 116
Brazil/Brazilian 8, 10, 12, 14, 92, 94, 96, 104–5, 107–9, 111, 113–16; Agency 109, 112; and China 107, 109; cities 111, 115; political spectrum **109**
Brazilian Development Bank (BNDES) 112
Brazilian Digital Surveillance Markets 3, 104–5, 107, 109, 111, 113, 115
Brunetti, F. 60
business: associations 61, 64; expansion 39, 42, 45; interests 12, 35, 41; models 35; operations 2, 33, 35, 43, 47, 49; partnerships 41, 48; practices 36–7, 45; registration 45, 49; relationship 80; strategies 33, 42, 48

Cairo 77–8
Cheney, C. 34
China/Chinese 3–5, 12–15, 19–26, 33–7, 39–42, 44–9, 66–7, 72–80, 83–4, 90–1, 94, 96, 98–100, 112, 114–16; actors 3, 7, 11, 13–16, 21, 23, 25–6, 91, 99–100; approach 13, 21–2; authorities 15; belt and road initiative 92, 114; capital 11, 36; companies 12, 20, 25, 39, 42, 45, 90–1, 97, 99–101, 105–7, 114–16; contractors 11, 15; digital and global engagements *8*; and digital authoritarianism 106; digital efforts 116n2; digital platform companies *39*; Digital Platform Companies Expansion 32–3, 35, 37, 39, 41, 43, 45, 47, 49, 53, 55; e-commerce platforms 12, 16, 26; and Ecuador 92, 95; embassy in Brazil 104, 114; engagement 6, 115; enterprises 78, 112, 114; exceptionalism and identicalism 3, 24; expansion 3, 104–7, 109, 111, 113, 115; exports 3, 16, 104, 107, 116; exports of surveillance technology 19, 107; Fintech 41, 46; firms 2–3, 7–11, 13–20, 22, 32–7, 40–2, 44–8, 79, 81–3, 91, 93, 99–100, 108, 111, 114–16; funding 67, 98, 113; Global Investment Tracker 36, 40; government 2, 12, 16, 19, 32, 34–5, 40, 42, 48, 94, 114; and Indonesia 41, 42, 45;-invested platforms 40, 47; investments 34, 40, 42, 46, 74, 114; investors 42, 45, 81; market 8, 13, 40; mobile 9, 11, 24, 41; OEMs 76, 81; overseas investments 33; partners 45, 49; players 34–7, 44; providers 96, 99–101, 111; state 2–3, 7–8, 10–16, 19–21, 25–6, 33–5, 48–9, 50n2, 68, 78–9, 114, 116; state funding 98–9, 114, 116; suppliers 81, 100, 115; tech companies 19, 108; tech giants 2, 74–6; technologies 3, 14, 25, 73, 93, 99, 106, 108; technology stack 9, *10*, 23; Telecom 9, 11, 24; telecommunications firms 35, 96; telecommunications infrastructure projects *9*; users 11
China Development Bank 41
China Digital Expansion 2–4, 6–25, 34, 36, 38, 40, 42, 44, 46, 48, 58, 60, 62, 64, 66
China Global Investment Tracker (CGIT) database tracks 36
China National Electronics Import & Export Corporation (CEIEC) 94–6
China-Pakistan Economic Corridor's (CPEC) 39
Chinese Communist Party (CCP) 19
Chinese currency (RMB) 33
Chinese ICT 32, 72; companies 8, 11, 33; corporations in North Africa 2, 72; firms 24, 33–4, 36, 76, 78, 83
Chinese platforms 16, 23, 33–4, 36–7, 39–49, 82; companies 33, 37–40, **40**, 48–9; expansion 50n5; investing in local capacity building 46–7
Chinese surveillance:-related digital projects *18*; state 91–3, 95–9, 103; systems 90–2, 98–9, 107; technologies 17, 91–2, 96, 99–100, 105, 110–11, 113–16
Chinese tech firms 2–3, 5, 8, 11–13, 15, 24–6, 26n7, 36–7, 58, 73, 75, 78–81, 83, 113, 115–16; ability of 2, 13; in developing countries 74

commercial interests 19, 33–5, 40, 42, 48, 82
communication technologies 23, 72, 106
competitive markets 14, 34
comprehensive strategic partnership 92
Coordinating Ministry of Security 94
Correa, President 92–3, 95–6; administration 93–4
counter-hegemonic approach 57
countries 2–3, 5, 7, 9–19, 25–6, 37, 39–43, 46–7, 56–7, 64–6, 68, 75–7, 79–81, 83–4, 92–7, 100, 105–7, 112–16
Cross-Border Inter-Bank Payment System (CIPS) 10
cutting-edge technologies 75, 82
Cyberspace Administration of China 20

Dahua 20, 91, 111–13, 115–16
data centers 23, 25, 44, 46
data localization 44
democratic countries 99, 106–7, 111
democratic governments 21, 106
democratic political forces 111
Democratic Staff Report 90–1, 96, 99
destination countries 37, 48
developing countries 21, 34–5, 43, 45, 56–9, 65–6, 68, 72, 74, 81, 83–4
developing economies 33, 73
differentiated approach 90, 100–1
Digital Currency Electronic Payment (DCEP) 26n5
digital/digitalization 15, 17, 24, 57–8, 62–4, 67; activities 2, 8–9, 11, 15, 17, 24; actors 3, 12, 15; authoritarianism 2–3, 6, 17–18, 20, 90–2, 104–9, 114–16, 117n3; authoritarianism model 18, 92; benefits of 17; Cold War 4, 25; companies 15, 23, 26, 67, 72; component 5–6, 41, 72; connectivity 22, 81; design 24, 26; development 6, 13–14, 21, 24, 59; ecosystems 65, 81; engagements 7, 67, 115; expansion 2–3, 5–8, 11, 15–18, 20, 22–6, 33–4, 48–9, 68, 105, 107, 109–10, 113–15; expansion of Chinese firms 91, 114; firms 2, 10, 14, 66, 73, 76; governance 2, 6, 20–2, 26, 106; inclusion 59, 77; investments 12, 16; levels of 62, 67; MNCs 73–5; platform companies 33–5, 37, 39, 41; platforms 33–4, 37, 40, 44, 48, 82; policies 22–3; projects 2, 12, 14, 25; sectors 37, 44; sovereignty 20–1; systems 6, 15–16, 18, 24–5, 57, 61–2, 75, 83, 107, 114; technologies 3, 7, 10, 17, 24–5, 56–7, 62–3, 65, 83, 90–1, 105–6; trade 5–6, 21; transformation 73, 77
digital economy 5–6, 8, 16, 32, 34, 43–4, 49, 77, 81; collaboration 32–3; component 33, 35, 48; sector 43, 45; stakeholders 2, 43
digital infrastructure 9, 15–16, 18, 20, 22, 33, 35, 44, 74–5, 80–1, 83; projects 9–10, 16, 83; and systems 18, 20
Digital Silk Road (DSR) 1, 2, 6–8, 10, 12, 16–18, 23, 32–3, 35, 41, 48, 72–5, 77–9, 81, 83–4; investments 26n4
digital surveillance 20, 105, 109; cameras 106, 115; markets 105, 107; systems 107, 115; technologies 105, 107–9, 113, 116
Digital Villages initiative 2, 56–7, 59–68, 71; to Latin America 2, 56; in Mexico 60–1, 65
direct training 58, 67–8
domestic market 13–14, 35, 74

e-commerce platforms 2, 9–10, 16, 25, 40, 57, 61, 65
economic development 17, 72, 76
economic growth 7, 21, 43, 77
economic inequalities 16, 56
economic interests 13, 115–16
economic value network 65
ECU 90, 92–6, 99
Ecuador 3, 12, 90, 92–6, 98–101; technicians 94–5
e-government systems 3, 11
Egypt 2, 14, 73, 76–84; and Algeria 76–7, 79, 82; ICT 77
Electronic World Trade Platform (eWTP) 2, 35, 57, 59
El-Kadi, Tin Hinane 2
Ellis, Evan 92
emerging markets 32–6, 39–40, 43, 48–9
emerging technologies 7, 23
empirically-grounded research 48, 90, 92
empirical research 7, 17, 25
enterprises 2, 56–7, 61, 63–8, 104, 106, 111
entrepreneurs 57–8, 62–3, 68
Ericsson 74, 76, 79
Ethiopian government 18–19
existing literature 33–4, 48, 57, 105
expansion 2, 5, 9, 11, 32–7, 39–45, 47–9, 53, 55, 82–3, 91–2, 98–9, 111, 113–14; of China's surveillance systems 91, 107; Chinese digital platforms 33–4, 48; Chinese surveillance technologies 96, 116; digital authoritarianism 92, 106; in Indonesia 33, 37, 41
explicit surveillance technologies 17, 106
exports, of surveillance technologies 3, 22, 91, 106

facial recognition 17, 104–6, 108–9, 111–13; software 111–13, 115; surveillance technologies 112, 116; systems 19, 111; technology 111
federal government 105, 107–9, 111–12, 114
fieldwork interviews 33, 81
foreign: actors 36, 77, 91, 93, 99–100; affairs 7, 20, 32, 107; companies 74, 80; direct investment 8, 37, 43, 73; firms 39, 43, 73–4, 76, 80, 82, 84, 99–100; investment 37, 42–4; investors 40, 43–4; markets 105, 107; multinationals 79, 116; ownership 43–5; policy 5, 42, 92–3, 95, 107, 114; providers 92, 99; relations 8, 104, 106; subsidiaries 74–5; suppliers 98, 107; tech firms 39–40; technologies 43, 116; workers 46–7, 49, 74, 98
forward linkages 74, 80–1
Foster, Christopher 1, 50n6
Fu, X. 81

Gagliardone, I. 36, 75
Gao, Ping 1
geographic proximity, to China 39–40
global digital governance 4, 21–2, 26
Global Digital Talent (GDT) 61; training 61–2
global expansion 13, 33, 35, 48
Global South 2–8, 10–18, 20–6, 33, 48–9, 56–8, 65, 67–8, 84, 90–2, 99–100, 104–7, 114–16
government/governmental 15, 34, 36, 42–6, 49, 61, 63–4, 66, 77, 81–2, 84, 92–8, 104–6, 109–10, 113–16; agencies 45, 61, 114; of Jujuy 97–8; leadership 64; officials 37, 60, 76, 115; services 113–14
Greitens, S. C. 107
Guanajuato, state government 61, 63–5

Han, Xia 1
Heeks, Richard 1
He, Yujia 2
higher education institutions (HEIs) 60, 62, 64–5
high-tech firms 35, 75
high-tech investments 37–8
horizontal integration strategies 113
horizontal linkages 73, 75–6, 78–9, 82–4

host countries 33–7, 39–40, 42, 48–9, 74; governments 14, 33, 36, 73, 84
Huawei 8–12, 14–15, 17, 20, 24, 74, 78–80, 82–3, 91, 97, 111–13, 116; certifications 74, 82; device 80–1; factories 80; and Hikvision 12, 112; ICT Academy 82; technologies 82–3; and ZTE 2, 9, 11–12, 14, 67, 72–3, 76–81, 110, 113, 116

IDEMIA 117n7
inclusive digital development 56, 84
inclusive globalization 16, 35, 57–60, 65, 67, 68n1
Indonesia/Indonesian 9, 24, 26, 33, 36–7, 39–50, 82, 104; companion employees 46; conglomerates 41–2; FinTech 41; firms 41, 43; government 43–4, 49; Investment Coordinating Board 42, 45; ownership 44; policy 49
industrial development 109, 111–12
information and communication technologies (ICTs) 106; academies 82; engineers 82; industry 42, 76, 79, 82; infrastructure 15, 74, 77–8, 80; products and services 106; sector 33, 35, 79
information-and communication-technology-for-development (ICT4D) 9
information silk road 5–6
The Information Society 1
information technology 77–8
infrastructure projects 12, 42, 93
Instituto Tecnológico y de Estudios Superiores de Monterrey (ITESM) 61
integral security concept 93–6
interactions 11, 26, 49, 63, 67, 72–3, 107
international/internationalization 12, 33, 74, 84, 90–1, 96, 99; business 7, 42; capital 35, 48–9; development 13, 16; markets 34–5, 42; OEMs 79; organization 10, 21, 23; sources 112, 114; standard-setting bodies 75, 83; strategies 14, 24
International Telecommunication Union (ITU) 75
internet connectivity 63, 77
Internet Corporation for Assigned Names and Numbers (ICANN) 20
internet-enabled inclusive globalization 12, 33
investments 2, 8, 11–12, 15, 23, 32, 34–41, 43–4, 46, 48, 113, 116; destinations 38–9; policies 40, 44

Jakarta Post 46–7
Jepson, Nicholas 1
joint technology training center 3, 76
joint venture 16, 41, 44–5, 47, 77, 80
Jornal Grande Bahia 112, 114
Jujuy 93, 97–9; government 97, 99; Ministry of Security 98; policy makers 97
Jujuy eguro e Interconectado (JSeI) 90; in Argentina and ECU 92; projects **93**

knowledge transfer 3, 49, 73–4, 81, 83–4, 95

labor market 2, 33, 43
large developing economies 38–9
Latin America/Latin American 2–3, 6, 8, 13–14, 56–7, 59–60, 62, 66–8, 90–1, 93, 95–7, 99–100, 103, 106
linkages 72–5, 77–8, 80, 82–4
local actors 2, 19, 25, 60, 64–7, 96, 99–101
local agency 3–4, 22, 25–6, 84
local businesses 37, 49; operations 33, 40, 44; strategies 37, 43
local capacity building 2, 15, 33, 46–7
local companies 16, 79, 82
local criticisms 91, 100
local data centers 44, 46
local economies 15, 58, 73–4, 81
local employees 46, 79, 83
local engineers 74, 79–81
local enterprises 16–17, 64–5, 78, 109, 111–12
local entrepreneurs 10, 58, 60
local firms 16, 23, 25, 43–4, 47, 49, 60, 73–4, 79–81, 84, 98–9; digital 4, 26
local governments 35, 64–5, 92, 94, 105, 110, 114, 116; allies 108, 114
local ICT: actors 73, 75, 78, 83; firms 13, 81
localization strategies 40, 78, 84
local markets 10, 14, 16
local officials 18, 25, 107–8, 112
local operations 37, 46, 48
local partners/partnerships 2, 16, 41, 43, 45, 47, 49, 61, 74
local players 37, 42
local policies 2, 26, 49
local small enterprises 57, 59–61
local stakeholders 23, 26, 60–1, 66–8
local subsidiary 41, 44, 57, 59, 61–2, 65, 67
local universities 23, 73, 77, 82–3
local workers 25, 46–7, 49, 76, 79, 84; and managers 79, 84
local workforce 46, 49; development 47, 49
Lugt, S. 106

major investments 36–7, 39–40
management and operation 91, 95, 97–100
managers 79–81, 84
Mao Zedong 76
market players 33, 49
mass surveillance 106
medium enterprises 41, 44
Mexico/Mexican 2, 10, 26, 56–7, 59–68, 71, 97; Digital Villages **66,** 67; projects 62, 65
middle-income countries 2, 5, 75
Ministry of Communications and Information Technology 77
Ministry of Manpower regulations 46
Minority Staff 8, 104, 106
Moreno administration 95–6
multinational companies (MNCs) 72

National Integral Security Plan 94
national policies 2, 26
Negative Investment List 43–4
new digital ecosystem 64–5, 67
new technologies 34, 36, 72
new value networks 58, 64–5, 68
New York Times 92
non-BRI countries 36, 38–9
North Africa 2, 72–3, 77, 79–80
Northeast region 108–9, 111, 113–14

Open Door Policy 77
opposition politicians 42, 97–8, 100
optic network 73, 97–9
Ospina, Angelica 1
outward foreign direct investment (OFDI) 36, 38
overseas: expansion 33–7, 40, 48–9; foreign direct investments *38*; investments 33, 37, 48; markets 35, 45

partial opposition 108–9, 111
partners 36, 49, 81
physical infrastructure 57–8, 66, 83
Pisanu, G. 106
platform companies 35–7, 48
policy: environment 43–4, 48; implementation 33, 43, 49; makers 90–1, 97, 99–100; recommendations 73, 83–4
politics/political 11, 73, 75–6, 114; capital 12, 65, 67; economy 24, 33, 73, 77, 83; forces 79, 104; illiberalism 8, 18, 91; interests 13, 16, 35; opponents 18–19; opposition 108, 111, 116; parties 91, 100, 104; relations 109, 114; spectrum 3, 19, 108–9, 114–15; statuses 105, 107; systems 99, 107; tensions 107, 109, 114
private firms 33–5, 44, 48, 96
privately-owned enterprises (POEs) 34
private sector 17, 42; firms 33, 41
pro-active policies 73, 84
provincial government 97, 99
public officials 94–7, 99
public safety systems 96–7
public security 94, 104–5, 107–8, 111–16; systems 12, 105

Qingna Zhou 5
quantitative data 33, 37, 44, 76–7

"R&D centers" 16
recipient: countries 12, 16–17; governments 13
research agenda 5–6, 23
research design 6–7, 108
research questions (RQs) 33, 57, 60, 65–7
Rousseff, Dilma 105

safe city projects 17, 91, 111
Schindler, Seth 1
security: cameras 92, 109, 113; sector 93, 95
seeking local partners 33, 44
Seoane, Maximiliano Facundo Vila 3
small enterprises 2, 35, 57–68; digitalization 57–8, **59**, 60, 62, 67; in Mexico 61, 67
smart cities: in China 91; projects 11, 94, 112
social media 10–11, 23, 41, 43
socioeconomic risks 36, 42
software platform 94, 100
South Africa 7, 26
Southeast Asia 9–11, 32, 36, 40–3, 47, 49
spillovers 72–3, 80–1
state governments 60–8, 108, 110–13, 115
state-owned companies 16, 41, 83, 115
state-owned enterprises (SOEs) 11–12, 19, 34, 90, 94, 96
state-owned firms 9, 24
structural transformation 72–3, 77, 81, 84
subcontractors 75–6, 80
sub-national governments 107, 115
surveillance: cameras 104–6, 108, 111–13, 115; equipment 92, 115; infrastructures 112–13, 115; projects 90, 92, 111, 113; systems 3, 7, 90, 92–3, 97, 99–100, 112–14
surveillance technologies 3, 18–20, 22, 91–2, 98–101, 104, 106–9, 112–13, 115–16; adoption of 108–9; origin *19*; sale of 91, 100; selling 90–2; supplying 3, 111; use of 18, 22
systematic literature review 5–6
systems 3, 6–7, 9, 17–18, 20, 58, 67, 75, 91–100, 105, 111–12

Tagiaroli, G. 111
Taobao Village Model 56, 58, **59**, 60–6, **66**, 67, 68; in China 58, 62
Team China monolith 3, 24
tech firms 2, 12, 24, 40, 44, 75, 79, 83
technical design 99–100
technical standards 21–2
technical support 95–6
technologies/technological 3, 6–7, 17–22, 34–7, 42–3, 45–6, 49, 56–7, 72–6, 80–1, 83–4, 90–2, 94–5, 99–101, 104, 106–8, 112–16; capabilities 91, 98, 100; competition 83, 107; dependency/dependence 81, 83, 91, 96, 100, 116; latecomers 82–3; learning 73–4; spillovers 72–7, *78*, 80, 83, 85n1; stack 9, 10, 20, 24; standards 75, 83; transfer 2–3, 13, 15, 46, 72–8, 80–1, 83–4, 116; upgrading 3, 73–4, 78, 82–3
techno-politics framework 72, 74–6, 82, 83
"techno-totalitarianism" 107
telecommunications infrastructure 7, 9–10, 13, 34, 98
Thomas-Noone, B. 34
Three World theory 76
trainee consultant 60–1
transferred technologies 16, 75
trickle-down model 63, 65
Tugendhat, H. 79

United States (US): and China 4, 25, 107; -China Economic and Security Review Commission 107; government sources 91–2, 98; Senate Committee on Foreign Relations 106; USD 32, 36–41, 43–4
United States-Ecuador Partnership Act 96
University-FDI linkages 82

van der Lugt, S. 18
Velasco, Carla Morena Álvarez 3
venture capitalist (VC) 40
video cameras 17, 96–7
video surveillance 94–5, 98–9; cameras 91; capabilities 94, 99; system 17, 94, 97–9, 112

Wen, Y. 8
Western countries 22, 91, 99–100
Western firms 3, 13, 19, 47, 91, 99, 115
Western powers 22, 83
Woodhams, S. 106
World Bank 32, 39, 57, 78, 112; and Alibaba Group 58–9
World Economic Forum 77, 107
World Trade Organization (WTO) 77

Yi, Wang 32

Zanatta, B. 117n8
Zhou, Qingna 1
ZTE 2, 8–12, 14, 67, 72–4, 76–83, 92–3, 96–9, 110, 113, 115–16; and Huawei 74, 78–80

FSC
www.fsc.org
MIX
Papier | Fördert
gute Waldnutzung
FSC® C083411

Kolibri 360 GmbH
Ferdinand-Jühlke-Straße 7
99095 Erfurt, Deutschland
produktsicherheit@kolibri360.de